# WORSE THAN HE SAYS HE IS

## White Girls Don't Bounce

# WORSE THAN HE SAYS HE IS

## *White Girls Don't Bounce*

### by *Anicka Rodman*

### with *Alexander Scott*

DOVE
BOOKS

ISBN: 0-7871-1517-7

Printed in the United States of America

Dove Books
8955 Beverly Boulevard
Los Angeles, CA 90048
(310) 786-1600

Distributed by Penguin USA

Interior design, layout, and photo insert by Michele Lanci-Altomare

Photos courtesy of Anicka Rodman, private collection.

First Printing: May 1997

10 9 8 7 6 5 4 3 2 1

*To Monique, my friend;*
*to Mom, my guide;*
*and to Alexis, my light.*

# Contents

-- -- -- -- -- -- -- -- -- -- -- --

# Acknowledgments

DESPITE WHETHER OR NOT YOU BELIEVE THIS INSANE TALE OF MY LIFE with Dennis, I have worked very hard to make sure it is as accurate as possible. I have gone through medical records, psychiatrists' notes, birth certificates, marriage documents, court papers and depositions, police reports, letters and cards from Dennis, newspaper and magazine articles, and even a scrapbook my mother put together for my daughter, Alexis, about her father.

While little in life is perfect, and in spite of the many years since some of the events occurred, I do have a good memory, and to the best of my recollection, this is a pretty darn reliable account. A few of the names have been changed at the behest of my legal advisers, but everything and everyone else is true and complete. Hey, Dennis didn't even get our wedding date right in *his* book (he was off by a *year*).

Some of those mentioned below had an actual hand in the birth of this book, some made life easier while I lived it, and some of them lived it with me. I would like to recognize their participation.

My gratitude goes to Harry Langdon for being such a pro in every sense of the word.

My thanks to the folks at Dove for their kindness, patience, and professionalism:

Rick Penn-Kraus, for his keen eye; Michele Samet, for her persistence; and Jay Woodruff—sorry I didn't call you back. I also want to give a big thank-you to the other Dove-ettes who have done their utmost to make this book the best it could be: Mary Aarons, Chris Hemesath, Richard Dooda, Stefan Rudnicki, and Doug Field.

I want to thank Dove's Beth Lieberman and Paul Pirner for their opinions, most of which I agreed with; for their accessibility, which made life easier; and for their philosophy and humor, which helped steer this story. I am also grateful to have shared that moment when Beth discovered the miracle of cordless telephones.

I want to thank the big Dove, Michael Viner, for stepping up to the plate, then applying the lash, knowing it was for the best.

Thanks to Jimmy Vines, who, while everyone else passed me by, saw through the three-ring circus to the human story within.

My warmest appreciation goes to my new friend, Alexander Scott, who walked in my shoes for a few months, made me laugh, made me cry, and ultimately made me happy. And remember, what I'm wearing is *my* business.

Thanks to the Sacred Heart School for protecting my baby from those who would make her part of Dennis's sideshow: to Alexis's principal, Ms. Douglass, and her teachers, Mrs. Tuerpe, Ms. Herbert, and Ms. Tarrico, for seeing a little girl, not the offspring of a cartoon character.

My thanks and love to the Flores family, particularly Maria, for taking me and my daughter in when we were at our lowest. To Crista Sandoval, who for fifteen years has never forgotten my birthday—I love you. And my love goes to my friends, particularly Anthony, who look past the tattoos and wild hair, past the idea I'm *Dennis Rodman's ex-wife*, past my past, to see the inner Annie.

My love goes to my brothers for being there, and to Dad, who found his way back.

My heart goes to my baby, Alexis, who let her mommy lock herself away for so many hours at a time and fly here and there while writing this book. I want her to read this book someday when she can understand it. When she's about seventy will do.

And I want to thank in advance the reader, who, after reading this, will be inspired to make a change for the better in his or her life or the life of someone else.

# Why I Wrote This Book

As they say, there are two sides to every story. In his book, *Bad As I Wanna Be*, Dennis got to tell his side.

Now, I get to tell mine.

In his book Dennis wrote about how he came from poverty and ended up with riches. He complained about how underpaid he is. He said the NBA likes to market itself and its players with a certain image, and he doesn't fit that image. He talked about what a free spirit and a renegade he is.

All of that is true enough.

But it's not the whole story—it's not even close. What Dennis wrote in his book was carefully planned to reveal just enough to intrigue but not enough to let you really get a peek into his life. Despite how he presents himself, Dennis is a very private person.

Dennis and I have known each other since 1987. We lived together, on and off, for more than six years. We have a beautiful daughter, Alexis. He got me pregnant six times. He talked me into having several abortions. He married me. He made me abandon my career by promising financial security. He abused me verbally, then physically. And then he tried to leave me broke and broken. He almost succeeded.

The interesting thing about Dennis's side of the story is that in his book our relationship gets a total of about 5 pages out of 250. As of this writing, Dennis is almost thirty-six years old, so the time we've known each other makes up more than a quarter of his life. It seems as though Alexis and I should have had at least, say, sixty pages in his book. But for obvious reasons, he decided to leave out the parts that showed the real Dennis.

The part that might discourage commercial endorsements or another one-night stand.

That's one of the reasons I wrote this book. To tell the truth. To let people know the other Dennis. The one who beats women. The one who is so lazy he gets strangers to take his daughter to the bathroom in exchange for an autograph. The self-centered, compulsive liar who...

Well, read the book for yourself and find out.

Did I write it for the money? I'll answer that with another question: Would you put your life, warts and all, on the printed page for all the world to see for nothing?

No way.

Did I write this book just for the money? Absolutely not.

I have a story to tell. My life's been an interesting journey so far, and I think it makes for good reading. In a way it's like a car wreck: horrible, but you just have to look.

Finally, I want my baby, Alexis, to know the truth. Much of it is unpleasant, and I won't want her to read this book for many years, until she's old enough to understand how people's lives can go wrong.

I don't want her to have misconceptions about her father. I don't feel Dennis is a monster or even a bad man, though you may think differently after you read this. But as they say, love is blind.

Do I still love Dennis? Yes.

Did I pull any punches in this book? No.

What you read here is what happened, to the best of my knowledge, from the time I was born, through the time I met Dennis, through our years together, to the present.

Whether or not you care about Dennis Rodman, I think you will find my story a compelling, sad, insane, and often hilarious tale that definitely will not bore you.

Enjoy.

> — *Annie Rodman*
> *Sacramento, California*
> *March 1997*

# WORSE THAN HE SAYS HE IS

## White Girls Don't Bounce

# **C H A P T E R**      **1**

## *In the Beginning...*

IT WAS A LITTLE AFTER 11 P.M., A FEW DAYS AFTER VALENTINE'S DAY, 1991. I was four months into my fourth pregnancy, and, as usual, I was waiting for Dennis to come home.

I knew the Pistons, Dennis's team at the time, hadn't had a game that day. That meant he had gone out after practice that afternoon. The question was, where had he gone? The options seemed limited. Either he was with one of the many sluts he kept on the side or he was with his groupies—young, white, video game-playing boys. I'd know the answer soon enough, though I would soon wish I hadn't asked.

Alexis, our three-and-a-half-year-old daughter, was asleep in her room upstairs. If ours had been a normal home, I would have been asleep, too, curled up next to the man I loved, safe and happy in our palatial home, dreaming about our wonderful future. But we didn't have what you'd call a normal home. At least it wasn't what I thought of as normal.

We were living in a beautiful, 9,000-square-foot, three-level mansion overlooking Gilbert Lake in Bloomfield Hills, Michigan, a very exclusive neighborhood in the suburbs of Detroit. But behind the modern white facade and the spectacular floor-to-ceiling windows of this not-so-normal house, there was an endless stream of screaming, fighting, and lying. There were also abortions, miscarriages, and sexually transmitted diseases. There were other women, though I don't know how many. And there were young boys, though they seemed to be mainly adoring, if obnoxious, fans.

Granted, the life of a professional athlete isn't the same as that of a nine-to-five office worker, but I kept hoping (especially on nongame days) that Dennis and I could have something closer to the life of Ozzie and Harriet than life with Ozzy Osbourne. I knew going in that Dennis would be on the road half the season and that he wouldn't be "off work" until ten or eleven, even when the Pistons played at home. On days when he finished practice at two-thirty in the afternoon, however, I didn't think it was too much to ask of him to come home to his family at a decent hour.

Looking back, I think that might have been my biggest mistake: expecting something normal. It took me forever to figure out that Dennis had his own ideas about family life, especially now that he was Mr. Big Shot. I mean, when I first met Dennis he was a benchwarmer. Now he was the league's premier rebounder, having led the NBA in boards the year before. On top of that, he had earned himself a position on the All-Star Team. The Pistons had increased his contract to $3.1 million a year, and he had just signed a lucrative deal with Nike. But the money and fame came without any instructions on how to use them properly, and Dennis wasn't prepared for any of it. He was just a naive boy from the ghettos of Dallas who, through his athleticism, hard work, tenacity, and the good fortune of being 6'8", had become not only famous, but a millionaire as well. He had too many options and not enough self-control. The pressure was more than he could handle. I hoped I could help Dennis deal with his success better than I had dealt with my own when I had become a successful model before I even graduated from high school.

Another big problem was that I loved Dennis too much. No matter how many times I caught him cheating and lying or how many times we fought, I always thought my love for him would solve any problem. I had the notion that I was addicted to him, as if he were a drug. I guess it's the only way I could justify staying with him after the way he treated Alexis and me.

That evening in February 1991, Dennis and his crew got home late and settled into the game room. I waited until he came upstairs for something, then confronted him. I asked him point-blank where he'd been after practice. While Dennis was good at hiding his guilty body language, we'd been together long enough for me to recognize it. When he told me he and the boys had been to a local restaurant I knew he was full of it.

All I could see was Kathi the Stripper.

I did something Dennis didn't expect me to do: I went downstairs to the entertainment room and asked the boys where they'd been. Dennis hadn't had the foresight to coach them, and they all hemmed and hawed with six different stories. I had my proof. Dennis was lying.

I went back upstairs, armed and ready.

Years later Dennis would tell me I had "given him too much freedom" and that was the reason he had cheated on me. When he told me that I remember thinking back to this evening. *I* gave him *too much* freedom? I wasn't a parole officer or private detective, I was his spouse. All I wanted from him was his loyalty, his fidelity. When it came to me, Dennis lived by the philosophy *out of sight, out of mind.* If I wasn't there to police him, he claimed, then he had no choice but to fool around. That's pretty weak.

So when I confronted Dennis about where he *really* was that evening, the fireworks began.

When we fought we sometimes hit each other, but we always screamed, guaranteed. Dennis didn't hit me that often, but when he did it wasn't much of a contest since I'm 5'10" and 130 pounds and he's 6'8" and 220 pounds. And if I hit him back, it pissed him off. This night, though, our fight involved mostly screaming, with just a little shoving and slapping, probably out of Dennis's deference to my being eighteen weeks pregnant.

Our screaming got so loud it woke Alexis, who had been asleep upstairs in her room. As soon as I heard her crying, I realized how crazy and stupid the whole situation was, so I turned my back on Dennis and headed for the stairs.

Dennis always wanted the last word or last blow in a fight. By the time I'd gotten to about the fourth step, he lunged at me. He grabbed for my shirt, which was loose, and missed. Instead, his fingernails dug into the skin of my back. The pain shot through me, causing me to arch my back. Due to the added weight of my developing baby, I lost my balance. Before I could catch myself, I tumbled backward and hit the marble floor with a sickening, gut-wrenching thud right at Dennis's feet. We both paused for a moment, Dennis because he was surprised, and me because the wind was knocked out of me. Then he said what he often said: "Why do you make me do this?"

I just lay there, partly in pain, partly in shock. I was horrified at the thought of what the fall had done to the baby. I can't describe the sorrow I felt: for the baby I carried, for Alexis, for me. Maybe even in a strange way for Dennis and what he'd become.

Then I snapped back to my grim surroundings when Dennis, looming over me, unleashed a verbal attack, apparently trying to minimize the terrible thing he had just done. "Get up, you're all right!" he yelled. "Get off the fuckin' ground, you fuckin' baby! That baby is okay!" To this day I don't know whether he was referring to our crying child upstairs or to the baby I was carrying. If it was the latter, he couldn't have been more wrong.

I was lying on the floor, my ears filled with Dennis's screaming and Alexis's crying, and all I could think of was: *How in the hell had I gotten here?*

■ ■ ■

I was born in Allentown, Pennsylvania, at 1:15 A.M. on February 26, 1965. I was the youngest of five children and the only girl of John and Carolyn Bakes. My mother's family originally emigrated from Europe, but a couple of generations ago a branch of the family tree moved and settled in Chile. I've been told more than once that I inherited my short temper from the Chilean side of the family, hence my childhood nickname, Chili Pepper.

Both my parents were very athletic in their youths. Mom was 5'9" and active in school sports. Because of her height, she played center on the basketball team. She was also the pitcher on her softball team. She gave up sports when she became a housewife and a mother. After all her kids were grown, she returned to work as a school secretary. Dad was six feet tall. In fact, he played minor league baseball for the Tiger organization, but I don't remember what city they played in. He also pitched for the official U.S. Air Force team when he was in the service. He played until he lost three fingers on his pitching hand in an accident, the details of which still are not clear to me. There were a couple of stories told around the house to explain it—one was that while he was in the air force, he stuck his hand out the window to signal that he was making a turn and his fingers got cut off by the propeller. Even I didn't believe that one. The other had something to do with an accident while he was working as a plumber's assistant, but no details were given.

When I was about a year old we moved to Sacramento, California, where we lived in a small two-bedroom house on 61st Street in south Sacramento, on the fringes of the worst part of town. It was a lower-middle-class neighborhood that was racially mixed and very friendly. All of the dads were blue-collar, and the average education level was high school with a college degree or two here and there, like my dad. Most had diplomas from the school of hard knocks.

Growing up, I assumed my life was just like everyone else's. I had three brothers: Christopher, Matthew, and Bill. We had another brother, but he died when he was five months old. His name was Andrew, and he would have been the oldest if he had lived.

At any rate, life seemed perfectly normal. I played with my brothers all day, every day, and learned to fend for myself. I became a certified tomboy and almost never played indoor "girl" games. I was always outside playing sports or fighting with my brothers. I really loved them.

During the summer Mom would take my brothers and me to the local public swimming pool with sack lunches. She would also take us to Little League and volleyball and basketball and softball games. I loved my mom more than anyone or anything, and sometimes I made her promise that she would never leave me. Mom was the only person who could get me to show my soft, feminine side. She tried to dress me like a little princess, sewing beautiful dresses for me to wear, but I hated dresses and froufrou outfits. Mom used to say that after she got me all dolled up, I would go out to our treehouse, change into hand-me-downs from my brothers, and stash the pretty dress.

For some reason my mom seemed to think I was strong-minded and independent, rough on the outside and a sad little girl on the inside. Some of that was true. I was strong willed, but with all the love she gave me, I could never be the sad little girl for long, no matter how much other shit was going on at home.

My dad was an alcoholic. He had been as long as I could remember. I think he started drinking after the death of their first child, Andrew. Andrew was just a few months old when doctors discovered he had a fluid buildup on his brain. Back then they didn't have any surgical procedures to deal with this sort of problem. In fact, my parents later told me that Andrew was the first baby to have this particular operation done on him: a draining tube was inserted into the back of his skull to relieve the pressure on his brain. The doctors told Mom and Dad that Andrew's chances of surviving the surgery were slim, but they had to do something for their "little angel," as they called him, so they consented to the operation. Andrew was in the hospital for two months following the surgery and it was touch-and-go the whole time.

Our parents would tell my brothers and me about Andrew. They said that every day during the two months after Andrew's operation, they would come home and find three little ducks on our front porch. They didn't have any idea where the ducks had come from, since there weren't any ponds or lakes near where we lived. But there they were, each day, waddling around on the porch, as though they were waiting for an update on Andrew's condition.

Despite the fact that Andrew received good medical care, the operation failed and Andrew died when he was just five months old. My parents told my brothers and me that when they came home from Andrew's funeral, the three ducks were gone, and they never came back. I've never asked if the duck story was true. I really don't care if it is or not. I think they just wanted to give us some image to remember our older brother by, since we never got to see him. Now, whenever I see fuzzy little ducklings at a pet store or paddling after their mom on a pond, I think of Andrew.

Though I don't think it's in any of the medical journals, the doctors told my parents that the operation on Andrew led to some breakthroughs in the treatment of this type of disorder. Now the operation is being done successfully, and I like to think that it's all because of my older brother, Andrew, whom I never got to meet.

They say experiences like that either bring a family together or drive them apart. I'm not sure it did either of those things, but I think it caused my dad so much pain that he started looking for relief in a bottle. I hardly ever remember him being around unless he was passed out or yelling at my mother. I can't speak for my brothers, but my dad definitely wasn't able to show his love for me. I needed his love and approval, and since I never got it, I think I ended up subconsciously looking for someone like my father (athletic and abusive) to give it to me.

My dad's drinking was just another part of my childhood. I love my dad and I know he has a disease. He couldn't help how he behaved at the time because he wouldn't admit that he needed help—and that's the first step any drug addict has to take before he or she can start recovering.

I've noticed a lot of cycles in my life, cycles that started long before I was born and which led me and others, like my mom and my dad, to make the choices we made. My dad's mom died when he was five, and he was left with his father, who was an alcoholic. I'm pretty sure that's where my dad learned the behavior.

My dad used to wake up at five every morning and take the number 15 bus to work. He worked until five in the afternoon and he rarely missed a day. I used to love to take the bus downtown to visit him after school. He worked at the Metro Main Post Office, and I thought it was the most spectacular building anyone's dad could work in. I'd go in and stand in line until he saw me. Then he'd buzz me through the locked door and I was allowed into the inner sanctum. That was so cool to an eleven-year-old, being allowed "backstage" where all the post office secrets were kept. Of course, there weren't any secrets, but to me it seemed like there were. Anyway, he'd let me watch as he dealt with customers and solved all the postal problems that came up. I thought he was so smart, being able to take care of whatever came up.

A lot of the regular customers would stand in line a little longer than necessary just so they could do their transaction with my dad. I was so proud of him when he was at work—it was the only time I saw him sober. After work he'd go to a bar and start drinking. Mom didn't allow alcohol in the house, but she let Dad drink at the bar. Maybe she knew there was no stopping him and she just didn't want us to see him do it. At any rate, Dad eventually would call Mom and tell her to come get him, so she would pack us all in the car and off we'd go to get Dad. When we got to the bar, Mom sent in my oldest brother, Chris, to get him. If Chris wasn't with us, Matt and I were sent in.

Dad wasn't going to the Four Seasons for drinks either. One of the bars he frequented was called the Sea Shanty, a dive in every sense of the word. It was the sort of place where serious alcoholics hunkered down at the bar and drank. Lots of pathetic, toothless men sucking on unfiltered cigarettes, coughing, and swilling cheap booze. I can't point to anything specific, but I always got the distinct impression that my dad was acutely embarrassed whenever I showed up to get him. He'd pay his tab and hustle Matt and me out of there. Once we were back in the car he'd light into my mom: "Jesus, Peaches, why'd you send Annie in after me?"

Mom wouldn't answer, but I'd say, "She didn't send me. I did it." Nevertheless, he'd turn it around, and by the time we got home he made it sound like it was my mom's fault that he was at the bar in the first place.

One weekend, when I was only about six years old, my dad told my mom that he was taking Matt and me to the flea market. Mom said what she always did on the rare occasion that Dad took us any-where: "Don't drink with the kids, Johnny. Don't drink with the kids."

With his back to her, Dad would sort of swat at the air and mut-ter, "Oh Jesus, Peaches." And off we went. Naturally Matt and I were excited about going to the flea market. But we never got there. Instead, we went to a place called Perkins at Perkins Station. Perkins was another of Dad's hole-in-the-wall bars. After parking the car in front of the bar he got out and said, "I'll be right out." And he left us in the car. Every fifteen minutes or so, he would come out of the bar to bring us beef jerky. "I'll be right out," he'd say again. Then he disappeared back into Perkins.

We were there for an hour or so that day, and I remember Matt doing his best to keep me occupied, trying to protect me, I think, from understanding exactly what was going on. Dad finally came out with one more load of jerky and we went home. I never really thought about that as an unusual event; it was close enough to the rest of my life that I assumed it was completely normal for dads to feed their kids beef jerky in such a manner.

I have a lot of scattered, unrelated memories about my dad during that time. I remember him coming home on the bus from the bar, having missed dinner. Mom would reheat his plate and serve him, and she'd sit with him while he ate, not speaking much. I remember waking up in the middle of the night and finding Dad passed out or drunk in the living room, and I'd help him get to bed. I remember writing him little notes that said, "Daddy, please stop drinking. If you love me, you'll stop!" I must have been around ten or twelve years old when I wrote those notes. Unfortunately they didn't make him stop.

Dad wasn't *always* drunk, but it seemed he was that way more often than not. When he was sober my dad was the most special person. He was sweet even though he had a hard time showing me affection. It would be years before I felt I ever got his genuine approval.

When he got drunk he usually got violent. At that age I didn't realize he had a disease. I just thought he didn't love me. I wanted a dad who didn't get drunk all the time, someone I didn't have to make excuses about when my friends wanted to come over. I started to realize that maybe my life wasn't so normal after all. I noticed that my friends' fathers weren't like mine, and that made me want what they had.

My dad went through stages as he got more and more drunk. First he'd be funny, then he'd get sullen, then he'd get outright mean. He was a badass you did not want to mess with, especially when he was drunk. One time my whole family actually went to the flea market where Dad had said he was taking Matt and me that other time. While we were there some asshole made the mistake of giving my dad some shit about his post office uniform. They argued, and the asshole made a derogatory comment about my dad not having all his fingers. Now, if my dad had been sober, he probably would have walked away. But since it was near the end of the day, and since they sold beer at this particular flea market, Dad was drunk. He beat the guy to a pulp. I think I watched that incident with a weird mixture of fear and pride—I hated the violence, but I was proud to see my dad defend himself.

Another time Dad came home from the bar and his hand was bleeding badly. Some other drunk at the bar had been harassing some woman and Dad had come to her defense. He hit the guy so hard in the mouth that his teeth broke off on my dad's hand. I remember trying to bandage it up before Mom got home.

I eventually came to understand that it was the alcohol that was so horrible, not my father. If my mom confronted my dad about his drinking, he would fly into a rage. He screamed and threw stuff around the house. He was always verbally abusive to my mom, and I grew up thinking that was normal. I saw him raise his hand to her more times than I like to remember, but I never actually saw him strike her. He not only threatened her with violence but, maybe worse, he also threatened to leave her. The thought of trying to raise my brothers alone was so overwhelming that Mom usually backed off from confronting Dad about his drinking. She would forgive him and take him back, and then it would happen all over again. Cycles repeat themselves. Since I was raised with this sort of stuff going on all the time, I think I was destined to repeat it.

When Dad would start getting violent—screaming and throwing things—Mom would try to protect us. She would take me and my brothers out to sit in the car. We used to look at the stars, and she'd tell us all about the Big Dipper. We'd stay out there, looking up at the night sky, until it was safe to go back inside. Again, for the longest time, I thought all this was normal.

My father worked for the post office for thirty years before retiring. At one point near the end of his career, they fired him because of what they claimed were budget cuts. They later rehired him, but at a lower salary. I can't imagine how that must have made him feel. After all those years of dedication to his job, they treated him like shit. He did his best to provide for us—in fact, he worked his ass off to send us to good schools—but we still had to go on financial aid sometimes, and my mother ended up having to work as a maid, cleaning the houses of some of my classmates' families.

Kids at that age can be cruel, and the kids I went to school with were no exception. After having five children and settling into middle age, my mother lost her athletic figure and put on some extra pounds. The combination of her weight gain and the fact that she was forced to work as a maid gave my classmates plenty of ammunition. I got into a lot of fights defending her and myself from all the taunting. The school would call my mom because I'd beat up yet another boy who was making fun of her. She would cry and tell me I didn't have to stick up for her. That was just like her. She wasn't very good at sticking up for herself, so I felt it was my job to do it for her. Nobody messed with my mom and got away with it!

My mom came from a very sad background. She had two sisters—Joyce and Jackie. Their father walked out on them when the girls were pretty young. Their mother, whom we called Nanny, couldn't support them, so she sent them to St. Patrick's Orphanage in Sacramento. Periodically Nanny would meet a man who seemed willing and able to support them all and would retrieve the girls. But when those men left, Nanny had to give the girls back to St. Patrick's. When my mom was about twelve, Nanny retrieved them for the last time and they lived together until my mom got married. Even after she married Dad, Mom actually lived with Nanny while he was attending college.

I think Nanny felt guilty for abandoning my mom and her sisters, and she tried to make up for it by being a good grandmother to me and my brothers. When things would get bad at home I'd go to Nanny's house sometimes for safe haven. My mom would call ahead, and Nanny would be waiting for me on the front porch. I have nothing but fond memories of her.

Mainly because of my father's drinking, my mom's home life wasn't exactly a Norman Rockwell painting. Despite the hardships, though, she kept my brothers and me going. We didn't have much growing up, but my mother did her damnedest to see that we were happy. I was always envious of the rich kids, but I never told my mother. I kept things like that inside. My mother taught me to be thankful for whatever I had, regardless of how little it was.

In high school, I had to work in the school cafeteria as part of being on financial aid. I remember the rich girls coming through the food line and snubbing me. I just knew they were laughing behind my back about how my family was poor and my mom was fat and had to work as a maid, and that pissed me off. But while I was thinking how much I hated them, deep down I wished I was one of them. I never let them know that. Instead, I held my head high. I've always had a sort of kiss-my-ass attitude toward people like that. My mother was a proud woman and I learned that from her.

Ironically my mother may also have been the one responsible for the mistake I made with Dennis, the mistake being that I stayed with him for so long. I saw my mother berated and belittled and otherwise abused by my father, and I saw her forgive him and stay with him and try to make it work. It only makes sense that I learned that behavior from her, but I can't blame her. That's not what she was trying to teach me, and I finally learned—the hard way!—that I have to take responsibility for my own actions.

Except for phys ed, school was a struggle for me. I had to study harder than most just to keep up. I was basically a C and D student. I can remember sitting in algebra class wondering what in the world the teacher was talking about. My algebra teacher, Mr. Colvard (bless his heart), tried so hard to explain quadratic equations and all the other stuff to me, but I just couldn't understand it. He moved me to the front of the class so I wouldn't miss anything. He tried explaining it in sports terms since I excelled in athletics, but even that didn't work. I would stay after class and Mr. Colvard would patiently go over everything we had covered, but I just couldn't get it through my thick head. I think because I worked so hard, Mr. Colvard gave me a D, even though I probably deserved an F. I always tried to do my best, though, and that's all that mattered to my mom.

In biology I sort of shot myself in the foot gradewise when I flat-out refused to dissect a frog. I even held my own little protest against the practice. I've always been an animal lover, and I think that may have been the reason I used to bring a lot of stray animals home. Once I brought home a ragged little cat that had lost all her fur. I named her Curly, and I wanted to take her to school for show and tell. It was wintertime, and my mom said it might be too cold for that, so I made Curly a sweater out of an old sock and took her to school. Some of the kids were cruel, making fun not only of me but also of my poor hairless little cat. I couldn't understand it. I ended up in the principal's office that day after I punched out two boys for making particularly disparaging remarks about Curly. I can't stand bullies, and even back then I wouldn't put up with such unkindness.

I also talked a lot in school and got into my share of trouble (mostly because I was sticking up for the kids who were always getting picked on). I never really got along with other girls. My three best friends were boys: Jack, Ronald, and Tom. We understood each other's problems and connected the way friends for life do. There weren't any hidden agendas or fake loyalties, only common enemies and interests, and we knew how to make each other laugh. These were real, genuine friendships that I hoped would last forever. But that's not the way it worked out.

Guys used to tease me about being flat-chested when I was in eighth grade. I'd tell them to shut up and leave me alone, but that would just encourage them to tease me further. If Jack was there, he'd make them stop. Jack was big and athletic, and when he told a group of guys to shut up and leave me alone, they did. He was my personal protector. My guardian angel.

He was also the first guy who kissed me. It happened one afternoon in eighth grade. Jack was at my house, and we were in the living room, looking out the window. I don't remember exactly how it happened. It was sudden and surprising and I was *so* embarrassed, but I liked it. One innocent kiss, and it led to my first crush. The next year, as high school freshmen, we crossed the threshold into the French kiss. Jack never went for second base, however. He found a new girlfriend in our sophomore year, but we remained good friends and I'll never forget that first kiss.

Even if Jack and I had tried to take French kissing a step further, I'm not sure we would have gotten very far. My brothers and I were raised Catholic and went to Catholic school. I was taught—both at home and at school—that sex was a bad thing and that all parts of the human body were considered nasty. Mom and Dad were extremely strict with my brothers and me. I wasn't allowed to date until I was seventeen. I wasn't even allowed to have boys over to the house except for my tomboy buddies Jack, Ron, and Tom. Believe it or not, I was a virgin until I was twenty-one, when I finally went to bed with a dancer from Chippendale's. (Turns out they're not *all* gay.) I guess it's possible that some of the sexual behavior I later engaged in was my way of rebelling against my strict upbringing. And I'm sure that same upbringing is the source of my guilt about all the abortions I later had.

Anyway, like I said, I wasn't a very good student except for phys ed, where I got my only A's. I was always a tomboy and I guess I inherited my parents' athleticism, so I was into sports 24-7 and loved every minute of it. In high school I was a starter on both the volleyball and softball teams. I earned MVP honors in volleyball. On the diamond they called me Stretch when I was covering first base, but I preferred being catcher. There is nothing better than the feeling you get after you've practiced and practiced with your teammates until you thought you'd drop, and then, during a game, you make the slightest eye contact with a teammate, and in that moment you communicate something to them and *wham!* you make the pass or set up the spike shot or pick off the guy trying to steal second. It feels like magic, but you know it's because of all the hard work you've put in.

Because my grades weren't so good and I barely passed algebra, I ended up in math fundamentals, a remedial math class. It turned out to be my favorite class for two reasons—first, because I could understand the subject better, but mainly because of my teacher, Sister Assumpta. She knew my home life was hard. She understood me and my problems, and she took the time to get to know me instead of just judging me. I loved and respected her. Along with my mother, Sister Assumpta was my mentor and my shoulder to cry on. Whenever I got into trouble and got sent to my counselor (who happened to be Sister Assumpta), she'd smile and take me along on errands and we'd just talk about things. I will never forget how kind and sweet she was to me.

During summers I mucked stalls at Camp Sacramento at Lake Tahoe. Even though shoveling horse shit wasn't the most glamorous job in the world, being able to work that close to the animals made it worthwhile. Our family's money situation was always tight, so I worked lots of odd jobs and saved as much money as I could, and eventually I bought myself a quarter horse for three-hundred dollars. I named her Erin. Taking care of Erin is how I first learned about responsibility. Horses need lots of care and attention every day, and Mom made sure I was out there doing my duty.

Another reason I saved money was because I wanted to move my mother away from my dad. It wasn't a very realistic idea, but she made so many sacrifices for me, I just wanted to do something for her. I thought she deserved better than what she got. I never saved enough to do everything I wanted to when I was a little kid. Later, when I became a fashion model, I was able to accomplish some of it. If my parents taught me nothing else, they taught me a good work ethic and that's something I still have.

Through my sophomore year at St. Francis High School I was just another tall, skinny, flat-chested girl. But during my junior year, I finally developed breasts. I also started my period. I was, I think, the last girl in my class to do so. My mother even took me to the doctor the previous year to see if I was all right in that department. I was, as it turned out, just a late bloomer. Anyway, before I knew what was happening, I blossomed from a tomboy into a young woman. My mother wanted to break me of my old habits, so she signed me up for a charm and modeling school called Mannequin Manor. She thought it would be good for me to polish my feminine side (something Dennis seems intent on doing to himself nowadays).

One day the director of the modeling school told my mom she wanted to take me to New York with her. I didn't think anything of it, but little did I know that my life was about to change. All the things I had ever wanted were about to become mine, and all because I was 5'10" and weighed only 113 pounds. Plus I was—all modesty aside—one hell of a beautiful sixteen-year-old!

I had no idea of the power that my beauty gave me. I especially didn't realize how much sexual power I had. But I would soon find out.

# CHAPTER 2

## *The Model Was a Tomboy*

THE YEAR WAS 1981, AND I WAS ALL OF SIXTEEN YEARS OLD. Meanwhile, down in the Lone Star State, my future lover, husband, and living nightmare, Dennis Rodman, was a twenty-year-old janitor working the graveyard shift at the Dallas–Fort Worth Airport. He was making $6.50 an hour. One night, while he was sweeping the long, tiled corridors, he noticed a bunch of wristwatches just on the other side of one of the security gates that roll down in front of the shops. He also noticed that he could reach them, and he did.

Dennis wasn't your run-of-the-mill thief. He didn't steal the watches in order to resell them and make a profit. In what was a perfect example of "the young Dennis," he gave the watches away like Halloween candy. He was just seeking approval from his homeboys. He wanted to feel like a big shot. Unfortunately, while he was out playing Robin Hood, his supervisor was watching the surveillance camera videotape that had captured Dennis's crime. When his supervisor confronted him about the stolen watches, Dennis agreed to return them. Chagrined, he went back to all his friends, collected all the watches, and gave them back. Not surprisingly, he then found himself unemployed.

When he graduated from high school, Dennis was only 5'11". By the time he reached age twenty, he had grown to nearly 6'8". He never played on the high school team, but with his new stature, he decided to give basketball a shot. He enrolled at Cooke County Junior College in Texas and started playing ball. In his first game at Cooke, Dennis scored 24 points and grabbed nineteen rebounds! Dennis played in only sixteen games at Cooke, but he did all right for a kid who never played high school ball. He averaged 17 points and thirteen rebounds each for those sixteen games, but he was having trouble academically, so he dropped out and went back to Dallas. There he got a job cleaning cars at Henry Butts Oldsmobile for $3.50 an hour. His future looked grim.

As for me, I felt like my future was going to be a bed of roses. I was going to be a big-time fashion model. After all, I was in New York for an annual convention where modeling school instructors from around the country brought in the fresh young faces who they believed had the best chance of getting signed by New York or foreign agencies. I had been chosen along with one other girl from my school.

The other girl, Mary Jane Klisowitz, was already a friend from modeling class in Sacramento. During the week when we were put up in the Waldorf-Astoria, we became even closer. We did everything together. Whenever we were left unchaperoned we hit the streets of the big city. Mary Jane and I were quite a sight as we strolled the streets and shops of Manhattan, window-shopping and gawking like the small-town girls we were. That was such a great time for me—being sixteen, feeling beautiful, and being loose on the streets of the most famous city in the world! We were so young and naive and full of energy and high hopes, and at that age, of course, everything seemed so dramatic and exaggerated. Each small success was likened to winning the lottery, and every little failure made us feel like jumping off the Brooklyn Bridge.

I was the one who got the lucky break. Toward the end of the week we were told the big day had arrived. Tables were set up in a large ballroom, and seated at those tables were agency reps from around the world. The models then went from table to table with their portfolios in the hopes that someone would "hire" us. I was at my second table when a petite Japanese woman stood up and walked around the table. Her name was Yoshie and she was president of the Liberty Modeling Agency in Tokyo. She asked how old I was and whether I was interested in going to Tokyo to model. I didn't hesitate for a second and said, "Uh, yeah!"

Just like that, I was signed. Mary Jane wasn't, so we had to say good-bye. She was proud of me and gave me a necklace to commemorate the occasion. I remember telling her the day I left that I was going to send for her and get her into my agency. I also remember that I hated myself for being the one who got picked.

My mother did a thorough investigation of the agency before she'd let me get my passport and visa. She also had a long talk with Sister Catherine, the principal at St. Francis. Sister Catherine decided that it was a great opportunity for me and guaranteed that if I wrote an extensive paper about the entire experience, the school would accept that for all of my junior-year studies. When I returned I could slide right into my senior-year classes. After everything was settled, I was off to the Far East!

The modeling business is just that—a business. Models are a big investment, and the agencies work us hard to make their money back. When we first arrived (whether from Europe or Australia or the United States) they sent us on auditions all day, every day, until our faces became familiar to the people who did the hiring. I must have walked a hundred miles a week going from audition to audition. Once they got to know us and began talking to each other about the latest crop of foreign girls, we were in business.

I landed some of the biggest and best modeling jobs in Tokyo. I did commercials for everything from Channing Cosmetics to a fancy cigarette filter company. I also did a lot of runway modeling, including fur coat fashion shows and dozens of other glamorous (and sometimes not so glamorous) jobs.

There I was, a gullible, naive little girl from Sacramento accustomed to making minimum wage mucking horse stalls or raking leaves or selling yogurt, and suddenly I'm raking in five thousand dollars per commercial. Talk about culture shock. The other American girls and I were like kids in a candy shop. We were young and on the loose without adult supervision in one of the world's busiest cities.

Sure, I was homesick, but I could make myself forget about that for a little while by going out on the town. We spent a lot of time hanging out in the Roppongi district, where all the nightclubs and restaurants were. In fact, it was there one night that we partied with the Scorpions, who were touring the Far East at the time. What a blast!

That first trip to Tokyo lasted seven months. Although I was dazzled by being in this wild, exotic place, making more money than I thought I'd ever see, I was still a fairly unsophisticated little girl a long way from home, away from my mother for the first time. I was homesick. Extremely homesick. I wrote to my mom and to Mary Jane often. Mom kept in touch, but I never heard from Mary Jane, which I thought was weird. I suspected that she was jealous or mad at me. Whenever I asked my mom if she knew what was wrong, she acted strange and changed the subject. After I got home my mom sat me down and told me that Mary Jane had been killed in an automobile accident. Mary Jane's mother and my mom thought it was best not to tell me while I was overseas without any support system. I still wear the necklace Mary Jane gave me.

Now that I was home from Tokyo, I had to finish high school. After all those years of being tormented and treated like a loser, I was now the envy of every girl who had ever snubbed me. I thought I was the shit. All those snobs who used to make fun of me and my mother were now bragging that they went to school with me, the big-time fashion model.

The most important thing of all was that I finally won my dad's approval. He had never come to any of my softball or volleyball games. He might say something like, "Hey, your mom says you had a good game yesterday." But he was never there in the stands nudging the guy next to him, saying, "That's my girl over there at first base!" After I started modeling, though, he was so proud of me. He loved taking pictures from my portfolio and showing them to all his coworkers.

I graduated from high school in 1983. Earlier that year Dennis enrolled at Southeastern Oklahoma State in Durant, the place where he eventually would be discovered. In his first year, he was a First-Team NAIA All-American. It was the first of a lot of awards Dennis would earn in his newfound sport. In fact, he would go on to win just about every award given in the NBA except for League MVP.

After graduation, I decided to look for a modeling agent on the West Coast so I could be close to my family. Mom and I went to Los Angeles and met with Elite and Nina Blanchard. Blanchard said I should come back after I lost all my baby fat. Elite invited me back to meet the president of the agency. She suggested I get a nose job in order to enhance my best features, namely, my eyes, lips, and cheekbones.

Models learn quickly that unless one happens to be born perfect—and I mean perfect—one has got to be willing to sacrifice oneself physically. And I was willing. The first plastic surgeon I went to took way too much cartilage out of my nose. The healing process resulted in a mass of internal scar tissue, so the doctor began injecting cortisone into the scar tissue. The second doctor told me that whoever did the first surgery had botched it badly. More work would be required to repair my nose completely, but outwardly, at least, I looked okay.

One day I got a call from a friend named Dennis Henning, whom I had met at Mannequin Manor. We had stayed in touch, and he was now in New York working as a model and actor. He said I should forget the West Coast, come back to New York, and stay with him and his roommates in their huge loft in Manhattan's East Fifties. So I went. I ended up living with these five guys, who basically took care of me. They were all starving model-actors and uniformly good guys who more or less treated me like their little sister.

I signed with the Ford Modeling Agency and got a little work, but not enough to keep up with the cost of living in New York. I needed money fast, so I called my old agency in Tokyo, Liberty Modeling. I was welcomed back with open arms. Liberty Modeling later became Yoshie, Inc., the most exclusive agency in Tokyo. They loved American models and now, ironically, after my botched nose job, I had a rather exotic look, so I was even more prized than "normal" American models. Go figure.

Once again I had to be willing to sacrifice myself physically. I was instructed to drop ten pounds. I ended up losing twenty-five!

My boobs were sagging down to my belly button, my cheekbones jutted out like a starved prisoner's, and in the nude I looked like a skeleton with flesh stretched over my frame. The result was the busiest schedule I'd ever had. (Nothing like rewarding an eating disorder!) Oddly enough, I felt great. I was eating nothing but popcorn and chocolate Ex-Lax, a model's best friend.

It was during this phase that I did my most memorable photo shoot. I was flown to Sri Lanka to do an Estée Lauder ad. It was the most beautiful country I'd ever seen, more breathtaking than I ever imagined a place could be.

I sent photos with some of the letters I wrote to my mom, and she panicked over my weight loss. When she called me on it I immediately became defensive. I told her I was in complete control and did not have a problem. (I think this is the same thing alcoholics, drug addicts, and others with behavioral problems will tell you.) Then I got a telegram: Mom was flying to Tokyo. I was pumped! I canceled every job that would conflict with her visit. My mother, my hero and protector, was coming to Tokyo, where I was a big cheese. I would get to show off and make her proud. I was so excited.

I picked her up at the airport. When mom saw me in person, she just about fainted. I had never seen her look so scared in my entire life. I remember waiting for her behind a big glass wall while she went through customs. I put my hand up on the glass and she put hers up on the other side. She mouthed, "I'm taking you home, angel." Later she told me that when we finally hugged it felt like hugging a skeleton. I was nothing but bone.

I didn't let her take me home right away. I rescheduled all my jobs and took her to each and every one of them. Seeing the look on her face as I worked—her unbridled pride—was the most rewarding thing I'd ever experienced. It meant so much to me to be able to make her proud. But as soon as the lights went down and I was her little girl again, not the big-time fashion model, her concern returned.

Finally she convinced me to see a doctor at an American military base in Tokyo. I had stopped having my period, my blood pressure was dangerously low, my hair was thinning, and going to the bathroom had become a chore. "Ex-Lax to disengage, Kaopectate to stop the flow" was my working motto. The doctor advised my mom to return to the United States immediately and seek treatment for anorexia.

We did as we were told. After being more or less force-fed I slowly regained my weight. My period resumed and my hair grew thick again. Anorexia was a way for me to have control. I had the power to do whatever I wanted with my body. Don't eat anything, and you can achieve a whole new look just like that! And not only did I get a new look, I got more work than I could handle. What could be wrong with that?

I was pissed that I had to come home. I was pissed at myself. I really never did have control over what I was doing. I was deluding myself about that. If my mother hadn't come to take me home, I hate to think what would have happened to me.

Despite all the cortisone injections, my nose wasn't healing properly, so I went to see another plastic surgeon. Dr. Bernstein literally sculpted my damaged schnozz into a work of art. After a little postoperative rehabilitation I was ready to forge the dangerous waters of the modeling world once again.

I signed with Model Management in San Francisco. When I went in to be weighed and measured, my agent gave me the news. "There's an Italian agent who is interested in you," she said. So we met.

His name was Tony. His English was better than my Italian, but that's not saying much. I managed to figure out the gist of what he was saying, which was: Will you come to Italy to work? I thought it over for about two seconds. Yes, I'll come!

One week later I was on my way, represented by the Toni & Tony Modeling Agency, with offices in Florence and Milan. I was put up in a huge flat with ten other models from Finland, Sweden, Germany, and the United States. I became friends with the two other girls from the States: Heather, who was from Dallas, and Dana, who was from Carbon Hill, Alabama. We had an absolute blast! Heather and I grew especially close. On our off days, we would hitchhike all over the country. The Italian men loved American women.

I soon discovered the modeling world was much more aggressive in Italy than it was in Japan or the United States. Photographers were constantly making passes at us. One photographer promised me the cover of an exclusive Italian magazine if I would have sex with him. At the time I wasn't willing to trade sex for professional advancement. But if I knew then what I know now, I'd have done it. I mean, I wasn't going to be a virgin forever, and instead of losing it to some silly boy from Sacramento who I'd probably never see again, why not get more for my trouble than just a case of teenage guilt? But my good Catholic upbringing, combined with the image of my disapproving mother, kept me from giving in and giving it up to the photographer. Needless to say, someone else got the cover of the magazine.

Soon Tony started sniffing around. He began asking me out to dinner and taking me to the countryside. At first I assumed it was just agent–client bonding, then I realized what was going on. It was a pattern. Many of the older models had fallen for Tony's seduction routine and expected to be rewarded with both career advances as well as loyalty. They got neither.

Tony tried and tried to get in my pants, but to no avail. I finally told him that I was there to be a model, not his paramour, and if he didn't like it, he could send me home. I was bringing in enough money to prevent him from doing that—sex is second to money for some people.

Without batting an eye, Tony turned his attention to Heather. She was a couple of years younger than me and twice as naive, if you can believe that. When I came home one day and found her crying, she told me Tony had put the moves on her and more or less threatened her career if she failed to cooperate. I had become somewhat protective of my friend, and I blew! I stormed into Tony's office and tore a strip off the son of a bitch. He freaked. He said Heather had overreacted and had gotten it all wrong. I told Tony he had better stay the fuck away from Heather or I would take every one of his clients and bolt to another agency.

Surprise, surprise. From that point on, Tony was all business.

Once we had our arrangement straightened out I worked all over Europe, doing mainly catalog work. I worked in Frankfurt,

Innsbruck, Paris, Nice, Monaco, and all over Italy. I traveled mainly by train and was leading what I thought was a glorious and glamorous life.

That's not to say it was easy. I worked my ass off—all of the models I know work as hard as anyone on Wall Street or on a road crew. But the pay was good and the perks, like all the attention and the special treatment, made it worthwhile. My biggest problem was that I loved spending my money. I saved some, but it was going out almost as fast as it was coming in.

When my visa was about to expire, I had two choices: I could zip to a neighboring country and have it renewed, or I could go back to California for some home cooking. I missed my mom and her TLC, so I decided to pay a visit, get rested, and then return to Europe. Once I returned home, I gave my dad thirty thousand dollars and bought my mom a new wardrobe. I wanted to pay them back for the costs of modeling school and my portfolio. I felt I owed them so much. After all, I wouldn't have made it without their help. I also bought myself a new sports car, a brand-new Triumph TR-7, bright green with a black racing stripe. That left me with a pretty skinny savings account, so I decided to get back to work. Instead of heading to New York or back to Tokyo or Europe, I decided to test the waters in La La Land. I went to Los Angeles and signed with Judith Fontaine and with the Playboy agency. American models are hot items in Europe and the Far East, but when you pull into Southern California you're just another pretty face, so the jobs in L.A. weren't quite so easy to come by. In addition, there are plenty of women willing to go that extra mile.

Like a lot of other models, actors, and dancers in L.A., I was living in a crummy, roach-infested apartment on Franklin Avenue in Hollywood. The neighborhood was fraught with drug dealing, prostitution, and muggings. It was quite a letdown from my glamour years in Tokyo and Florence, where such things were almost unheard of. But it was, after all, L.A., home of the star-making machinery. And if you wanted to get churned through the machine—and I was absolutely sure that's what I wanted—you had to live there.

For some unknown reason, I was still clinging to my virginity. Maybe it was my Catholic upbringing, or maybe I just hadn't met a person special enough to make me want to give it up. However, I would soon meet that person at one of the jobs I held between going to auditions. I was working at the juice bar in a health club during the day and as a cocktail waitress at Chippendale's at night. At Chips, as we called it, I hooked up with a girl named Eileen, who became my new best friend. Auditions were coming less and less frequently, and Eileen and I were going to more and more parties in our spare time. There's an amazing party circuit in Los Angeles that you can get tapped into if you're a television or movie star, a big agent, a producer, a director, or just a beautiful girl with no entertainment-industry credits. The parties are extravagant and loud and peopled with lots of influential men and sometimes women who might be able to help you out. Occasionally they offer out of a genuine interest in helping you get ahead, but usually it's at a more personal cost to you.

This was around 1986, the same time Dennis's basketball career at Southeastern Oklahoma State was coming to a close. He had earned First-Team NAIA All-American honors for all three of his seasons there. He had led all NAIA players in rebounding as a junior, averaging 15.9 per game, and he did it again as a senior, averaging 17.8 per game. During his college career, Dennis averaged nearly 26 points and sixteen rebounds per game. He had an unbelievable .637 field goal percentage. Most remarkable of all, given those numbers, is that he lasted until the twenty-seventh pick in the second round of the NBA draft. Still, for a kid who didn't start playing organized hoops until he was twenty, he was doing all right for himself.

Meanwhile, I started running with a big-time L.A. crowd, Lakers owner Jerry Buss among them. I met Jerry through an agent named David Wilder. There were parties and games at the fabulous Forum and more parties at Pickfair, the famous mansion owned by Mary Pickford and Douglas Fairbanks during Hollywood's Golden Era and later purchased by millionaire Meshulam Riklis and his wife, actress Pia Zadora. These were exactly the sorts of parties I had heard about and imagined: bowls of cocaine set out for all to enjoy, and celebrities coming and going like next-door neighbors at a backyard barbecue.

I went to a great Halloween costume party at Max Baer's place in Beverly Hills. It was an exclusive little soiree, so exclusive that you couldn't get in unless you were on "the list." I was used to lists at nightclubs, but at someone's house? David Wilder made sure Eileen and I were on the list, and boy, did we feel like we were on the inside track. Max Baer, the former *Beverly Hillbillies* cast member (he played Jethro) was by this point a successful producer. Eileen and I were dressed as Chippendale's waitresses, complete with fishnet stockings, garters, and spiked heels. We spent most of the night wandering through Max's beautiful mansion, trying to figure out who was who.

Not a night went by that I wasn't hit on by at least a couple of guys. But after a day of scurrying from audition to audition and a night of schlepping cocktails, I was too tired to get involved with anyone. The parties were a fun diversion, but I wasn't looking to fall in love or even in lust. I was just having fun.

When Eileen and I weren't attending private parties, we were prowling L.A.'s hottest nightclubs. It was almost surreal: rooms filled with TV, movie, and rock stars. Getting hit on by rich, powerful, and famous men and the occasional woman, too. Laughing, drinking, flirting, hot-tubbing, skinny-dipping, and just about anything else you can imagine.

Eileen and I were in the fast lane, where a waitress's salary doesn't go too far. But for some reason, Eileen always had enough cash. At first I didn't ask, but finally I had to. She clued me in by taking me to a mansion in Bel Air. The place was a fortress with security cameras everywhere and guards patrolling the grounds. Inside, about fifteen girls were sitting in the living room. I remember one of them: Her name was Heidi. Eileen then ushered me into the master bedroom, where another ten girls were sitting around. There, she introduced me to Alex, the infamous madam! She was sitting up in this huge bed, surrounded by a dozen or more cats and talking to clients on the phone.

So there I was, standing in a whorehouse. And I was there to apply for a job. Pretty weird circumstance for a virgin. But I was damn near broke, and my friend had made it sound so reasonable:

"Hey, you're going to lose your virginity someday, right? Would you rather do it for free or make some rent money in the process?" Well, I couldn't think of any good counterarguments, so I just followed Eileen's lead.

Alex asked me to do a turn so she could check out my body. Then she told me the rules. Dress professionally, never look like a stereotypical hooker; call in before and after each job is finished; give the men whatever they ask for; be willing to go anywhere and do anything at any given time; get the money up front; and, if you see anything suspicious, get out!

"Are you willing to abide by these rules?" Madam Alex asked.

I said yes. And what's weird is, it didn't seem like that big a deal. I was working my ass off at the juice bar and at Chippendale's, and I was barely getting by. I saw all the nice things Eileen had, and I wanted nice things for myself. If I could make a real living by going on some "dates," well, why not? Besides, at that point it was all theoretical. It wasn't as if Alex was about to send me into the next room where I would have to do the squat-and-gobble for the next forty-five minutes. Sure, I'd follow the rules, no problem.

My first job was at the Beverly Wilshire Hotel. Another girl and I went to a room and waited. The other girl, whose name I can't remember, could tell I was nervous, but she had no idea I was still a virgin. She told me to relax, that it was no big deal. "You just close your eyes and think of the cash," she said. It seemed like a reasonable thing to do.

Eventually we were escorted into another room, where we were greeted by a short Arab man. My only thought was, *Gotta do it, get it over with, the first time's the hardest, make money, money, money.* I was doing everything I could to make myself go ahead with it, but then I pictured the guy naked. That was all it took. I excused myself and went into the bathroom, where I stared at the mirror. I kept seeing my mother and I knew I couldn't go through with it. I went back out, got my purse, and held up my index finger. "One minute. Be back," I said, assuming that made sense to the man. I drove straight home, crying the whole way. I couldn't believe how disappointed I was in myself. I had a guaranteed way to make good money, but I just couldn't bring myself to do it.

After this first incident, Alex decided to give me one more chance. She apparently thought I had it in me somewhere. My second job was to fly to Switzerland and accompany a wealthy businessman on a two-week ski trip. It paid fifteen hundred dollars a day. I was packed and at LAX, ready to go. About five minutes before the flight boarded, I called my mom to tell her good-bye. I told her I was going on a modeling job. The last thing she said to me was, "I'm so proud of you, honey."

After I hung up I left the airport. I was angry and embarrassed. Angry that I lied to my mother, and embarrassed that I was almost willing to become a hooker, or a call girl, or whatever it was. My luggage is probably still circling the baggage claim carousel at some airport in Switzerland.

It was back to the juice bar and Chips and the endless series of auditions. Nothing was coming through. I considered calling my Japanese agency again and I even thought about Tony in Italy, but ultimately I decided to stay where I was and tough it out.

I started dating a film producer named Jimmy Welsh. He was a nice guy but a lot older than I was. I soon grew accustomed to dining at the city's best restaurants and riding around in limos and Rolls-Royces. Jimmy and I were at a party one night when a friend of his came up and asked, "Is this your date, or are you baby-sitting?" Jimmy got a little embarrassed and I wanted to knee the bastard in the groin. It was awkward enough without the wisecracks. Later, back at Jimmy's house, perched high in the Hollywood Hills, he asked if I would go with him to the Cannes Film Festival. Three weeks, all expenses paid, on the French Riviera. Tempting. I knew the time had come for me to put out or get out. I told myself I could do it, just fuck him and get it over with. Then, out of nowhere, the strangest thing popped into my head. Jimmy had ear hair. Lots and lots of ear hair, sprouting out like shrubs in an unkempt garden. And that was all it took. I couldn't go to bed with him any more than I could go to bed with an azalea bush. *Au revoir* to the French Riviera.

Of course, it really wasn't the ear hair. I guess I needed to give myself some sort of excuse not to go to bed with this guy, simply because I didn't want to. Why I couldn't just say no is beyond me. Call my psychiatrist and ask her.

Jimmy was soon going out with Eileen, who was willing to do whatever it took. As far as I know, she said oui to all his requests. That was the end of the great Los Angeles restaurant tour for me, but I still have fond memories of Jimmy. He was quite kind. In fact, I sometimes wish he had been my father instead of a potential lover.

I was still working at Chips and was soon swooning over one of the dancers there. His name was Doug Compton, and he was the most gorgeous man I had ever laid eyes on. We started getting romantic. I decided the time had come. I was finally ready to lose my virginity—and to a man who wasn't promising me anything in return. Doug was sweet and gentle, but I didn't think the sex we had was anything to write home about. The relationship ended when I discovered Doug was trying to bed all the women who worked at the club.

In 1986 I left Los Angeles, tired of all the partying and scarcity of modeling work. Back in Sacramento I met Roger Nichols, a guy who played football at Cal State Sacramento. He wasn't flamboyant or cocky and didn't have any of the characteristics normally associated with athletes. He was just a nice guy and had a great body—he was, after all, a college football player. Now that I had finally gotten over the hump, so to speak, of losing my virginity, I was in bed with Roger in fairly short order. He taught me how to enjoy sex and showed me subtle ways to satisfy him. I knew in my heart that I would never be content with someone as normal as Roger, but it was nice while it lasted.

I dated Reggie Theus for a while after that. Reggie has gone on to become a basketball commentator for TNT and TBS, but at that point in his career he was playing for the Sacramento Kings. Reggie treated me like a lady, and everything was moving along nicely until I found out he had a steady girlfriend—and it wasn't me. So I broke it off.

I'm attracted to athletes. Simple as that. Ever since my first crush, Jack, I've always found myself attracted to athletic men. Why? I can't say. Could be that I'm just superficial, but that would indicate that all athletes are dumb as rocks. They're not. I've known my share of athletes, and their IQ range is as wide as it is in the general population. But when it comes to physiques, you've got to admit that athletes have cornered the market on great bodies. I'm sure someone with a trunkful of college degrees will have a better answer than that (or at least one that's more complicated and sounds better), but quite frankly I don't care. I don't need to know why.

At any rate, I've never been willing to play second fiddle to anyone, and I wasn't about to start. All I was looking for was a man who would treat me with the respect I deserved and who would be loyal to me. You'd think I was asking for the crown jewels.

Things were really looking down. I hadn't had a modeling gig in a long time and I was almost broke. I finally decided to go on the wet T-shirt and leg contest circuit. Yes, there's actually a circuit. There'd be a "Hot Legs" contest at one bar on Thursday night, a wet T-shirt competition somewhere else on Friday night, and yet another T-shirt event at a third bar on Saturday night. In an average week you could make five hundred dollars without breaking a sweat. Was it degrading? Not to me. It was fun. It was competitive and it helped pay the bills. Was it intellectually stimulating? Not to me, but that's not why I was doing it. Hell, working at the Department of Motor Vehicles probably isn't intellectually stimulating, but it's still a job. And a legs contest doesn't take up forty hours a week.

I didn't see it as a fall from grace, going from the runways of Europe and Tokyo to wet T-shirt contests. I was simply trying to support myself while trying to get my modeling career back on track. I'm practical that way. You do what you have to do to fulfill your responsibilities.

It was a rough time for me. I learned that my best friend from high school, Jack, had died of leukemia. I was crushed. He had been diagnosed with the disease a couple of years earlier. There was always the hope that it would go into remission, but it never did. I couldn't understand why this sort of thing happened. He was my best friend, and now he was gone forever. It was the saddest thing I'd ever been through in my sometimes pretty sad life. I still think about Jack and I miss him a lot.

A month after Jack died, my Nanny passed away. I was in the midst of a lucrative three-week modeling job in Switzerland that had come from out of the blue, and I was planning to use it as my reentry into the European market. But as soon as I got the bad news that Nanny was sick and had been put into a rest home, I packed my bags and headed back to Sacramento. When I got to Nanny's room I saw she had pictures of me taped all over the wall. By that time she wasn't the spunky, perky grandma I remembered. She was weak and frail, and she knew as well as I did that the end was near. She and I were cut from the same cloth, for she had also relied on her looks as a young woman and was not afraid to show her hot Chilean temper. My mom and I, however, were total opposites. She never drank or cursed. She dressed conservatively and went to church every day of her life.

First my best friend died, then my Nanny. My support system—hell, it seemed like my whole world—was falling apart. I heard somewhere that there are five stages in the mourning process, but I seemed to bypass all of them and go straight into a sort of numb oblivion. I came to believe it was God's way of preparing me, strengthening me for what lay ahead.

The modeling job in Switzerland turned out to be my last one overseas. Though I never reached supermodel status, I thought I'd done pretty well for a girl from a lower-middle-class Sacramento neighborhood. I decided to try and make a go of it in my hometown. I took a job teaching at a local modeling school and did TV commercials now and then. I was also thinking about going to college and maybe pursuing a degree in criminal justice.

Because I had been away from Sacramento for a while, I'd lost touch with most of the people I had grown up with. Some of them had moved away, others were married and cocooned out in the suburbs. So I started exploring Sacramento nightlife from the consumer side instead of the wet T-shirt side. It wasn't exactly the Roppongi district, but it was fun. Flirting with guys at the local bars, meeting new friends, dancing. It was the same thing a million other people my age were doing—at least it was until Dennis Rodman came up to me and asked if I would dance with him.

# C H A P T E R 3

## The Way We Were

ONE NIGHT IN JANUARY 1987 I WAS AT A PLACE CALLED CONFETTI'S, having a drink with some friends. It was one of my hangouts, and as usual it had a pretty good crowd. The place attracted a lot of yuppies as well as basketball players from the Sacramento Kings and players from visiting teams.

People assume that because I had dated Reggie Theus, I must have been an avid sports fan. I wasn't. I mean, just because you date a plumber doesn't mean you're interested in clogged drains, right? I followed sports enough to know that the Kings had played a home game that night, but at that moment I couldn't have told you who they played. I was about to find out.

I was standing at the bar with my friends, just watching the crowd, and suddenly I was tapped on the shoulder. I turned around and saw this tall black guy. He was nervous, but he was trying to be cool. He was actually kind of cute as he struggled to muster the courage to talk to me. "Hi, I'm Dennis," he finally said. "I play for the Detroit Pistons."

I looked him up and down, then turned back to my drink. "Hi, I'm Annie," I replied, "and I don't give a flying fuck."

It wasn't that I didn't think he was cute; it's just that I wasn't impressed simply because he played professional basketball.

But he was persistent. He responded to my snub by buying me a drink.

After he bought me drinks and followed me around for a while, I decided he was harmless enough. When he asked me to dance for the fifth time I gave in. We ended up dancing all night. In between dances we'd talk, and he came across as kind of sweet, kind of shy, and definitely not too sure about how to handle who he called "this gorgeous woman" he had just met in a bar.

By last call Dennis and I had danced a lot and talked a lot, and I'm sure he figured he was going to get me to come back to his hotel. He followed me out to the parking lot and asked if I would come up to his hotel room to talk. I said no. Then he asked if we could at least go to the hotel and talk in the lobby. Again, no. Then he mentioned the word "bed," and I put him in his place by telling him the only bed I'd be sleeping in that night would be my own. Alone. But then I gave him my phone number and told him to call me next time he was in town. I sort of liked him, and even though I hoped he would call before his next West Coast road swing, I had to be cool about it. Then I left.

I bet it drove him crazy to meet a chick in a bar who wouldn't go back to his room and "do" him. I imagine that the veterans on the team had told him all he had to do was ask and women would comply with his every wish. To say the least, he looked surprised when I turned him down, as if he had gone into McDonald's and ordered a hamburger and they told him sorry, no. It wasn't supposed to work like that. I think the challenge appealed to Dennis. I was forbidden fruit, and he wanted a bite.

My confidence was through the roof at that time because of my success in modeling and life in general. I had plenty of men competing for my attention, but there was something about this gangly young guy from Detroit that stuck in my mind. I think it was his willingness to overcome his shyness and approach me. I found that refreshing compared with some of the slick guys who seemed to hit on women professionally. On the one hand I really didn't care if Dennis called me or not, but on the other hand I was intrigued for some reason. Turns out I didn't have to wait long for the phone to ring.

As I literally walked in my front door, having left Dennis in the Confetti's parking lot less than half an hour before, the phone rang.

It was late, so I quickly grabbed it to keep it from waking my folks. It was Dennis. He said he was calling because he wanted to make sure I had given him the right number. I thought it was sweet that he was so attracted and so insecure that he called right away to find that out. We talked a while, then I said good night, hung up, and went to bed.

The next day he called again, wanting to know when he could see me. He asked if he could fly me to Detroit. Now, during the course of my modeling years, I had enough rich guys offering to fly me here and there that I wasn't impressed by it anymore. I knew they wanted only one thing, and I wasn't interested in that trade. Besides, I really didn't know this guy, so I said no. He kept after me. He asked if we could get together in San Francisco next month when Detroit would be playing against Golden State. It didn't take long to think that over, because I did want to see him. I agreed to meet him.

Dennis and the Pistons came back the next month to play the Warriors. I went to the game as his guest and we got together afterward. We hit it off right away. He made me laugh like I hadn't laughed in a long time. He was silly and cute and unaffected by his professional stature. He was smitten and I was smitten right back. Why? It didn't matter why. It just mattered *that*.

While the Pistons were still in California, I came out to Oakland on the afternoon of a nongame day and went straight to Dennis's hotel. Now, I was less than a month away from turning twenty-two, and Dennis was about twenty-five. We had urges and desires, and we finally had one another. I had great expectations. Unfortunately they were not met. Even then, Dennis wasn't shooting much. He got off only one shot, and there were still about ten seconds left on the twenty-four-second shot clock when that happened. No rebounds, no assists. Two loose balls. He didn't want to do anything weird, but what he did do, he did with enthusiasm. The weirdness would come later.

He then jumped out of bed and grabbed a camera. He said he wanted photographs of me that he could take with him. I obliged and posed for some cutesy nude cheesecake photos and a couple that were slightly more salacious. He loved it and so did I. It was slightly naughty and therefore titillating. I hoped the photo session might encourage him to get back in the game, but no luck. He was definitely done for the afternoon, performance-wise.

That night we went into San Francisco with Pistons teammate John Salley for dinner. When we returned to the hotel, we did it one more time before he fell asleep. The sex hadn't rocked my world, but Dennis had. He had completely charmed me with his innocence and his ability to make me laugh. I couldn't wait for the next time.

From then on we were hooked on each other. The attraction between us became tremendously strong. He was shy and nervous in a way that made him irresistible. He didn't want to let me out of his sight, and whenever we parted I didn't want to say good-bye. He flew me to Seattle and Portland and anywhere else I could go. I was still a modeling instructor in Sacramento, but it wasn't a problem getting time off for these excursions.

I was pretty sure he had women in Detroit and maybe elsewhere; after all, he'd had a life before we met. But I had this deep feeling that we were soul mates and meant to be together. Love makes you think all sorts of things.

Our relationship progressed, and we became closer and closer. My first orgasm *ever* was with Dennis. He treated me like his love slave, and I did anything he wanted. We experimented sexually, and with us there were no limits. I'd do anything he wanted, anytime he wanted. I had fallen so deeply in love that nothing else seemed to matter. The modeling jobs I was getting were now just events to fill the time until I could see Dennis again. The work was local television and print advertisements and some fashion shows that my agent at Model Management in San Francisco arranged for me.

Dennis was still in his first year in the NBA and was mostly "riding the pine" with the Pistons, but I didn't care. I honestly think that if he had told me he was a janitor at the airport, I still would have fallen for him.

He loved showing me off as his girlfriend, the model. He was very possessive and protective, and when I told him I had been asked to go back to Europe to do some modeling, he pleaded with me not to go. I had received a call from my old Italian pal, Tony. He had a nice gig lined up for me and wanted me to stay for the long term after that.

But Dennis had other things in mind. He said we should move in together, in Sacramento, Detroit, or wherever I wanted. I was tempted but played coy. I wasn't quite ready to give up my life as a model to play house with this guy. As a compromise, I told him I wouldn't move in with him—yet. But I also said I wouldn't go to Europe if he didn't want me to. I'll never know if I blew a huge opportunity by passing on Tony's offer, but I did pass on it, and not without some regret.

I had spent six years of my life modeling and had enjoyed it so much that I still couldn't let go completely. Despite the natural high I felt with Dennis, the attention and the money from modeling was good for my self-esteem and my checking account, and that independence of body and mind was important to me.

But all that was about to change.

Just when you think you have it all figured out, life throws you a curve. Dennis was flying me here and there to be with him, and our love affair was in full swing. But I wanted to keep working, and moving to Detroit was not part of the plan. I thought it might happen eventually, but at that point I was content just to fly off to see Dennis and to continue taking whatever modeling jobs turned up.

One day in May I called my agent in San Francisco to talk about upcoming jobs. We decided to meet that Saturday to go over some possibilities. On the morning of May 16, 1987, I got into my little Volkswagen Cabriolet and headed out for the two-hour, hundred-and-some-mile drive to my agent's office in Mill Valley. I jumped on I-80 and headed southwest out of Sacramento. My route would take me south to Richmond, where I'd cut over to the 580 and proceed over the Richmond–San Rafael Bridge, right past San Quentin Prison, and on into the beautiful little town of Mill Valley, about forty-five miles north of downtown San Francisco.

About an hour into the drive I crossed over the Carquinez Bridge, where the Sacramento River empties into San Pablo Bay, and was passing through Pinole, a little town ten or fifteen miles north of Berkeley. Since it was a Saturday, traffic was light, so I was lulled by the monotony of the drive.

Suddenly I came around a sweeping curve and saw nothing but a wall of taillights. I was approaching a huge traffic jam at about 65 miles an hour. I hit the brakes and was about to swerve onto the shoulder when a car smashed into me from behind, and it was all over. The impact slammed me into the cars ahead, and the last thing I heard was the grinding and tearing of glass and steel.

When I woke up in the ambulance they kept asking me what my name was and what year it was. I guess they were worried about brain damage. And they should have been. I slipped back into unconsciousness and didn't come out of it again until the next day, when I woke up in Pinole County Hospital. Even then I was still too disoriented to understand the extent of my injuries, which were catastrophic.

My skull was fractured in two places, and the skin and underlying tissue of my forehead was pushed up from my eyebrows to my hairline. I also had a major subdural hematoma, that is, a dangerous collection of blood from broken vessels that causes a swelling under the skin of the skull. The doctors were concerned about that for a few days. My vision was also pretty blurry (it went to 20/40 in my right eye and remains unchanged to this day), and on top of all that, my right ear had nearly been sliced off. My thanks go to the doctors who not only saved my life, but also managed to sew my ear back on without any horrible scars.

When I came out of my haze and found myself lying in that hospital bed I went into a panic, followed by a deep depression. My looks, my career, my cute little car...all gone! And I was scared to death what Dennis would think when he saw his Bride of Frankenstein. Mom was at my side, and Dennis called frequently and sent flowers, but I worried about the day we'd finally see each other...or should I say, when he finally saw me. What would he think? The Pistons were in the midst of losing to the Celtics in the Eastern Conference Finals, so Dennis wasn't able to come visit, but his phone calls were enough to keep me going.

After being in the hospital for three days, followed by a couple of weeks of being laid up at home, I started physical therapy at the Crowl Sports Center. The therapy consisted mainly of applying an ultrasound device to my head to help break up the blood that had collected to form the subdural hematoma. Then I began seeing neurosurgeon after neurosurgeon. I had taken a vicious blow to the head, and the doctors were not only trying to figure out how to put me back together cosmetically, given that I was a model, but they were also concerned that I might have sustained permanent brain damage.

After I had healed enough that the doctors could survey my injuries, they told me I had a massive indentation in my forehead. They said if I wanted to continue modeling it would have to be fixed. That was obvious when I finally got a look at it. I was horrified. My forehead had a major dent in it!

During that time of the recovery and rehab I found a plastic surgeon who said he could fix me. He proposed a complicated operation that involved shaving me bald, then making an incision that went across the top of my head, literally from ear to ear. The doctor would pull my scalp down, and tissue taken from somewhere else on my body would be inserted into the crushed part of my forehead. I was absolutely terrified about having the operation. On the phone, Dennis told me that if I didn't want it, I should speak up, since I wasn't having it to save my life. As soon as I heard him say the operation wouldn't change how he felt about me, I said no to it. Dennis assured me I wouldn't have to model anymore. He told me he would take care of me. He said he didn't want me modeling anyway, because he always wanted me to be with him or waiting for him at home. Although I found that notion somewhat appealing, I wasn't ready to give up on modeling just yet.

When I had healed to the point where I could have some new pictures taken, my agents encouraged me to do it. So I made an appointment with a photographer, and he took some head shots. In every one you could see the indentation. As soon as they saw the shots, my "loyal" agents dropped me like a hot potato.

I could have submitted to the skull operation, but there was no guarantee that it would restore me to my former self; besides, it was a major surgical procedure, and there's always a risk involved with that. I decided my modeling career was over. But my future with the love of my life was just starting, and I walked away from modeling without looking back. Dennis was infinitely more important than modeling so the choice was easy and I gladly accepted it. I think he was actually relieved I couldn't model anymore.

He could now become my whole world.

I called Dennis to tell him my decision. Since he was in the middle of the play-offs, I wasn't sure if he would be at home or at practice, so when I called, I expected to get either him or his answering machine. What I got instead was a woman's voice. I was startled. I asked who she was. She stammered and sounded kind of nervous, maybe even evasive. Before she could say her name, Dennis came on the line. At that point in our relationship, if I had known he was such a dog, I would have cut it off right then and there. But he insisted that the girl was in from Seattle and was the girlfriend of one of his best friends, Zollie Stevens. He had mentioned Zollie's name before. I was a little suspicious, but I bought it. Probably because I wanted to.

(Eventually I met Zollie in Detroit. He was one of the few black friends Dennis had, and he hung out with Dennis and Isiah Thomas. He had played some college ball but never made it into the NBA. He was a great guy who respected me and who, I later learned, didn't approve of Dennis's fooling around. He used to come over on evenings Dennis was out all night and just keep me company. There was never anything between us, just friendship.

Anyway, at some point when I had gotten to know him and vice versa, I asked him about that night and the girl from Seattle. Zollie just threw up his hands and said, "I don't want to get in the middle of this." Right then I knew I'd been had by Dennis. It turned out that was the first in a series of a few thousand other lies.)

By June 1987 the season was over for the Pistons. I had healed quite a bit and I felt like traveling, so I flew out to Detroit at Dennis's request. I thought I still looked pretty bad, but to my huge relief, Dennis didn't even flinch when he saw me. He even talked about our future together. I had been scared for no reason.

Dennis was living in a little one-bedroom apartment in Southfield, Michigan, a suburb of Detroit. He was making around

$85,000 a year at that point and the rent was only $620 a month. He had only one car, a Chevy Blazer. He had even rented furniture. I had planned on just a visit, but almost as soon as I got there he was asking me to move in, so I finally agreed. I called Mom and asked her to send my stuff. Just like that.

Mom wasn't exactly happy about it. I would be living in sin, and to her that wasn't just a figure of speech. She meant it literally. But she didn't say anything. It didn't matter to her that Dennis was black. Sin is color-blind. Still, she sent my stuff and I moved into the apartment. As for my brothers, they didn't seem to care one way or the other. As long as I was happy, they were happy.

In a few short months my whole life had changed. I had left modeling and California and my family for a new life in Detroit with the man I loved. It was a great time for both of us in that little place with the rented furniture, because we did what the average young couple did: We mainly just played. We went bowling, we went to video arcades, and we ate out a lot. We were still a couple of years away from the poisoning effects of too much money, power, and fame.

On the court, Dennis was trying hard to make his mark. And off the court, he still had his feet on the ground. Like I said, we were just your average young couple in love. Average except for one area.

Sex.

Picture a black man who is 6'8" and a white woman who is 5'10". He's a super athlete and she's a total jock. He's proportionally equipped (or more) and they're both horny as hell. Sex for us was not like two bunnies fucking. It was more like two grizzly bears wrestling. We tried all the basic positions, and a few that weren't so basic. I remember one time when we tried it with me standing on my head with my back against the wall. Dennis seemed to like it, but I ended up with a headache. Next! Had anyone been standing nearby watching us go at it, they probably would have been injured.

I had been with only two men before Dennis, and despite his having been on the road in the NBA, he wasn't tremendously experienced either. But what we lacked in experience we made up for in enthusiasm and creativity. For Dennis, it was "the rougher the better." It seemed like the more pain I could endure, the harder and farther he wanted to take it. He once said to me, "You are my bitch. I love fucking you 'cause you can take it." That was all I needed to hear, because then I knew that despite the pain, as long as I could take it, he'd never have to look for someone else who could. And by that time I knew there were lots of NBA groupies who fit the bill.

If you've ever seen Dennis play basketball, you know how strong, fast, and relentless he can be. He was all that and more in bed. That is, whenever we *used* the bed. Our sex was totally savage. I remember him ramming me so hard I thought he'd actually come up into my throat. The pain was exquisite at times, and looking back, I think I thrived on it and wanted it to hurt.

Then one day he announced we were going to have anal sex, and the Catholic girl in me slammed on the brakes. I had all sorts of hang-ups about anal sex, but I didn't tell him half of them for fear of alienating him. Finally I gave in again, knowing if I didn't, he'd quickly find someone who would. He wasn't even gentle the first time, and later when I went to draw a bath, I stood in the bathroom feeling like Amtrak had gone up my ass. When I got into the water, it turned pink and that scared me to death. I was bleeding and I began to cry. I cried my eyes out, and all I wanted was to be comforted by my mom. But I knew she would never in a million years understand what I had just done. That made it worse.

Dennis loved anal sex, and we continued it, but it never got any easier for me. When were having sex the "traditional" way he liked to say to me, "Your pussy is stretched to fit only my dick. If you ever get fucked by another man, I'll know. This big black dick is gonna stretch you out so bad that no other man will want you. Only me!" He could be such a romantic.

I finally decided to turn the tables and screw *him* until he couldn't take it anymore. By this point in our relationship, Dennis was able to sustain his erection for more than the twenty-four-second shot clock. In fact, he could keep it up for quite a while. I tried to screw him so hard he would finally declare me the winner. We soon became obsessed with who could top who at sex, and the kinkier the better. I did everything I could to blow his mind, and I thought we were doing great until one day his mind was apparently a little too blown. "Where'd you learn that?" he demanded. "Who's been in my shit? What other dick you been suckin'?"

I couldn't believe it. Now he thought I was fooling around on him just because I was trying so hard to please him. We'd eventually get around to having sex and he'd forget all about his suspicions.

Sometimes he'd sing the U2 song "I Still Haven't Found What I'm Looking For," only he'd change the lyrics to "I've *found* what I'm looking for." I was so passionately in love with him, I know that if the need came up, *I would have died for him.* I realize now how very sexual our relationship was. Everything we did seemed to have some kind of sexual twist to it, whether it was sitting on his lap to play arcade games or sitting on his lap while he played the mega–drum set I later bought him.

We were so horny it was almost ridiculous. I think when you're young and haven't had a lot of sexual experience, and you're with someone who has as many hormones churning as you do, you go a little crazy. Dennis used to love to examine my bare body from head to toe—we were like kids playing doctor, only we were adults at the peak of our sexual drives. There was a lot of kissing and licking, but he refused to go down on me, which was all right, since that was never my favorite thing anyway. Years later he finally did it in an attempt to curry favor, but he didn't have a clue as to what he was doing. I think I finally just asked him to give up and do the one thing he was good at. And he did. We were quite a team. But we couldn't do it forever, and every now and then we went out for dinner or a movie instead.

One night, after seeing *Beauty and the Beast,* Dennis decided that it was "our" movie. I was Beauty and he was the Beast. I didn't argue with him. Despite his feelings about his looks—he was completely insecure about his appearance—the whole notion of us being Beauty and the Beast actually was romantic to me.

Dennis grew up hating the way he looked. The other kids teased him about his ears and his bad complexion. He had acne as well as rashes on his face, and the fact that he picked at his pimples didn't help. Next to the chip Dennis has on his shoulder about his mother, he also has one about his looks. Of course, I never saw him as a kid. I always thought he was handsome in a unique way. I think his hair coloring and tattooing and body-piercing extravaganza is part of an attempt to improve what he sees as his ugliness.

After the 1986–87 season was over, there was no reason to stay in the sprawl of Detroit, so we packed up and headed for the wide-open spaces of Oklahoma. Dennis explained that he liked to go to Oklahoma because he had family there. That's about all he told me about them.

On the way there, driving day and night, we'd find a deserted stretch of highway and sail along at 115 mph. The drive was like our whole relationship—fast and dangerous. Once in a while we'd make a pit stop to grab something to eat or use the rest room, but mostly we stayed on the road. Sometimes Dennis would pull into a rest stop, and as soon as I saw the look in his eyes I knew why we were stopping. The second the car had stopped moving we'd jump in the backseat for a quickie. Good thing we were both so athletic, because backseats generally aren't made for people as tall as us—especially doing what we were doing!

Dennis was a serious country music fan back then. He was completely Nashvilled out. Growing up in Texas, I imagine he heard a lot of that music as a kid. He had cowboy boots and jeans and the whole rodeo wardrobe, including hats. I wasn't crazy about country music, so I introduced him to Van Halen and Rush and some of my other favorites. He loved them. He trashed the country discs and went U2 crazy, eventually becoming a fan of Pearl Jam and the other grunge groups. I thought it was weird, though, that he never cared about rap. It seemed to me that rap was very much about where Dennis had come from, so I thought it would appeal to him. Maybe it was precisely because rap reminded him of where he came from and what he was trying to escape that he never listened to it.

Sometimes, when Dennis would be at the wheel and we'd be listening to Randy Travis on the radio, I'd look out the window and watch the pastures and farmhouses race by, and I'd count my blessings. I was so happy. Occasionally I'd take a nap, and when I woke up Dennis would be staring at me. Thinking I'd been drooling or something, I'd put my hands to my face. "What? What's wrong?" I'd say, alarmed.

He'd just shake his head. "Why are you with me? You are so beautiful, man. I'm so ugly. You can have anyone, why me?"

I'd kiss his cheek and whisper in his ear, "Because I love you. I'm here to take care of you, Dennis."

When we got to Oklahoma we headed south to a little town called Bokchito near the Oklahoma–Texas border. Bokchito was not much more than some ranches and farms and very few paved roads. He said we were going to the Riches'. Imagine my surprise when Dennis's "family" turned out to be white. And rednecks to boot.

Four years earlier, when he was playing at Southeastern Oklahoma State in Durant, Dennis met a kid named Bryne Rich, a white kid about eight years younger than Dennis. One day after shooting baskets, Bryne invited Dennis home to nearby Bokchito for dinner. Pat Rich, Bryne's mom, was used to Bryne's friends, all small white kids. I'll just bet she shit a brick when a 6'8" *black dude* walked into her living room that night. Pat was somewhat friendly to me, but there was more than enough to indicate she was a serious racist. She told me that while he was in college Dennis would bring white women back to the house, and she'd tell him he was "acting like a nigger." She was pleasant to Dennis, but I think she put up with him because Bryne idolized him.

Also, the year before he and Dennis met, Bryne had suffered a major tragedy. The story was that Bryne and some other kids, including his best friend, had been out shooting at stuff with their shotguns—generally just farting around like typical thirteen-year-olds do—when Bryne's gun accidentally went off, killing his best friend. Apparently Bryne was so traumatized he crawled into a shell for a long time.

He came out when he met Dennis.

And that's why Pat Rich, a woman who was afraid to be seen alone with a black man, tolerated Dennis.

Anyway, we were allowed into the Riches' home and given Bryne's room. Bryne took the sofa in the living room. A separate mattress was placed on the floor for one of us, while the other slept in Bryne's bed. Pat said she wouldn't have us sleeping together in her house. We agreed to respect her wishes, but as soon as the door was closed, we jumped in bed together. One night we made a little too much noise and Pat busted us. We were quiet after that.

While staying in Oklahoma we'd drive the fifteen miles to Durant and work out at a place called Charlie's Gym, then dine at the Branding Iron, a local steakhouse. After dinner we'd cruise down the main drag in Dennis's cherried-out Mustang. Summer in Oklahoma can be pretty muggy, and I remember the nights as hot, sticky, and totally magical.

We started palling around with this other couple, doing things like waterskiing and horseback riding. Dennis was good at anything he decided to take on. He was fearless and seemed to master everything he did very quickly. Whether it was waterskiing, Rollerblading, riding horses, playing the drums, or something completely different like driving an 18-wheeler or a tractor, if he put his mind to it, he would do it and do it well.

And Dennis loved video games. He told me he cut his teeth on pinball as a kid, and when he got older and video games were invented, he turned to those. We used to spend hours at the arcades, and I'd watch as he ran up huge point totals on all the machines. His favorites were Mortal Kombat, Indy 500, and golf. He wasn't just good, he totally kicked ass. Dennis Rodman is a natural.

We had a wonderful time in Oklahoma. We woke up when we wanted, we ate when we wanted, and we made love when we wanted. We had no schedule, and our only job at that point was to have fun. I was having the best time of my life because I didn't have a care in the world, and I was madly in love with a man who was totally into me.

Only one ugly thing was in our lives during that time: prejudice. Sick, mindless racial hatred. I had been with black men, including Dennis, in many public situations before, but that was in large, sophisticated cities where no one thought anything of it. Here, we might as well have been on another planet.

There are a lot of open-minded, decent people in Oklahoma. Unfortunately there are also a whole lot of small-minded hillbilly idiots who make comments when they see a white woman and a black man in public, or just stop and let their jaws hang open as you pass. Those pea-brained hicks really used to piss me off. I'd let my feelings show, and Dennis would get uncomfortable and move away from me. That made me want to mess with their empty little heads all the more. I have a real mouth on me when I get ticked and I'd let 'em have it! If I caught someone staring at us, I'd let loose with "You got a problem you wanna talk about?" or "What's the matter, never seen a black and a white eat dinner together?" or "Do I know you from somewhere? No? Then quit staring at me!" Dennis used to say, "Watch out! Her bite is as big as her bark!"

While we were hanging out in Oklahoma, Dennis decided to buy an old ski boat that caught his eye. It was small and had seen some serious use before he laid out four thousand dollars for it, but it was his pride and joy. We used to spend hours washing and Armor All–ing it and talking about where we'd take it.

One weekend we hooked up the trailer and went to nearby Lake Texoma, a big reservoir on the Texas–Oklahoma border, to try the boat out. Lake Texoma is a popular place because it's not too far from Dallas–Fort Worth, and it seems like half the people in Oklahoma go there, too. We got out on the lake and were cruising around when a guy and his girlfriend pulled up next to us in a slick-ass new ski boat and said, "Hey, why don't we race? Let the girls do the driving."

Dennis looked their boat over and turned to me in a really low voice, "Shit, his boat'll blow us outta the water. We can't race him."

I gave their boat, then the guy and his girl, the once-over. "Let me race her," I said.

As we sat there, our boats bobbing in the chop of the water, I put my hand on the throttle and waited for the guy to drop his flag. One look at the girlfriend at the wheel and I knew I'd smoke her. The guy dropped the flag and *boom!* I was gone! The chick in the other boat was still sitting there, trying to get in gear, so the guy waved us back, saying she wasn't ready. We lined up again, and this time when he dropped the flag I came out faster than the previous time. I punched the gas, and we left them in our wake.

Later on at the ramp, as we snapped on the towline and winched the boat onto the trailer, Dennis turned to me. "You made me proud of you," he said. That was the first time he had ever complimented me like that, and I was pumped. But if I had known then it would be the *only* time he would ever compliment me, I would have been very, very sad.

Too soon, our perfect summer came to an end. I had to go back to Sacramento to attend the arbitration for my lawsuit regarding the car accident. I didn't know how long I was going to be gone, but I hoped it wouldn't be too long. Dennis hated to see me go—at least I thought he did.

Turns out that as soon as I went back to Sacramento, he brought a girl down from Detroit to be with him.

From what I understand, right after I got on the plane at Dallas–Fort Worth Airport, Dennis must have walked down the concourse a short distance and picked up a girl named Kathy. Kathy sold Kool cigarettes, so I call her Kathy Kool because Dennis had another Kathi, a stripper whom I refer to as Kathi the Stripper. But more on her later.

Meanwhile, Kathy Kool has landed, and I'm back in Sacramento, blithely thinking everything is fine. I called Dennis one day at the Riches' and Pat answered. Dennis was out. Pat seemed nervous and I got suspicious. She hemmed and hawed, but finally I got her to throw Dennis under the bus and tell me about Kathy Kool. He had brought her down to spend Fourth of July with him. I asked Pat sarcastically whether she was going to make them sleep in separate beds. She had no answer. I hung up.

I was totally stunned. So much for that line of crap he gave me about me being the only one and all those promises about growing old together. I was devastated. I called him later and broke off our relationship.

He was taken off guard, but I'll tell you one thing about Dennis Rodman: The man can lie very convincingly. He told me that Kathy meant nothing and that she'd be out of there ASAP. I didn't buy it at first, and he kept after me. One day he called me and said one of the Rich boys, Mike, was getting married, and Dennis wanted me with him at the wedding.

Women are suckers for weddings.

Next thing I knew, I was on my way back to Oklahoma and into his arms again. I really missed him, and despite the setback to our relationship, my love for him was as strong as ever.

Not long after I had come back to Oklahoma, we went out for a drive and had stopped to fool around a little. Pretty soon we ended up on the hood of the car with Dennis playing doctor. Without any warning, he pulled out a two-carat diamond ring and handed it to me, saying, "This is for you. I want you to be my wife. I want you to have my children. You are the reason I'm playing so well. I don't ever want to live without you and your love. Will you be my wife?"

Now it was my turn to be taken off guard. A week before, I had been in the pits of despair, our love affair over. But on that day, with those words, I was suddenly trembling with joy. Our lives together were just beginning, and the promise of the future was so bright it hurt my eyes. I said yes with all my heart.

We didn't set a date. I didn't think it was necessary. I thought he was sincere.

As time went by Dennis told me he didn't want to get married "until the next season was over." The season melded into the play-offs, which became the finals, which became his postseason and then training camp. I was beginning to wonder if we were going to get married at all. He always had some excuse as to why we couldn't tie the knot.

When he proposed, though, I believed he would eventually be my husband, and I decided a makeover was in order. I took him shopping. Out went the flannel shirts and beat-up jeans, and in came the polo shirts, designer slacks, sweaters, and nice jeans. He hadn't developed a taste for wedding gowns or dresses yet, and I think he really liked the new look. I know I did. This change in image seemed to work magic on Dennis in that his self-esteem seemed to change for the better. He even walked taller. He was becoming a new man.

We went back to the little apartment in Detroit. I took care of the place, and Dennis went to training camp. His enthusiasm about being in the NBA had waned. He didn't hate it yet, but he never said anything to indicate he was looking forward to his second season. The 1987–88 season would turn out to be a big one for him. In fact, it was going to be his best year with the Pistons. He was going to start making his name in the NBA and in the world. It was also going to be a big "season" for us. I was going to get pregnant with Alexis.

And our relationship was going to begin its long slide into hell.

# *C**H**APTER*      **4**

## *Battle Lines Bein' Drawn*

ALMOST FROM THE TIME WE MET, DENNIS AND I HAD TALKED ABOUT having children. We both wanted kids for entirely different reasons, but I was just happy that we both wanted them. So in January 1988, when I found out I was pregnant, I was overjoyed. Dennis was happy, too. Unfortunately he already had two major things on his mind: basketball and partying.

The 1987–88 season was Dennis's second in the NBA, and he was playing at the highest level of his career. On January 24, 1988, about the time I found out I was pregnant, he had a monster game against the Trailblazers, scoring 30 points and pulling down eighteen rebounds. He used to tell me that he wasn't in it to score, that rebounding was his art form and he was the best, and that the NBA only rewarded showboating point-scorers. But I think he was secretly pretty proud of that game.

When Pistons star Adrian Dantley got hurt in February of that year, Dennis came off the bench to start twenty-nine straight games, a huge change from his rookie season, when he started a grand total of *one* game. The 1987–88 season was a good one for the Pistons, and it eventually became clear they were headed to the play-offs. They finished the regular season tied with Denver for the third best record in the league. In an interview, Chuck Daly, the Pistons' coach, said that without Dennis's rebounding the team was not effective. Dennis was on his way to stardom.

Maybe his success on the court went to his head. Maybe it was just all the attention he was getting. Whatever it was, I saw Dennis start to change. He began exhibiting a new type of behavior. It coincided with my pregnancy, so that probably had a lot to do with it, but it was something I had not expected, something that would later grow to insane proportions: abuse.

It started as verbal abuse. A snipe here, a spoken jab there. Comments that, taken individually, didn't matter much, but cumulatively they started to hurt. I began to realize he was looking at me differently ever since I became pregnant, and rather than celebrating the beautiful event that was happening—our creation based on our love—he found it ugly. Dennis was good at pulling things back from the brink, though, and just when I was beginning to think he hated me, he'd turn around and convince me of the exact opposite.

On February 26, 1988, my twenty-third birthday, Dennis surprised me with a car: a brand-new Saleen Mustang, an outrageous present for a guy who spent $620 a month for our apartment. The Saleen Mustang was based on a run-of-the-mill Mustang, but it was custom-built and a lot faster and a whole lot more expensive than a regular Mustang. I was blown away.

I think Dennis gave me things when he couldn't give of himself. Sometimes I'd get jewelry or furs (which I didn't want because I'm an animal-rights activist) and other stuff when he was either trying to make up with me or feeling guilty. Usually the gifts came after we fought over one of his chippies and I'd leave, but once in a while they came without any fireworks beforehand.

Once it sank in that I was pregnant—Dennis actually went to the doctor with me a few times—sex between us ended. He decided he didn't want to have anything to do with me sexually. I had heard that was a problem with some men, but I was shocked and hurt when it happened to us. I was young and worked hard to keep in shape. I knew I was competing with all those pretty, naked young girls in the strip joints, and that spurred me on to stay fit. I gained only *fourteen pounds* while carrying Alexis.

Despite my program to stay desirable to my man, Dennis treated me as though I had leprosy. He wouldn't touch me no matter what I did to entice him. This was a huge letdown from our all-too-recent animal-like sex life, and I didn't know what to do. I had gotten used to bonding physically with the man I loved, and now I felt like we were worlds apart. In combination with his abusive remarks, his rejection caused me a lot of mental anguish, as I didn't know which to blame: his weirdness over the pregnancy, or his lack of energy after all the tramps he was nailing on the side.

If Dennis wouldn't accept me as a sexual being during the pregnancy, I thought I might at least get him to focus on our child. I would pull up my shirt, show him my distended belly, and tell him to touch it. Forget it. I'd even grab his hand and try to put it on my belly, and he'd pull away, saying, "I can see it. I don't need to touch nothin'."

But in spite of his odd behavior toward me and our developing baby, he was excited about one thing: having a boy. That's all he talked about, having a baby boy. He was almost obsessive about it. Of course, I didn't care if it was a boy or a girl, I just wanted one thing: a *healthy* baby.

About this time I got a phone call that completely threw me. On the other end a young woman introduced herself as Robie. She asked if I was Annie. I said yes, curious as to why she was calling. Suddenly she took a real harsh tone and proceeded to tear a strip off my butt. She told me she had been Dennis's girlfriend since he was at Southeastern Oklahoma State, and they were still together. Then came the dagger through my heart: She said they were engaged.

Then she started grilling me on what I was doing with her man. I couldn't believe what I was hearing. She told me that Dennis had said I was just a friend who needed a place to stay and that he had been generous enough to let me stay there. I listened for a while, then finally said, "I don't know who you are, but you'd better leave Dennis alone. He and I are engaged, I'm having his child, and you can go fuck yourself."

I hung up. I was shaking. Despite my tough words, I was pretty rattled. I knew I was having Dennis's baby and I knew he had asked me to marry him, but who was this woman? She sounded like she really *did* know Dennis. Did he really tell her I was just some welfare case? I didn't know what to believe, so I went to the source.

When Dennis got home I asked him who Robie was. I told him she'd called and had said she was his girlfriend and that he had proposed to her. And she was still under the impression they were going to get married.

What did Dennis do? Throw a fit? Deny it all?

No. He just shrugged and walked away. Just what I didn't need to hear.

Life is sometimes good at piling things on. Some people say life never gives you more than you can handle. I'm not so sure. I had to deal with this crank call from a woman claiming to be Dennis's fiancée, Dennis and his other infidelities, his abusive turn, the cessation of our sexual relationship, my pregnancy and all the heightened emotions that brings. Then one more traumatic event was added to the pile: My beloved Sister Assumpta died. Aside from my mother, she was the one guiding, loving figure in my life who gave me more than I put in. I was devastated.

While I was in this state of grief, the Lakers sunk the Pistons in the finals, and Dennis came back to our Southfield apartment in a deep funk. He took the loss as hard as any committed professional would, but where he differed from most committed professionals was in the way he took out his frustration. He took it out on me.

That night, in June 1988, we got into an argument about a girl he was seeing, and he chased me into the bathroom. Our relationship was about to hit a new milestone: physical abuse.

Keep in mind, I'm six months pregnant.

He cornered me in our tiny bathroom. We yelled at each other for a moment or two, and then he decided to take action. I was wearing my hair long at the time and had it tied back in a ponytail. That was a perfect leverage point for Dennis. He grabbed it and yanked my head down hard. I was pulled off my feet and nearly fell into the tub. Still maintaining a solid grip on my hair, he slammed my head into the porcelain wall of the tub. I started screaming and he held my head down. "Shut the fuck up! Would you *shut the fuck up*?" Finally I shut up. He let go.

Nearly knocked unconscious, I remember lying crumpled on the floor next to the tub in a daze while the winner of the bout left in triumph. I finally got up, took some Tylenol for the massive headache I had, and crawled onto the bed. As I lay there, I began to seriously question who I was. I felt I was losing who I was, what I believed in.

I had to get out of there.

I had seen the rage in Dennis's eyes as soon as he had gotten home from getting stomped by the Lakers, and I knew now that smashing my head into the tub wasn't going to siphon off all his hostility. I decided to go home to Sacramento. To Mom.

Sometime in early July I went back to Sacramento. It was the first time I left Dennis, and I was heartsick. I loved him deeply, but I felt our baby was in danger. Mom comforted me, but it was becoming clear her daughter was with an abuser, and she cautioned me about going back to Dennis.

Dad figured I could take a few lumps since, after all, Dennis was a star. It was all confusing to me, and I missed Dennis. He called often and begged me to come home, but by then I was under the care of a local doctor for my pregnancy and decided not to do anything until our baby was born. On top of that, Mom wanted to take care of me, and I was in need of her loving arms.

It was at about this time that the proud residents of Auburn Hills, a suburb north of Detroit, were getting ready to unveil their newest attraction: the Palace of Auburn Hills. No longer would the Pistons have to share a bedroom with the Lions in the Silverdome in east Pontiac. The Palace was their new home. A modern arena with a capacity of a little over twenty thousand fans, it officially opened on August 13, 1988. Less than four miles north of the Silverdome on the 75 freeway, the Palace must have been some kind of boost to the players' morale, as the Pistons won the championship a year later. It might also have had something to do with the man I was living with off and on.

Dennis was the Pistons' Sixth Man that season, and he would end up being voted the runner-up for both NBA Defensive Player of the Year as well as NBA Sixth Man of the year. He also led the league in shooting percentage at .595 percent.

As my late September due date approached, Dennis came to Sacramento to be with me for the birth of our baby. For the time being, my mom welcomed Dennis despite the image of his abusing me in the back of her mind. Mom loved Dennis because I loved Dennis. She saw what was good in him and embraced that, but she couldn't forget the fact that he had hurt her baby girl.

Late in the evening of September 27, I went into labor and Dennis took me to the hospital, where Mom joined us. Once I got situated in the room, I told Dennis it would be a long night and that he should go home. I knew Mom wanted to stay with me, and I was concerned about Dennis getting his sleep. Dennis kissed me good-bye and took off, and Mom and I talked and waited for the contractions to increase. According to the doctors, I was probably not going to deliver until sometime late the following morning, so Mom and I settled in.

A little while later, at 1:05 A.M., I got up to pee and my water broke. Suddenly I was on the fast track, and my baby was going to come out on *her own* schedule. In minutes I had dilated to eight centimeters. Mom called Dennis. The drive from our place to the hospital normally took ten to fifteen minutes.

He made it in four.

Dennis burst into my room, winded, nervous as hell, a video camera in his hand. He was tremendously excited and started getting everything on video, but as soon as the baby's head appeared, he was overcome by emotion and handed the camera to Mom. Dennis got tears in his eyes and briefly I reveled in this perfect moment. I was in labor only two hours. It had been a breeze, and knowing it was all about something Dennis and I had created together made the whole experience easier. This was probably our best moment together, very personal, deeply touching, and we were both overwhelmed.

Dennis got to cut the umbilical cord, and despite his comments about wanting a boy, when they wrapped our baby girl and handed her to him, he was the happiest I have ever seen him. He wouldn't have traded our baby, then or now, for anything.

We named her Alexis. During the pregnancy the doctors had told us we were definitely going to have a boy. I had asked Dennis if he wanted to name the child Dennis Jr. He said no, he hated his name. So we settled on Milan, for reasons I can't recall. But we also talked about a girl's name just in case the doctors were wrong. I lobbied for the name Alexandria after St. Alexandria. Dennis wanted something more African, like Kahnesha, I think. We settled on Alexis and everyone was happy. Except the doctors; they were still expecting a boy.

As I cradled Alexis in my arms, Dennis couldn't take his eyes off her. He kissed me on the cheek and the forehead. "You okay, Momma?" he asked. My baby was healthy and my mom and my man were at my side. I was definitely okay.

They moved me down to postpartum while Dennis and my mom stayed with Alexis in the nursery. I was pretty groggy, partly from the delivery and partly from the painkiller they gave me. I had had to have an episiotomy (though Dennis claimed to have stretched me out, he wasn't *that* big), and I was still punchy.

At some point I had to go to the bathroom, and I staggered out of bed and promptly fell and hit my head. The next thing I remember was Dennis's worried face as a nurse was administering smelling salts. I realize how strange that moment was, given that just a couple months before he had slammed my head into a bathtub and walked away, and now he was holding my hand and saying, "Is she all right? Is she all right?"

Later that day I was released and Dennis told me he had to get to training camp right away. I hated to see him go, wanting so much to spend that first night with Alexis cuddled between us. But he left, and my family gave me all of their love. My brothers went nuts over Alexis and took turns holding her. They jokingly promised me they wouldn't terrorize her as they had done to me. They are wonderful uncles to Alexis. She loves them and they love her.

The Pistons played their first game in the Palace on November 5, 1988, against Charlotte. They beat the Hornets 94 to 85. A new era was beginning for the Pistons. At home in Southfield, a new era was beginning for us, too.

— — —

Long after I moved to Michigan to live with Dennis—much too long, in fact—I simply didn't have any friends. I was living a very weird, very secluded life. Dennis preferred it that way. He didn't want me to have any friends. Sometimes he just wanted me to stay at home so people couldn't see what he had done to me.

Ironically, it was Dennis who introduced me to the person who would become my best friend. Her name was Monique St. John. She was a great-looking lady, tall with long black hair. People called us Salt and Pepper because of our contrasting hair colors. And I guarantee when Monique and I swept into a room, all eyes turned to us.

When I met Monique, she was seeing Isiah Thomas. She and I became fast friends. That's when I started turning the tables on Dennis, because now I had someone to go out with while Dennis was out admiring strippers. Monique was the companion I needed. She stayed with me through it all. She witnessed a lot of the shit I went through with Dennis. She made a couple of those drives from Michigan to California with me. She moved in with me for a while in Sacramento, and she really helped me raise Alexis.

Next to Alexis and my mom, I've never cared about another female the way I cared about Monique. She helped me through the roughest parts of my life, and I owe her for that. She saw Dennis hit me, and she heard him smack me around while she was staying with us in Michigan. Monique was with me, holding my hand, as I went through two of my abortions. She was there to pick me up every time I fell. And it was Monique and Alexis who pulled me out of my depression after my mom died.

I trusted her with all my heart and soul. She taught me to have self-respect. She taught me I didn't have to use sex to get approval from men. Monique was almost like a second mother to Alexis, and she was like a shrink to me. She knew me inside and out, and I doubt I'll ever have another friend as good as her.

She despised Dennis, and she wasn't afraid to let him know how she felt. The best parts of the worst years of my life were spent with Monique. We got into and out of a lot of trouble together, and we were one another's support group.

I remember when Monique and I went to see a couple of guys who played ball for the Detroit Lions—Chris Oldham, who I knew from Sacramento, and Ray Crockett. They were in training camp and were staying at a hotel in Auburn Hills, so we had to sneak into their room after bed check. Like most guys (and like Monique and me), they were looking for some fun with no strings attached. It was innocent fun, though, no sex. We were just kids getting a thrill by sneaking around.

Monique and I also hit the concert scene for a while. As Rodman's "woman," I was allowed backstage automatically. I knew some of the members of the L.A. Guns from when I lived in L.A., and we partied with them when they came through Detroit. We also partied with the Scorpions, Ratt, and Van Halen. I became pretty good friends with Van Halen's manager, a great guy named Scotti Roos. Monique and I weren't star fucking, we were just hanging out, partying with these dudes who loved having exotic, fun women around them. We had a blast.

By 1991, after Dennis had proven himself to be a less-than-faithful partner, Monique and I started hanging out with players from opposing basketball teams. I secretly hoped Dennis would find out and get hurt knowing I was going out with someone else. My hidden wish came true when word got back to him that I was seen leaving a club with one of the Washington Bullets. When he confronted me about it I did my best Dennis Rodman imitation: "What Washington Bullet? I was nowhere near that club." Etc., etc., etc. After that, he started demanding that I stay at home. He said it wasn't right for me to be seen out in public, since people knew we were a couple. I replied, "You do it. What's the difference? Because you're a guy?" It reminded me of when Wilt Chamberlain announced that he'd slept with twenty thousand women, and people started talking about how society treats men like gods when they sleep around, but when women do it they're sluts. Dennis didn't want to debate the issue. He just didn't want me going out.

Monique and I stayed out late sometimes, forcing Dennis to be the baby-sitter on the rare nights he stayed home. When I'd get in he'd give me the third degree: "Where've you been? Who've you been with?"

I'd tell him I was tired and didn't want to talk about it, figuring he was just getting some of his own medicine. "Fuck that," he'd say. "Tell me where you've been!"

"Good night, Dennis."

He really didn't like that. Dennis continued insisting I stay home. By then, Alexis was already walking, so I really didn't mind. I started staying in all the time to take care of her. Monique came over and our friendship continued. I wasn't as isolated as I had been before she and I met. And since we had done some pretty good partying, we didn't feel like we were missing out on anything. Besides, all the cool rock 'n' roll dudes in the world can't compete with how cool Alexis was.

Unfortunately, after all we went through, my friendship with Monique almost ended over a guy. I had been dating him, and then one day I noticed he was more interested in Monique than me. Just like that, she snaked him. Or at least that's how it seemed at the time. I was deeply hurt and I figured Monique and I would never regain our friendship.

But then one night, while I was working on this book, the doorbell rang. It was Pepper. We patched things up and talked for hours. The part of my heart that was hers got repaired that night, and we agreed not to let anything stupid, like a man, come between us again.

--- --- ---

I bought Dennis a set of drums for his birthday one year. Sometimes at night, when things were going well between us, he would play them. I used to love to listen to him play; it made me feel so proud. Granted, I'm no critic, but I must say he was really good. He'd pull me onto his lap and teach me how to play. It was times like those that made me think, *This is how it's supposed to be.* I was so happy sitting there, banging away on those drums. We'd be laughing and having such a great time, so close, so perfect. Those were the kinds of moments that would draw me back after one of our fights. I'd forget the fight and remember only the closeness and the fun. My mistake.

Playing drums wasn't the only fun we had. We used to go roller-skating and horseback riding. Dennis and I used to have these great races on horseback, always competing, always having fun and enjoying one another. It reminded me of riding horses when I was young and working at the stables during the summer.

And, of course, Dennis loved his video games. He was like a twelve-year-old. We'd go to video arcades and I'd watch as he tried to master one game after another. I loved to see him having so much fun, feeling so carefree. No pressure from the media, no celebrity ego getting in the way and causing problems.

But as the money came in and he surrounded himself with his groupies, he started hanging out more often at strip joints than at the video arcade. Now, in order to get his attention, I had to compete with not only the groupies, but also the strippers. That was a battle I usually lost. And as if that wasn't bad enough, there was also Mike Gold, his strip-club buddy and a guy Dennis worked very hard to make happy.

Dennis met Mike Gold in late 1987, just before I got pregnant with Alexis. Mike was a rep for L.A. Gear. He had a great deal of influence over Dennis, and he eventually used that influence to take advantage of him. One mannerism of Mike's that really annoyed me was that he seemed incapable of looking me in the eye when he talked to me. The guy left a bad taste in my mouth.

Thinking back, it was a miracle that I got pregnant at all during that time. It seemed like Dennis was surgically attached to Mike Gold. That shoe salesman/hustler had Dennis out almost every night and often all night. I began to see Mike Gold as the Devil on Dennis's shoulder, whispering things in his ear. He was whispering things that would take Dennis further and further from me, both physically and emotionally. He was one of those guys with transparent character who didn't stand for much except making a fast buck and having a good time. Dennis was just starting on that upward curve toward superstardom, and he needed a mentor with strong ethics and a sure moral compass to help him find his way. Fate fucked Dennis over and gave him Mike Gold as a cruel joke.

During my pregnancy, Dennis and Gold lived in smoky strip clubs, watching naked girls gyrating. You would have thought Dennis and Gold *owned* these strip joints, they spent so much time in them. They were such pigs when they got together. They didn't have any respect for women and they acted like a couple of kids.

One night after Alexis was born, a large group of us went out to a local restaurant. Dennis had been making sexual comments about every woman in the place, particularly the waitresses. I was starting to lose my cool when he flagged down our waitress. "When do you get off?" he asked. The poor, confused girl looked at Dennis, then at all the expectant faces at our table. "Uh, six?" she answered. Dennis laughed. "Can I watch?" he said. The table exploded into guffaws.

That did it. I had been adjusting Alexis' high chair so I was standing up. I leaned over and smacked Dennis hard on the top of the head. The table fell silent as he winced. "The fuck you doin'?" he said incredulously.

I looked around the table, then at him. "It's one thing to act like a fuckin' pig when I'm not around," I said, "but don't you ever show me disrespect in public again." I sat down. The up mood around the table was pretty much shot after that, but I'd made my point.

That's an early example of one of the reasons why Dennis used to refer to me, usually behind my back, as "psycho." When Dennis and Gold were around me they sometimes spoke in pig latin, thinking I wouldn't understand. Pig latin. How appropriate.

The exploits with Mike Gold were a daily thing. Apparently they found each other absolutely fascinating, because they were inseparable. I began to feel jealous of Gold, almost as if he were another woman with whom Dennis was being unfaithful. Don't get me wrong—they didn't have *that* kind of relationship. On the contrary, they engaged in childish things like farting contests. I was concerned about what kind of father Dennis would make when one of his big goals off the court was beating Mike Gold at cutting farts.

During my pregnancy, Dennis must have realized he was neglecting me, because one day he brought home a Rottweiler puppy. I named her Willie, and as she grew older she became very protective of me because I was the only person she really knew. It seemed like the only time Dennis paid Willie any attention was when he was beating her. He'd beat her when she got excited and peed on stuff—which happened on only a few occasions—and one time I had to lay on top of her to protect her when Dennis tried to pound her for pooping on the carpet. I don't know why *he* got so mad. I was the one who cleaned it up.

Dennis had Mike Gold, I had Willie. Willie was pretty much my only companion, what with Dennis either on the road or shacking up locally with one of his ho's or just carousing all night with Gold. Willie did everything with me from going to the store to sleeping with me. She must have sensed my need for love.

One thing my pregnancy didn't affect was Dennis's social life. He and Gold were always out catting around, and Dennis probably figured, "Hey, she's pregnant, she's got Willie, what else could she want?" I wanted my man, at home. At least once in a while.

That's how I was feeling at 4 A.M. one morning, when Dennis had not come home. I wasn't too worried something had happened to him. If a Piston got hurt or in trouble, there probably would be ten people in line to offer donor organs or blood. I knew he was with you-know-who. I grabbed Willie and we got into the car and headed out into the predawn blackness to find my man and bring him home.

I went over to Mike Gold's apartment but didn't see any cars in the driveway. I then went on a sight-seeing tour of the Cribs of Dennis's Whores, trying to find him. By this time, I was all too familiar with where Dennis's ho's lived. But his car wasn't at any of those places.

It was now about 5:30 A.M. Frustrated, I went back to Gold's place. Bingo! Dennis's car was there. I went up to the door and knocked. I knew they were inside, but no one answered. I knocked harder. Nothing. *Okay,* I thought, *I'll give you a reason to come out.* I went over to Dennis's car and started to pound on the windshield as if I were going to break it. Suddenly the front door burst open and Dennis came running out—wearing only his boxers! He stormed over to me. "Would you just go the fuck home? You got no right bein' here. This is Mike's place!"

He went back inside. I got back into my car and Willie nuzzled up against me. I burst into tears. Driving home, blinded by my tears and with my emotions in full play, I wasn't watching the speedometer. Turns out I was driving over 70 miles an hour in a 30 zone, and though *I* really wasn't aware of my speed, the officer from the Southfield Police Department who pulled out behind me was.

I pulled over. He came up to the window and started to ask for my license when Willie went berserk. She wouldn't quiet down, so I got out of the car and shut the door. The cop noticed I was pregnant and had been crying. At first he thought I was in labor and asked what was wrong. I told him I had been looking for my fiancé. He ran a check on my license plate and realized who my fiancé was. The cop was kind and understanding, and though he didn't give me a ticket, he did remind me I had a responsibility to my baby to drive safely.

He was right, of course. As I got back into the car, calmer now, I realized Dennis may have had a lot of power over me, but if my baby was going to make it, I was the one who needed to take control and watch out for her. Even though I was sick with anxiety over the situation with Dennis, at that point I made a promise to my unborn baby I would never put her in harm's way again.

A funny thing about Dennis was that he worked harder at pleasing vague acquaintances than he worked at pleasing Alexis or me. By now Gold was Dennis's marketing and PR man and "best friend." So now I had groupies, strippers, and Mike Gold to contend with.

In the off-season, Dennis and I used to drive to Oklahoma to visit his friends and his surrogate family, the Riches. After he started hanging out with Mike, our trips to Oklahoma stopped—at least they did for me. Dennis kept going, only now he went with Mike. Before Mike Gold came along, Dennis and I would go out to dinner after games, usually with Alexis. After they became pals I was sent straight home with Alexis while Dennis and Mike spent the night on the town, usually coming home around three in the morning. Almost everything Dennis and I used to do together, he was now doing with Gold. Gold was Dennis's confidant and, it turned out, he was also Dennis's alibi machine. He covered for Dennis like a beach umbrella.

I didn't like Gold from the beginning, and it wasn't just because he monopolized my lover's time. There was just something snaky about him. I told Dennis, but he wouldn't listen. He and Michael were more like a husband and wife than he and I were. Some people even wondered if Mike was sucking Dennis's dick.

The Detroit Pistons organization shared my distrust for Mr. Gold. They seemed to sense the same thing I sensed about him, something that wasn't to be trusted. These suspicions seemed to be on target when Mike Gold was accused of embezzling twenty-five thousand dollars from Dennis's basketball camp. It was quite a scandal.

Honestly, though, I don't think it matters whether Mike Gold did these things. If he hadn't done them, someone else would have. That is a certainty in the world of professional sports and probably in the music, television, and film industries as well. Celebrity and money are magnets for the Mike Golds of the world. Sure, there are some straight-up people, too, but the good money is on watching your back and being sure about who you're dealing with.

Even after the alleged embezzlement, Dennis continued his friendship with Mike Gold, but they spent less time together than they once had. He was never short on "friends," however. There was a constant stream of young men, mostly under the age of eighteen, all white, who came and went. Dennis seemed completely unable to distinguish between genuine friends and people who simply fawned over him or just wanted a piece of his fame or his money.

There was one kid, about eighteen years old, who managed to gain Dennis's trust. I knew him only as P.J. or A.J. or something like that. He'd hang out like all the others, playing video games and telling Dennis what a great basketball player he was. Dennis fell for it every time. I saw how hard this kid was trying to wheedle his way into Dennis's life (and apparently into his wallet as well), and I warned Dennis about him.

But I was wrong. The kid didn't want to get into Dennis's wallet. He wanted to get into his checkbook. One day the kid stole a blank check from Dennis. Did he cash it for a hundred bucks and blow it at the video arcade? Nope. He bought himself a car! A brand-spanking-new 300 ZX!

Charges were filed, but Dennis was so embarrassed by the whole thing—embarrassed that he couldn't tell a friend from a thief—that he dropped the charges when the kid's father paid him back.

Dennis was also embarrassed that he had been warned and had not heeded the warning. The thing he hated most was that I was right. I never rubbed it in, but he knew I was thinking, *I told you so*. And eventually he'd let me have it for that.

The thing that was most surprising, and most revealing, was that he let A.J. or P.J. right back into the fold, just like Mike Gold. And I don't think it was a matter of Dennis being a forgiving kind of guy either. Rather, I think he was just naive about who to trust.

— — —

During the Pistons' championship season, Mike Gold had an ever-growing and always negative influence on Dennis's behavior and attitude. Dennis was no longer the sweet, shy young man who first put the moves on me at Confetti's a year and a half earlier. His confidence was growing, and the perks of the job were too tempting for him to resist.

One of the perks—at least that's how the players in the league see it—is that lots of women throw themselves at the players. Some of these women are pretty skanky, but there are some beauties out there, too. It's hard to compete with some of these young, hard bodies when you're pregnant or just after you've given birth, and believe me, it *was* a competition, especially in Dennis's mind. If my appearance didn't cut it, he was going to start looking elsewhere. This was another change that came over him after he started hanging out with Mike Gold. Dennis used to care about how I felt inside and what I was thinking. Now he just cared about my looks. The superficial was all that appealed to him. And what could be more superficial than a stripper's body?

Mike Gold got Dennis into the strip-club scene. I think that's where he gets his skewed idea of what a woman's breasts should always look like.

When I asked Dennis to spend more time at home with Alexis and me and less time at the strip joints, he'd look at me disapprovingly and say, "You wonder why I hang out at strip clubs? Those girls' tits are firm, yours hang too low now. Your body turns me off."

His severe lack of both tact and maturity led him to say things like that. I'm sure he'd attempt to defend himself by saying he was just being honest, thereby confirming the charge of tactlessness and immaturity. Regardless of the analysis, his statements about my body turning him off didn't do my self-esteem a lot of good.

Later, when I asked him to stop going to the clubs, he said, "I go to strip bars and that's final. I ain't giving it up, and if you don't like it, then pack your shit and go home."

He could be so sensitive and understanding.

As much as I'd like to put all the blame on Mike Gold, I can't. Dennis could have said no to Mike, but he didn't. Mike would say, "C'mon, Dennis, what's it gonna hurt?" Dennis, lacking the courage to tell this little shithead to fuck off, simply caved in to the temptation. He had a hard time saying no to anyone but me and Alexis. Maybe it's because he knew I loved him so much that he felt he could do almost anything, and I'd always be there for him.

Dennis's perfect-breast fixation became most evident when I was breast-feeding Alexis. He absolutely hated it. In his view the act was both "gross *and* disgusting." I tried to explain to him how breast milk helps build up an infant's immune system and helps ensure normal development. Dennis would counter with, "My momma fed me with a bottle, and look at how I turned out." Of course, that was all the reason I needed to continue breast-feeding Alexis.

Alexis's well-being was the only thing I ever put ahead of Dennis. Everything else in my cockeyed existence revolved around keeping him happy. He wasn't easy to satisfy. Except for brief moments, he didn't want to have much to do with Alexis or me. When he saw us, all he could see was responsibility, and that was the last thing he wanted as his fame began to grow. I also think that after I gave birth to Alexis, I began to represent motherhood to Dennis, and as a result he started to treat me the way he treated his mother. In other words, he started treating me like shit.

Dennis's dad abandoned the family when Dennis was three. By now I think everyone knows that the irresponsible coward's name is Philander Rodman. That's right, *philander,* as in "to make love insincerely." I see in the papers that he continues his indefensible behavior to this day, boasting that he has fathered twenty-seven children in the Philippines, as if that somehow could be a good thing. Just what the world needs, more of that reprobate's genes in the gene pool. I have often wondered how much better my life (and Alexis's) would have been if Dennis's dad had been a good father and raised his son to be a good man. Of course, since you get only one chance to raise your child, it's too late for Philander, just as it's too late for Dennis.

Growing up, Dennis's sisters got most of their mother's attention. They were better students than he was, and they were excellent athletes. He felt slighted by the way his mother treated him as a child, so when he hit the big-time and his mom called up looking for a big payday, Dennis was thinking pay*back*. He has a lot of chips on his shoulder, and one of the biggest is due to his relationship with his mom.

Dennis perceived Alexis and me as a weight around his neck, and his way of dealing with it was to reject us. We lived in the same house, but we didn't see much of him. He stayed out late after home games, slept late whenever he could, and of course was on the road for half the year. And I saw lots of credit card charges from strip joints coast to coast.

He used to say that my breast-feeding Alexis reminded him of something animals do. I'm not sure what he thought humans were—plants, maybe?—but I suggested that he could learn a few things from animals, things like loyalty and unconditional love. He always thought my affection for animals was a bit extreme. But in my experience they're more trustworthy than most people, especially those in the NBA.

Here's what I mean by that. After returning home from a visit with my mom in Sacramento, I was in the bathroom unpacking my toiletries when I found a little surprise in the cabinet under the sink. It was a half-empty bottle of prescription medication for killing crabs (body lice). The prescription was Dennis's. I walked out to where he was sitting and held the bottle out for him to see. "What the shit is this?" I asked.

For the life of him, Dennis couldn't think of a thing to say. He eventually cobbled together one of the world's lamest excuses, something brilliant like, "Oh, that? Well, I had a cough and so I asked the team doctor to call me in a prescription, and I guess they screwed up at the pharmacy. Can you believe that?"

No. I couldn't. "Hello?" I said sarcastically. "I am *not* one of your stupid-ass bitches who would buy an idiotic excuse like that. I'm the smart one, remember? I'm the one who always catches you doing stupid stuff. Want to try again?"

He shrugged. Like I said earlier, he hated being caught in a lie. I held the bottle of lice poison up to the light and looked at it. "So let me ask you, Dennis, when you drank half of this for your cough, exactly how did it taste?"

Once again, he didn't have an answer. I decided not to wait around to see if he was going to try a second excuse. I turned and went back into the bathroom to see if Dennis's little cootie friends were making themselves at home in my nether regions.

I spent the next day doing extra laundry, getting the sheets clean, disinfecting the mattress, vacuuming, and otherwise delousing our home. I don't know which of Dennis's sluts gave him the crabs, but I always suspected it was Karen Stewart, one of Dennis's favorites and a huge thorn in the side of our relationship.

# CHAPTER 5

## Welcome to My Nightmare

Aᶠᵀᴇʀ Aᴌᴇxɪs ᴡᴀs ʙᴏʀɴ ɪɴ Sᴇᴘᴛᴇᴍʙᴇʀ **1988,** Dᴇɴɴɪs ᴀɴᴅ I decided we needed a bigger place for the three of us. He was making more money, we had a child, and our $620-a-month apartment was looking pretty small, so we found a condo in West Bloomfield and leased it for $1,400 a month. The Pistons were now in their new digs in the Palace, and our move put us a few miles north of the old place and gave Dennis about the same commute time as before. We got settled in about the same time the Pistons played their first game in the Palace.

Moving into the condo after the confines of our little apartment was like getting out of jail. I had so much space to work with. It was a nice triplex with two huge bedrooms upstairs. It was great to have a large, separate room for Alexis. The next level down had a living room, kitchen, and dining room, each full of nothing but black leather furniture, as Dennis had insisted. On the ground floor was the entertainment area with Dennis's drums and all of his video gear, including his camera and tripod. That equipment was later used to record some things that made me go crazy, but right now, everything was fine. Sort of.

Dennis's attitude toward me began to change more and more. When I was pregnant, he let me know he was repulsed by my impending motherhood, and when I started to show he really tweaked out. He wouldn't even come close to me. After Alexis was born, I figured (and hoped) we would go back to the normal sex life that two people, who are living together *and* engaged, share. Wrong.

I think by then Dennis had so many bitches on the side—Annalisa, Tracy, Karen Stewart, and God knows how many others who I didn't know about—that he was spread too thin to keep me even marginally satisfied. He started to act like somebody who works three different jobs and answers the phone with the wrong company name. Dennis was juggling so many women that he started getting confused as to who was who. That's when he started referring to me as Yo. Yo was a good shorthand for him, because by calling *every* woman Yo, he couldn't fuck up and call me Annalisa or Annalisa Annie, which he had been doing from time to time.

He started barking, "Yo, you gotta wash my practice shorts. Yo, go fill up the tank, yo. Yo, get offa my back!" Pretty soon I got tired of being reduced to a street pronoun and would snap back, "Yo is not my name. Yo isn't on my driver's license or my birth certificate. My name is Annie. I answer to Annie." He'd just roll his eyes and chalk up my protests to bitchiness, and he kept calling me Yo, like some idiot street kid. For a while, that is. You see, I'm really stubborn and kept calling him on it. Finally I won and he went back to calling me Annie. I guess he figured he could put a little extra effort into remembering my name since I was his fiancée. I guess Annalisa and Karen and all of the others had to settle for Yo.

After Alexis was born I took a look in the mirror and decided it was time to kick some ass. I didn't want to give Dennis the tiniest excuse for not being attracted to me. What I didn't realize was that Dennis was a master at changing the rules without telling you.

I resolved to turn myself into the babe I had been before the baby, and not because of my own vanity. I figured the best way to assure that Alexis would have a father around the house was to make sure he found the mother attractive. So I got busy. I had yet to see my twenty-fourth birthday, and I didn't want to fall into the trap that a lot of women do after having a child—you start thinking of yourself as a middle-aged woman who can let herself go to seed. I didn't want to look fifty-five at thirty-five, so I came up with a plan.

I started going to the gym religiously and pumped weights for hours. I also went to a tanning salon a few times a week. I was starting to look like I lived in Venice Beach, California, instead of West Bloomfield, Michigan. I went back to the sexier clothes I wore before the pregnancy, and I cut my hair short and dyed it blond to look like Marie Fredriksson, the vocalist in the Swedish pop group Roxette, who Dennis thought was so hot. I thought the transformation would get him hot. Instead, it gave him more reasons to complain.

I'm a big-framed girl, and I've always been fit. My ideal weight was 140, and for 5'10" that's pretty darn good. When I started my training I watched what I ate, but nevertheless I was gaining weight. It was all muscle. Pretty soon I was bulked up to around 160, and I looked like a major Amazon. I loved it! The feeling of power and well-being I had was indescribable. And then Dennis noticed. He was at our gym one day, and my trainer said to him, "Man, your girl is strong! She's doing reverse squats with four 45-pound plates on each side!"

Was Dennis pleased? Not exactly. He came home and asked me if I was doing steroids. His accusation flattered me at first, then pissed me off. "You can't build that much muscle and not be takin' steroids, Annie," he declared.

I asked him if he realized how much I had been hitting the gym lately. I told him I was working out all the time, so it was no wonder I had bulked up. "I only did it for you," I said.

He just shook his head. "Regardless how much trainin' you're doin', this kinda result is not possible. You gotta be doin' steroids."

I felt like Dennis suddenly didn't know me, that our nearly three years together were wiped out by his suspicions. I thought he knew me better than to think I would ever put something like that in my body. I knew that steroids ruined your health, and the last thing I was going to do was destroy my liver, especially with a daughter I'd like to see grow up. I had prayed he would acknowledge all of my hard work, but when he did it came in an accusation.

I quit lifting and started doing cardiovascular workouts. Then I switched from my measured intake of high protein and low fat to a diet of Dexatrim. The Dexatrim was great. I had plenty of energy and no hunger. Problem was, I was burning up my own body. Pretty soon the muscle melted off and I passed my former ideal weight of 140 on the way to a sticklike 120. I didn't feel as good as I had, but I didn't want Dennis to think I was a steroid-pumped musclehead. I got what I wanted. As they say, though, be careful what you wish for, because you might get it.

When I had lost the weight and started becoming way too skinny, Dennis decided my weight loss couldn't be normal. Well, no shit, Sherlock. He didn't take into consideration any psychological reasons why I might have lost the weight, like trying to please a lover with impossible standards. No, Dennis came to the conclusion I was either on crank or cocaine or both. After two nose jobs I have had difficulty breathing at times. He knew that, but chose to link it to my "stimulant abuse." I've since heard that cocaine opens your nasal passages. I didn't know that little fact at the time, so I couldn't offer it in my defense. I copped to the Dexatrim, but it's hardly in the same universe as cocaine or methamphetamine.

The whole thing was ridiculous. He started going through my personal items: my purse, my jacket pockets, my car, and wherever else he thought I was hiding my secret "stash." Just like the steroid accusation, Dennis's belief that I was on stimulants was idiotic. He knew I wouldn't touch drugs any more than he would, so when I began to think he was half serious, I wasn't sure what to do. One night I realized he was completely serious.

He had taken one of his Mustangs in for some "very important" maintenance: He was having a TV and VCR installed. (I tried to picture him watching *Robocop* on his way to the Palace.) In the course of installing those items, the repair shop had to remove the passenger seat. When they did, they found something.

That evening I heard him drive up, and I went into the bathroom to check my hair. Suddenly I heard the door from the garage slam hard. Then Dennis started yelling, "Annie! Annie, get down here!"

I rushed downstairs, thinking it was an emergency. It was, and it was all in his mind. When I got to the kitchen he was hunched over the sink, upset. He turned to me and held up a small vial. "What the fuck is this?"

I shrugged. "I don't know. What is it?"

"You know what it is!" he screamed. "It's fuckin' cocaine!" Then he got my purse, spilled everything out, and started rummaging through it. My wallet, keys, hairbrush, and Kleenex weren't quite the drug paraphernalia he was looking for. He took a hard look at my Tylenol. Then he turned, grabbed me, and pushed me up against the wall. That's when it hit home that he really, truly believed I was doing drugs. "You are doing drugs, Annie, I know you are, goddamn it!" Then he yelled, "Why? I love you, damn it! Why?"

"Dennis, I don't know what you're talking about," I said. "I'm not taking any drugs and I never have taken any!"

I asked him where the vial of so-called cocaine came from. Turns out it was under the car seat when they pulled it out at the shop. I reminded Dennis that I rarely rode in his car. I also pointed out that I was sure there were "plenty of women who've been in that car a helluva lot more than me." He couldn't disagree. I told him that if he really thought I was on drugs, then I'd take a drug test, here and now, and put an end to the bullshit accusations. I suggested we go somewhere right then and I'd take a test. He let it go.

A few days later I think he found out where the vial came from. He didn't mention it again, nor did the subject of the drug test ever come up again. Then he did something that surprised me almost as much as the drug accusation. One night he arrived home with a bag full of stuff from a health food store: vitamins, protein powder, amino supplements, all kinds of things to help me gain the weight back. He gave me strict instructions what to take and when, and I did what he said. In a short time, my weight was back to normal, and I felt a lot better.

After the drug accusations, his trying to help me return to normal made me believe that Dennis cared, that he really did love me. I felt that separation from him when he seemed to lock out everything he knew about me. I was shocked to realize someone that close to me could get me so wrong—drugs have always been a foreign subject to me. As the child of an alcoholic, I vowed long ago never to let any substance run my life. If Dennis had found my true addiction, he would have been surprised: He was my addiction.

To escape the turmoil of my life, I would often drive over to Farmington Hills and visit St. Fabian's Catholic Church. Despite all the trying things that happened to me over the years, I could always find at least a little peace behind the walls of a church. I am a very spiritual person and believe in forgiveness, and I believe that God is loving and hears your words of prayer.

I would pray for Dennis.

I would pray for Dennis to love me more. I would pray for him to give up his women. And I would pray for our little family and its survival. I knew God would hear me, but God does not always answer you in the way you expect. I prayed for God to come to Dennis and to show him the blessings he had in his daughter and his loving wife and his great talent and all of his success. I prayed so hard that sometimes I would get the words mixed up and I'd have to start over. Somehow I think God knew what I was saying.

Dennis went to church twice that I know of: once when Mom died, and once right after I had had an abortion. He saw how the abortion affected me and accompanied me to light some candles. I went to ask for forgiveness for what I had done. As I've said, the abortions I've had will follow me always, but on that particular day I was at a low point. I knelt down, crossed myself, and started my prayers. I asked for forgiveness over and over. My shame was overwhelming. Then I prayed for Alexis. Then I prayed for Dennis.

I still pray for Dennis.

— — —

Christmas 1988 was more important than any previous Christmas because it was Alexis's first. We had just moved into the condo in West Bloomfield, and now we were about to have our first Christmas in our new home with our new baby. It was going to be magical for me.

I settled into my routine of taking care of Alexis and the house, then attending to my workout. This was just prior to Dennis's allegations that I was on steroids, and I was getting fit but hadn't bulked up yet. I missed Mom and the family and wished we all could have been together for the holiday, but I contented myself to celebrating it with my new family. I decorated the house in a festive way. Sometimes in the evening, before Dennis would get home from a game or late practice, I would just sit and gaze at our living room and its decorations and think about what a bright future I had with Dennis and Alexis. Tears would come to my eyes, I was so happy.

I knew about the other women Dennis was keeping on the side, but during these special moments that problem didn't seem as big, and I really thought we would work them through. I went shopping and carefully picked out gifts for Alexis and Dennis and my family and friends back home. I bought Alexis a bunch of little things, but the gifts were really more important to me (as she was too young to notice). I think any new mother would understand that.

When Christmas Eve rolled around, Dennis decided he wanted more exciting company and said he was going out. I had pictured a "perfect" Christmas Eve, the three of us sitting around in our new place, basking in the warmth of the season, but I guess that was unrealistic. So Alexis and I spent Christmas Eve alone while Dennis went out and did who knows what.

He came home late, or should I say early on Christmas morning, and wasn't interested in any Christmas activities. He announced he was going out again later. I told him I wanted him to stay home and at least spend Alexis's first Christmas with us. He said she wouldn't know the difference. Our discussion rapidly escalated into an argument, then into a full-fledged fight. Couldn't we have been—for once—like a normal family?

Dennis left. I sat down in the living room, looked at all the gifts I had carefully picked out, and started to cry. Later I composed myself and brought Alexis into the living room. I wrapped her in one of her blankets and sat her up on the sofa and we opened presents. Then I went ahead and cooked the Christmas dinner I had been planning for a while. I sat down and ate it while Alexis drank formula from her bottle.

At the end of the evening I went to bed. Later I heard Dennis come home. I turned over and pretended to be asleep. He got into bed and cuddled up to me. I started crying. He held me close and asked what was wrong. I said, "It was her first Christmas." Without saying a word, he just rolled over and went to sleep.

— — —

A lot has been said about Dennis's sexuality. Many people have wondered if he is gay or bisexual or whatever. All I can say is, I've never seen him have sex with a man. We used to take drives through Dallas during the summers, and one of his biggest thrills was parking outside gay bars and watching men come and go. I chalked it up to curiosity, which it was, and I never thought much of it because Dennis was heterosexual. At least he seemed that way.

I'm still a little naive about certain things, and I never figured he wanted to have sex with a man. But one time he asked me, "What if you caught me havin' sex with a dude? What would you do?" I thought it was Dennis being Dennis, and I just laughed it off. Now, maybe I'm not so sure. Maybe he is bisexual. I don't know. I don't care. At the time I didn't pay it any attention.

Someone once asked me if I've ever had sex with a woman. The answer is no. I like sex, but I like it with men. To me, there's nothing more beautiful than the male anatomy. I did things some people think are kinky, crazy, and wild. I did things some people think are immoral and dangerous. They may be right. But I did them, and what's done is done. But I've never been interested in having sex with a woman.

Except for some close friends, like Monique or some of the girls I modeled with, I don't have a lot of girlfriends. There are only four females I associate with who I know are down for me 101 percent: Alexis, Monique, my friend Shannon Reday, and Paula Wilhite.

Anyway, I prefer—or at least I used to prefer—the company of men. I've been that way since I was a tomboy. These days, just being alone or with Alexis is fine with me. After all my relationships I'm unsure whether I'm really suited for marriage. I have a hard time imagining waking up next to the same person every day for the rest of my life.

Sex isn't as important to me as it once was. I used to think it was the next best thing to peanut butter and jelly sandwiches. What does that leave? Masturbation? No thanks, I'm too busy for did-dling. Fortunately I've found a great guy with whom I'm in a monogamous relationship. So far, so good, but I'm being cautious.

As for Dennis? Someday, if he comes out and says he's been having sex with a guy or guys or maybe a whole team, I'll wish him well. And all of them, too.

– – –

I think the first time Dennis assaulted me was in June 1988, the time he slammed my head into the bathtub. I can't remember the first time he actually hit me, but I'm drawing a pretty thin line here between getting hit by Dennis and getting hit in the head by a bathtub.

The whole process started out with verbal abuse. Then he felt it was okay to shove me. That led to him hitting me. There were many instances of Dennis grabbing me by the neck and holding it tight until I was gagging for air. But his favorite thing was smacking me with an open hand. One time he left his handprint on the side of my face.

The first time I hit him was in 1988 or 1989, when we were liv-ing in the condo in West Bloomfield. I had just learned about one of Dennis's Texas fucks, a girl named Sherry. She called the condo. When I answered she was slow to respond, but eventually she said, "Sorry, I didn't know he had a girlfriend."

"Well, he does," I said, and I hung up. "At least for a little while longer," I muttered.

I was pissed. I wanted blood. I went looking for Dennis.

The first person I saw was a high school basketball coach sit-ting downstairs. He was waiting for Dennis so he could ask him to make an appearance at a high school game. I soon found Dennis sitting on the bed, watching TV. He was so arrogant and rude that he was making the guy wait until his show was over. I walked in and just slapped Dennis upside the head, not for being rude to the high school coach, but for giving Sherry our phone number. He didn't try to defend himself and didn't even flinch, like he felt he had it coming. He looked at me with hate in his eyes. "You are lucky there's someone downstairs," he snarled. Later, probably during a commercial break, he told the high school coach he was going to have to get back to him.

Dennis was stunned that I hit him. He was even more stunned that I started to make a habit of fighting fire with fire. But I was damned if I was going to go down without a fight. After I started fighting back, of course, the violence escalated. And it was always about women, never about money, or Alexis, or anything else.

This was fairly early in his career. He wasn't a real celebrity yet, but he was certainly more famous than he'd ever imagined. The Pistons were improving but weren't yet the champions they would soon be. Dennis, however, was changing right in front of my eyes from the sweet guy I met a year or so earlier into a real son of a bitch.

We both would have avoided a lot of pain if Dennis had had the sense or the decency (if that's what you call it) to cheat only when he was out of town. But no, he had to have some girls living practically down the street. He gave women our home phone number. He fucked them in the house where his wife and child lived.

I don't know how many times I walked in and could literally smell that he'd had some bitch in our bed. I'd find makeup on the pillowcases, and it wasn't Dennis's—he wasn't into that yet. He either didn't have the sense to wash the damn things, or he was so domineering that he wanted me to do it. Sometimes, when he was feeling particularly clever, he'd turn the sheets over in an attempt to cover his tracks. Or when he wasn't a fully functioning genius, he'd strip the sheets and leave them in the laundry room where I could find them.

One time, in 1989 or 1990, a woman named Tracy actually had the balls to call the police to my own house because I was harassing and threatening her. She wasn't lying! I had called Tracy's parent's house, where she was living, and I told her in no uncertain terms that she had better stay the hell away from Dennis. She stayed on the line the whole time. I was surprised she didn't hang up on me, but since she didn't, I simply let her know the danger she was in.

The next day, when the police showed up at our condo, I discovered why she hadn't hung up. She'd been recording the conversation on her answering machine. She then gave the tape to the cops and they were following up on the matter. I admitted that I had threatened her and, after talking to the police for a little while, I said I wouldn't do it again. I just did what I had to do. I was just trying to protect what was mine.

Another time I was so scared of Dennis after one of our fights that I called the police and asked them to stay with me while I packed my bags. I was afraid of what Dennis might do if he came home and caught me trying to leave. I don't recall why I was more afraid of him that time than any other, but it was the only time I ever called the police for protection like that.

I had to call the cops a lot when Alexis and I were living at the Adagio Apartments. One time my mom called while Dennis and I were fighting. He wouldn't let me talk to her, and Mom later said she could hear me crying in the background. She called the police. They arrived in fifteen minutes. I lied and said everything was okay. They asked to talk to Dennis. He came out and told them everything was cool, that we were just horsing around. The cops asked me if that was true. I lied and said yes. I don't think they believed me because they stayed parked outside for a while.

I wish I had earned frequent flyer miles for all the trips I took between Detroit and Sacramento during the course of my relationship with Dennis. I'd probably be eligible for a free round trip on the Concorde by now. I can't even remember how many times I went back to California. I would catch Dennis in a lie, or I'd find photos of him fondling a girlfriend, or I'd get word about him being with another of his many sluts, and I'd pack my bags and zip back to Sacramento.

Alexis must have thought everyone took cross-country flights at least once a month. She always liked going back to Sacramento to see her Nana and Papa, and she was always hoping to get a set of those Flight Wings that the attendants give out to kids. The one good thing was that Alexis was too young to understand the reasons for all the trips. She was just a good little traveler who liked to sit by the window and look at the little houses below. Whenever we flew out of Detroit she'd insist that she could see our house. "There's Daddy!" she'd exclaim. She's a cutie.

Anyway, after escaping to California, Dennis would eventually hunt me down. One time, in 1990, I was back in Sacramento and had started dating a guy named Mike Scholl. Dennis came looking for me, got into my apartment, and forced a girlfriend of mine to tell him where I was. After learning I was at Mike's, Dennis called.

"Why are you doing this to me, Annie?" he asked. "You're killing me." He pleaded for me to come back to my apartment so we could talk.

"You don't want to talk," I replied. "You want me to come back so you can beat me."

"I'm too low to hit you," he said. "I just want to talk."

Sucker that I was, I went back to the apartment, where he was waiting. I think my friend was so scared of Dennis that she left. I didn't get halfway up the stairs before he grabbed me by the arm and pulled me outside and to a nearby field, shoving me in front of him. He's unbelievably strong under normal circumstances, but when he's mad it seems like his strength doubles. I knew what he was capable of when he was like this, and I felt like I was being marched to my execution. He suddenly picked me up and threw me hard onto the ground. Then he kicked me like I was some stupid, disobedient animal. I was screaming for help, but since we were out in the field I guess no one could hear me.

He beat me up pretty good that night, all the while blaming me for making him do it, the way he always did. And, as I always did, I eventually went back for more. My behavior is why I convinced myself that I was *addicted* to Dennis. Why else would I return to a man who I knew would do this to me over and over? It's part of a cycle of violence that too many women get caught up in, and it's not easy to escape. It happens to women like myself and lots of other women who don't get the chance to write a book about it.

— — —

In January 1989 Alexis was just over three months old, and we were still at the West Bloomfield condo. Because I was still nursing her, somehow I got it in my head that I couldn't get pregnant so soon after having a baby.

I was wrong.

There were two things Dennis didn't know at that point: one, 1989 would be a huge year for him and the Pistons, and two, I was pregnant. When I confirmed the pregnancy with the doctor, I started planning how to break it to Dennis. I had no idea how he'd take it. In the back of my mind was the rationale that since we had once talked about having at least three kids, this would put us closer to that goal. But there was another thing that nagged me: Dennis's unpredictability.

When I finally told him I honestly wasn't sure whether he'd hug me or scream at me. He did neither. He paced around the room, then said with complete finality that there was no way we could take care of two children so close in age. I felt there was some logic to what he was saying, but who said having kids is logical? There are a zillion people with less resources than we had and with lots more kids. Since Dennis wasn't agreeing with me, there was only one option, and it scared me to death.

I was raised Catholic. As a Catholic, the word *abortion* is not in your vocabulary. When Dennis suggested it as our only way out, I froze. I thought there had to be another way since *I couldn't have an abortion.* But there was no other way. I suddenly felt like I was drowning. I had no good options. My only choice was to do something that terrified me both physically and spiritually. The joy of caring for Alexis was now overshadowed by this dark plan to end the existence of another life growing inside me. I had always despised the idea of abortion as a form of birth control, and I had no respect for women who stooped to that. Now it was my turn to walk in their shoes.

On the day of the procedure, Dennis went with me and we didn't have anyone to watch Alexis. So he followed me into the doctor's office, carrying Alexis as she slept in her car seat. I was led into a room with an examination bed and a bunch of equipment. I made Dennis wait outside with Alexis. I just couldn't look at her while I ended the life of her little brother or sister.

The doctor came in, and after a quick exam, he turned to a nearby machine and made some adjustments. Then he reached for a suction hose connected to the machine, pulled it over, snapped on a nozzle, and inserted it between my legs. He turned on the machine and said the procedure would take about five minutes. It was the longest five minutes of my life. I looked over at the jar attached to the machine and watched as fluid and blood and tissue began to spurt into it. The pain of the suction was extreme, but it was nothing compared to the agony I felt in my heart.

I swear to you I *felt* that living thing detach from me.

I remember thinking with sudden horror, Can *my baby* feel this, too? I looked at the jar and the remains of what would have been my second child. When the doctor was done he left the room for a while, and I lay there and stared at that jar with the spattered blood and pieces of tissue. Then I had a strange thought. I wondered if I were to drink the contents, would they go back inside me and return to where they belonged? It sounds gross, but I was very emotional and felt that jar held a part of me that I wanted to put back. I hated myself for what I had just done.

Soon Dennis came in with Alexis. Still on the table, I took her in my arms and cried. Through my tears I asked Dennis, "What have I done? Why did I do this? Why did you think it was best we do this?"

He just said, "You're gonna be okay."

I looked at him. "Am I? Am I gonna be okay, Dennis? Will I really? I'll tell you now, I'll never go through this again, with or without you, no matter what you say." He just patted my shoulder and told me I was going to be okay. He said it was just my emotions talking. But at that moment I promised myself I would never do it again. I later broke that promise.

I don't blame Dennis for everything that happened. A woman has control of her body and makes the decision to do what she does. Someone else may put pressure on her—be it a husband, boyfriend, or some advocate group—either to have an abortion or to not have one. But ultimately she decides: She makes the call, she lies on the table. She lives with it.

I have had four abortions. I am deeply sorry I did. Each one of those events is burned into my memory, and not a day goes by that I don't think about it and regret it. I think every woman should have the right to choose what she does with her body, but know this: *Be prepared to pay the price.*

Certain days of the year still haunt me. After each abortion I calculated the due dates of those babies, and on those days I do not
celebrate; rather, I say a prayer and ask for forgiveness. I ask God
to look kindly on me despite my sins. I ask that those little spirits,
who were on their way to becoming a son or daughter to me, forgive me for the terrible way I ended their journey toward life. Had
they become my children, I would have showered them with the
same kind of love I give Alexis. But unlike Alexis, I did not give
them a chance.

After each abortion, one of the ways I dealt with the pain was
to come up with names for what would have been my other children. I think about what kind of lives they might have had, and I
picture them in a beautiful place, free of all the tortures of this life.
I think about Alexis and cannot help but compare those pregnan-
cies to my pregnancy with Alexis. What if Dennis had decided *that*
pregnancy was unwanted? I picture an embryonic Alexis at one end
of that suction hose and I want to scream. I have those thoughts
sometimes late at night, and that's when I'll creep into her room
and see her sleeping peacefully, and my thoughts turn to what
might have been. I can't emphasize enough what an awful thing it
is to end a life just as it's gaining a tiny foothold.

During that period of my life, when I suffered both mental and
physical abuse, lost my mother, and went through the abortions, I
considered taking my own life. As all of that piled on top of me, I felt
absolutely lost and unloved. I had always seen suicide as a cop-out
for the weak, but when life's complexities pushed me to the brink, I
saw what a lot of women have seen. I was fortunate enough to come
back, unlike many of them. What saved me was my own little angel,
Alexis. I decided to live for her. She and I were a team, and I wasn't
going to let her down. After all, who would raise her? Dennis?

In the weeks after the first abortion, well-meaning friends told
me, "It was just tissue. It wasn't a real baby." They tried to comfort
me with those kinds of rationales, but I wouldn't hear them. My
guilt was so huge. My self-hatred ate away at me. Dennis didn't
have a clue as to what I was going through, and I can only blame
myself for that. I should have told him, screamed it if I had to, that

I wouldn't do it again. I should have said that I wouldn't have a living thing sucked out of my womb ever again. I should have told him how ashamed I was of myself for being too weak to stand up to him. I should have told him we would not kill another baby. I should have told him all of that, and it never would have happened again. But I didn't.

I went home right after the abortion and finished my housework.

— — —

That same year Dennis brought home an unwanted visitor: herpes. He had been on the road sleeping with who-knows-who. Whether he got it before and it hadn't shown up, or he picked it up from one of his groupies, didn't matter. Now I had to deal with it.

Up to that point Dennis and I did not use condoms. I knew he was having affairs, but that didn't hit home hard enough, I guess. One night it did.

Dennis was home, and since we weren't arguing about one of his women, we started to make love. In the course of foreplay I noticed a few small, swollen sores on his penis. When I asked him about the sores he dismissed them as having been caused by the chafing of his jockstrap. Sure, whatever you say.

I was suspicious and immediately checked into sexually transmitted diseases. I remembered Dennis had recurring cold sores on his lip, but I didn't associate it with herpes. There are four types of herpes viruses: HSV-1 and HSV-2, and oral or genital HSV-1 and oral or genital HSV-2 (HSV stands for herpes simplex virus). They are different, not only in how you contract or spread them, but also in how likely you are to get them. Most adults have oral HSV-1. By age fifty, upward of 90 percent of the population has it. You probably pick it up in childhood from being kissed, and you develop antibodies for it. No big deal. Occasionally you might get what is called a cold sore on your lower lip. That's oral HSV-1.

Genital HSV-2 is generally transmitted genitally during sex, but it can be transmitted to the mouth during oral sex. About 20 percent of the adult population has it. Herpes stays or spreads only where it establishes its site of preference. That means if it's genital herpes, it usually only spreads genitally. It can spread elsewhere, but the symptoms are generally milder.

Most people have a misconception that there is "good" herpes (cold sores) and "bad" herpes (genital herpes). That's wrong. They both are the herpes virus and are transmittable to other parts of the body. Maybe someone labeled oral herpes as "good" because in our sick society anything to do with the genitals is obscene. Or maybe it's because oral herpes creates antibodies that can actually ward off the effects of genital herpes.

The main problems with herpes for adults are discomfort during an outbreak and the general social stigma. The other problems are more serious. If a woman with genital herpes has a baby, it must be delivered by cesarean section, as a vaginal delivery could give the baby herpes, which can cause blindness, among other things. So even though herpes is hardly life-threatening and poses few problems for an adult, it's not something you want if you can avoid it.

I started asking Dennis to wear a condom after that, but I think the damage was already done. Herpes can lay dormant for a long time, and I didn't find out I had it until years later. Dennis told me many times, after I'd confront him about his promiscuity, that he was practicing safe sex and wouldn't ever "subject you to something and put you at stake." Just words.

One day in 1992 I was at my mom's in Sacramento when the phone rang. Mom answered the call in the other room, and soon I heard her voice rise in frustration. "Who is this? What do you want?" She was getting very upset. "Leave my daughter alone! Don't call this house again!"

I went into the other room and took the phone from her. "Who the hell is this?" I demanded.

"Annie?" It was one of Dennis's ho's, a woman named Linda. "I know you don't want to talk to me. I just thought I should tell you, Dennis gave me herpes."

My mouth dropped. I realized she was not trying to harass or irritate me. She was actually trying to warn me. The names, dates, and details all made sense. She wasn't lying. When I got off the phone I was dizzy. And sick.

I staggered into the bathroom, locked the door, and turned on the water to mask the noise. My stomach was churning as I lifted the toilet lid and leaned over. I was so tense I couldn't even throw up. I stuck my finger down my throat. I felt so ashamed and so dirty. I couldn't face my mother, who was so proper and clean she squeaked.

I underestimated her. Unlike the scene in my mind in which Mom went bananas and branded me with a Scarlet Letter, what she did warmly surprised me: She comforted me and showed complete understanding. That was my mom. Despite her conservative background, she had a huge heart and an open mind. She decided to call Dennis on my behalf and get to the bottom of the matter.

When she got Dennis on the phone and told him Linda had called and told me she had gotten herpes from him, he didn't say much. He liked, maybe even loved, my mother more than his own, and he probably didn't feel comfortable lying to her. He didn't deny it.

Linda's call kept playing back in my brain. I finally called my doctor, Dr. Womach, and made an appointment. I went in and had a culture done, and Dr. Womach called me back a couple days later and told me I was negative. No herpes.

I was greatly relieved, but the thoughts of Linda's call stayed with me. I started worrying about it. Your body tells you things if you just listen. A few days later my body shouted in my ear. Herpes can surface during times of stress, and what surfaced was a whopping outbreak. I called Dr. Womach and he told me to come in immediately. The doctor examined the lesion that had exploded on me and said it looked like HSV-2. I was subjected to more tests. The culture came back negative again. I was beginning to wonder if they were sending my cultures to the local Burger King for analysis.

Finally Dr. Womach decided the cultures weren't coming back the way he figured they would, so he ordered a full blood workup. This time we hit the jackpot: I was the proud carrier of *both* HSV-1 and HSV-2. Thank you, Mr. Rodman.

To this day I keep a strong, expensive medicine called Zovirax handy in case I have an outbreak. I haven't had one in a while, and according to my research, herpes attacks diminish over time. But if

I ever have another child, it will have to be by C-section, and I also have to live with the reality that whoever I become close to in the future will have to hear about this and decide if they want me and possibly the virus. I only pray that if someday I find someone I really care about, he will be understanding and love me enough to stand by me despite this problem.

— — —

In 1993 the shit hit the fan, so to speak. Lisa Judd, a cheerleader for the Atlanta Hawks, sued Dennis for giving her herpes. She was pretty enterprising, because according to what I heard, she found *eight* other women who would testify they slept with Dennis and contracted herpes from him. I was furious with this woman for (a) having the gall to fuck a married man (my husband), and (b) bringing a suit for what was essentially a consensual act. Well, except for the fact that she didn't consent to getting herpes.

After Dennis and I got married in September 1991, Ms. Judd started calling us at home all the time. Dennis's response to my questions about her was complete denial. She drove me crazy and was the source of a lot of fights between us. I finally changed our phone number to make her go away. Dennis just gave her the new one. So I changed it again. This time I didn't give *him* the number. I gave it to his agent, my mom, Monique, and the Pistons. But not to Dennis.

He came home one night and we got in a fight about the number. "This is my house and I pay the fuckin' bills around here and I don't even know my fuckin' phone number?" he yelled. "Gimme the fuckin' number!"

I stood my ground. "Yeah, okay. When you stop giving it out to your whores, I'll give you the fuckin' number!"

Answering the phone started to make me crazy. As I picked it up I'd say a little prayer, "Please God, don't let it be some loser ho of his." I changed the phone number during that time more often than Dennis changes his hair color these days.

The Hawks cheerleader and Dennis finally had a falling out and, like most parasites who get swatted off by their host, she tried to latch back on again. She found another reason to sue him. She was looking for millions and hired a hotshot attorney who signed her up with a fat contingency at the back end.

When she supposedly got herpes from Dennis and filed the suit, his high-powered lawyers went to work. The cheerleader's lawyer subpoenaed all of Dennis's medical records, but his lawyers managed to get a court order to have those records, and the whole case for that matter, sealed. They probably didn't want the *Enquirer* or some other tabloid getting their greasy hands on the juicy details. Unfortunately, this caused a problem for me later when I sued Dennis for giving *me* herpes. Because the records were sealed, I couldn't prove anything, so my only satisfaction is in telling the story here.

During the trial with the cheerleader, Dennis's lawyers went looking for dirt on her, and it turned out there was plenty of it. They found out she had slept her way through not only the NBA, but the NFL as well. When Dennis's attack dogs got wind of that, they told the court it was quite likely *she* had given *Dennis* herpes. Goes to prove once again that high-paid lawyers can get anybody off. The court's findings? Slut deluxe. The judge said they were two consenting adults and no one was at fault. Whoosh, she got blown out.

In the end, the cheerleader didn't get dick. Financially, that is. I guess she's appealing the case. I also understand she's paying back her lawyer in trade—if you get my drift. I learned my lesson. Once I quit sleeping with Dennis, I went and got an AIDS test, and now I take one every six months. I'm fine. As for Dennis? I don't know if he's ever been tested. So if you're reading this and you're an NBA or NFL cheerleader, a stripper, a rock star, or any other sort of cheap floozy with access to Dennis Rodman, watch out. You've been warned.

— — —

Despite the fact that Dennis treated me like shit at times, he would actually stand up for me on occasion. He was oddly loyal in that respect, and that was one of the things I loved most about him. And I was loyal to him.

Sometimes too loyal.

One time during a game—I think it was during the 1991–92 sea-son—Dennis was attacked by a player named Brad Lohause. I can't even remember the team Lohause played for (I think it was Milwaukee), but I remember taking the attack personally. I was fiercely protective of my family. Whether it was during a basketball game or just walking down the street, I'd give anything and every-thing to defend my loved ones.

After the game I was still fuming about Lohause's attack on Dennis, and when I saw him come out with his team to get on the bus, I went bonkers. Lohause was a white guy who stood around *seven feet*. So what did I do? Naturally, I went after his ass.

"Who the fuck do you think you are, you goofy-ass-looking piece of shit?!" I screamed at him. I started toward the big prick, but security stopped me before I could get to the pasty-faced beanpole. Lohause scampered onto the bus like a pussy as someone called for Dennis. In a minute he came out of the locker room, half-dressed, ice packs taped to his knees, saying, "C'mon, Annie, let it go!"

I didn't want to let it go. I wanted to go through the bus window and get a piece of the skinny little prick. But then Alexis showed up. She and Monique had been getting a bite to eat in the wives' lounge. When I saw Alexis I turned off my anger. I didn't want her to see me like that even if I was just being a mama puma, defend-ing her brood. I couldn't stand anyone going after my Dennis. People used to make jokes about how his ears stuck out, and if I caught wind of it, I'd shut them down right then and there!

Another time, Jerry Sloan, the coach for the Utah Jazz, gave Dennis some shit during a game. Afterward I got Sloan's attention and flipped him off. It was in all of the papers the next day. When asked about it, Dennis's comment was, "That's the way she is. That's Annie."

Like I said, in spite of all the grief he gave me, Dennis would usually stand up for me when the chips were down. And he knew I would always be there for him.

During the play-offs in 1989, Dennis got hurt. The Pistons had been on the road, and he flew back for overnight treatment at the Palace so he could play the next night. I remember him calling me at 12:30 A.M. from the locker room at the Palace. He was lonely and wanted me to come down with Alexis and spend the night with him. He was hurting and sounded really down. He needed us.

I gathered up all of his stuff, including his cereal and his boom box and his favorite tapes. Then I bundled up Alexis and we plunged out into the freezing cold and drove to the Palace in the middle of the night in a blizzard. When we got there it was dark and hard to navigate around because of the snow, but we managed to get in. In the middle of the night a place like that takes on a whole different character. I was kind of scared, walking around that huge, shadowy place with my little girl in one hand and Dennis's stuff in the other, but I kept reminding myself that Dennis was there and hurting and he needed me.

Finally we found a security guard who escorted us down to the locker room. There we found Dennis, lying on a table and hooked up to a bunch of wires and electrodes. He was undergoing some kind of electrotherapy to reduce the swelling. He was miserable. The first thing he said was, "Did you bring my Golden Bear cereal?" He seemed like a hurt little boy, and I just wanted him to get better. I told him I had the cereal and he brightened a bit.

That night was pretty rough for him. The three of us curled up on a sleeper sofa in the locker room office, but Dennis had a hard time sleeping because of the electrodes, and the medicine he had to take made him pee every half hour. Each time he got up I had to carry the electrical box connected to the wires with one hand and help him stand with the other. He was in so much pain he could barely stand, and he needed to use both hands to prop himself up against the wall. It was up to me to hold "it" while he peed. He was in a lot of pain, but he never complained. He also never thanked me or showed any gratitude. Deep down inside, though, I was certain he appreciated me and loved me.

Boy, was I wrong.

# CHAPTER 6

## Annie Gets the Rebound

B Y April 1989, Dennis and I were fighting constantly. We would fight, and then I would leave and go back to Sacramento. I've lost track of how many times I flew back and forth.

One time I returned from Sacramento to find a strange pair of shoes in my closet. I knew they were Karen Stewart's, since she was small and they looked like a size I wore in third grade. I came to hate Karen. I didn't even know her, but I hated her. She symbolized all that was wrong with my relationship with Dennis. I thought, *How could she do that?* How could she stay with a man who was already involved? A man with a fiancée and a daughter?

There was a reason.

Dennis was also playing around with Tracy, who'd recorded our phone conversation for the police, during that time. Tracy was getting thirds to Karen's seconds. When I'd leave town, Dennis was with Karen. If she wasn't available, or he just wanted variety, apparently he'd seek out Tracy. He probably had others, but Karen and Tracy were the locals I knew about. He didn't even have the decency to pork them in their own beds, for I'd find evidence of their "spoor" in my own bed. I'd find makeup and other things that led me to conclude they had been rolling around in *my* bed. And no, Dennis had not started using makeup at that point in time. And despite seeing my stuff all over the house, both Karen and Tracy got the mistaken idea that each of them was Dennis's main squeeze.

Eventually I found out how Karen and Tracy may have gotten that idea. Dennis lied to them. What a surprise. He told them, and probably others, that I was sort of a charity case he was "helping out." He threw in some true details to make the story sound better, including the fact that my father was an alcoholic and that one of my brothers had been in trouble with the law. He didn't mention that one of my other brothers was studying to be a physician's assistant and another was already an attorney. That wouldn't have been in keeping with the image he was painting of me.

He told them I was only at his place temporarily and that we slept in separate bedrooms. He made it sound like I had nowhere to go, so he had taken me in out of the goodness of his heart. I don't know if he tried to explain Alexis's existence. Maybe he told them I had been impregnated by an alien who happened to look like him. I wouldn't put anything past Dennis.

During the times when I wasn't visiting Sacramento and we weren't arguing or fighting, Dennis and I did have a somewhat active sex life. He and I always clicked during sex. I felt it was the only time I could have him all to myself. It's sad but true. Dennis liked to experiment. I now think he asked me to do things he'd tried on other women just to see if I'd do them. He liked to have me get a razor and shaving cream, and we'd get naked and I'd shave around his genitals. Then he'd shave me. He really liked that. He also started having me hold his dick when he peed—that really turned him on. I did what he wanted whether I enjoyed it or not. I just wanted him to be happy. I thought only he and I shared these "secret rituals."

Man, was I wrong.

During one of our lovemaking sessions, Dennis pulled out a Polaroid camera. At first I wasn't sure if I wanted photos like that floating around, but he laughed it off, saying I was just paranoid. Actually the idea was kind of a turn-on, so I went for it and the "photo session" became pretty racy. He kept those photos in his wallet, a place that wasn't exactly secure, it turns out.

One day I got a call that blew my mind. It was Tracy. *She* was irate. Yes, you heard me. Apparently she had been rifling through Dennis's wallet (I thought I was the only one who did that!) and found the Polaroids of me. I was shocked and embarrassed at first. Here's some ho of Dennis's, screaming at me, his fiancée, for making Dennis cheat on *her.* It was a hard-to-grasp concept that left me speechless for a few moments. Finally it sunk in what she was saying and who she was, and I told her to leave Dennis alone and hung up. I was steaming mad at that point.

And I just got angrier.

By the time Dennis got home I was ready for war. I was going to put his balls in a vise and turn the handle. Hold your dick while you're peeing? Sure, let me get some pliers. I was so pissed I was literally seeing red. I heard him come into the condo and I composed myself and went downstairs.

"Where are those Polaroids of me?" I demanded. I wanted to give him some extra rope to hang himself.

He looked a little leery. "Uh, in a safe deposit box," he lied.

I turned both barrels on him. "No, they aren't, you fucking idiot! Tracy has them, you fucker!" I screamed.

I admit, at times like that I would get a perverse satisfaction out of catching him. I look back now and see how sick I was. I had an overwhelming desire to hurt him physically. I thought for a moment that I could scratch his eyes out before he could stop me. Then I realized how far gone I was, so I simply turned and went upstairs. Later on I was still mad, but the murder in my heart had ebbed—slightly. I told him, "I don't care how you do it, just get those fuckin' pictures back from her."

I never saw the pictures again.

A few days before Mother's Day, I came across a receipt.

It was for a cocktail ring Dennis had bought for eight thousand dollars. I thought it must be an awfully nice ring. I also thought it must be for me, because at that time the only thing Dennis would've done for his mother is hang up on her.

Mother's Day came and went. No ring. Finally I confronted Dennis with the receipt, shoving it in his face and asking where the hell the ring was.

Let me explain something. I'd be the last person to "demand" a gift from anyone, but with all of Dennis's hijinks with his numerous women, I was all too aware of where that ring had probably ended up.

I actually caught Dennis off guard. He fumbled around and finally said the ring was being sized and yes, it was for me. I asked him how it was being sized if I hadn't even tried it on? Oops. He wasn't expecting me to use logic. I knew the truth but foolishly held out hope. I'd give him one more chance. I called the jeweler the next morning. The ring had been picked up. On the day it had been paid for.

That clinched it. I fumed all day, planning what I would say when he walked in. I was really gonna let him have it. He must have sensed something, because the afternoon became the evening and then midnight. I was furious at this point, but being angry all day had tired me out. I fell asleep. Around 4 A.M. I heard him come home. I jumped up and went downstairs, caution thrown to the wind along with my well-rehearsed speech. I lit into him about the ring and coming home so late and probably just his overall character flaws. He didn't take it well.

He slapped the shit out of me.

To get away from him, I turned and ran up the stairs, and he followed me. We stopped at the top of the stairs and continued yelling at each other. He lost it again. One minute we were arguing, the next minute he threw me down the stairs.

I tumbled down and landed at the bottom in a heap. That was it for Dennis. He had won the fight. I got up and painfully climbed back up the stairs past a scowling Dennis and went into the bathroom. I wiped the blood out of my mouth and looked in the mirror to survey the damage. I just couldn't understand why he didn't think having women on the side was wrong. To this day I still don't.

That incident stayed in my mind for the next few days while I thought about what had gone so wrong with our relationship. Dennis and I had been together nearly two and a half years, and it had been about a year since he started physically abusing me. I wasn't sure how much more I could take.

I found out that day.

I've spent a lot energy trying to block out this memory, but it's hard to do.What should have been the deal-breaker of our relationship, so to speak, was only one more in a series of explosions and reconciliations between us. I should have left for good at that point, but as they say, hindsight is 20/20.

On the very day I was wondering why there was so much anger between us, why we couldn't get along, we had another fight. It started with an innocent comment from me. I said something to Dennis that he took wrong. I can't even remember what I said, but he thought I meant something else and suddenly Karen's name came up. There she was, the subject of our conversation. Again.

I got angry. Dennis got angry.

We both started yelling, and then he hit me. I ran. He chased me outside as I headed for my car. I jumped in and was just about to pull my leg in when Dennis slammed the car door, crushing my leg between it and the frame of the car. I screamed in agony. He slammed the door again and walked away. I thought my leg was broken. I sat in the car for a few minutes, unable to move. I had a huge welt on my leg and in minutes a bruise began to form. I got out of the car and limped back inside the house. I sat on the bed and cried. After a while I got up and did the only thing I could think of.

I started packing.

On the flight to Sacramento I thought about what had happened between us. My decision to leave wasn't about trivial things like rings or flowers or Mother's Day or even Karen. It was about respect and honesty and consideration—of which I often felt I got little, if any, from Dennis. So there I was, on my way home with lots of sadness and regrets. I never wanted to leave him. In my dreams the only times I saw myself going home would be to see my family. In reality I was going home because of my tormented, upside-down life with Dennis Rodman.

I arrived in Sacramento with our baby on my shoulder. Mom was there, as usual, to comfort me. My troubles with Dennis took a lot out of her because she was so empathetic. She felt my pain, even on the phone from two thousand miles away. And when I would show up, the pain was written all over my face and in my body language.

Mom didn't give a rat's ass how much Dennis made or who he played for or what honors he got from the NBA. All she cared about was whether he was making her little girl happy. As much as my mom felt my pain, I lived in terror that somehow she would find out the *whole truth* about what went on between me and Dennis, and it would do her in. If my poor, beloved mother were alive today, I would not have written this book.

While I was emotionally recuperating in Sacramento, I felt a strong pull from Dennis to come home. He would call all the time and beg me to come back. "I miss you, Annie. I can't get you out of my mind. I miss Alexis. I miss not seeing you in the stands. You know I play for you and Alexis." He knew all the right buttons to push.

But Mom and my brother Chris had finally had it with my constant escapes to Sacramento. They sat down with me and told me I had to do something to change the horrible course my life was taking. "If you can't do it for yourself, do it for Alexis," Mom said. That hit home.

I asked them what I should do. Mom reminded me that if I was going to stay in Sacramento, I needed money to support Alexis. We discussed getting child support from Dennis. I believed hell would freeze over before he would give me a dime, and I told them so. Dennis wanted to keep Alexis and me under his control. Whenever we ran away, he didn't want us to have any money, and eventually we'd have to come crawling back. My oldest brother Chris is a corporate attorney in San Francisco. He said I needed a good family law attorney and promised he'd find me one. He did. He found me the best.

He introduced me to Marvin Mitchelson.

Mitchelson earned a nationwide reputation many years ago when he helped the girlfriend of the late actor Lee Marvin get a big settlement from him. Since then, Mitchelson has specialized in what became known as "palimony" lawsuits. He took only the high-profile, high-visibility cases. He himself was later brought down by a palimony suit, but when I met him he was the top dog.

Marvin assured me he would take Dennis to the cleaners. He was sharp and aggressive and more than ready to cut off Dennis's balls, fricassee them, and serve them right back to him. I wasn't quite ready to do that, but Marvin was very confident and powerful. As we discussed the case, Dennis started to take on a kind of abstract monster quality, like he was some sort of insect infestation Marvin and I had to take care of. I think really good divorce lawyers tend to make you feel that way just in case you have any second thoughts.

I gave Marvin a retainer of ten thousand dollars against a third of what he would get for me, and he went to work. Meanwhile, I returned to Detroit and pretended everything was cool. At the time the Pistons were red-hot and on their way to winning the NBA championship. Dennis was really caught up in playing at that point, so he didn't pay me much attention. Pretty soon Marvin wanted to meet with me again, and I flew back out to Sacramento, then down to Los Angeles.

Marvin and his team laid out the plan. They were going to ask for half of Dennis's earnings up to that point, or about $1 million, plus a $7,700 per month support payment. Then they told me I had to get out of the condo and move to the West Coast, preferably Los Angeles. I was shocked by the amounts they were going to ask for, mainly the $1 million, knowing that was more than Dennis had. He made a lot, but he also spent a lot. Today he's got that kind of money, but back then he would have had to live in his Saleen Mustang to afford it.

I didn't want to crucify Dennis. I just wanted to support my baby in something close to the lifestyle to which we had become accustomed. I wanted to have enough money so I could take care of her in an emergency. I know there are a lot of women with children who are separated from the father and suffer serious hardship, but those fathers probably aren't making $1 million plus a year.

What I really wanted was to be back with Dennis. That didn't seem possible, however, so I told Marvin to put together the paperwork. It was agreed that I would give the final word on if and when to fire the opening volley, that is, to serve Dennis with the official papers. I figured once I served him he'd probably want to kill me. I knew it was probably going to put an end to us once and for all, so I waited. I was both scared to lose him and scared not to end the turmoil. Then, when I was back in Sacramento, Dennis called me.

Unaware that I had hired the most famous palimony attorney on earth to plan his financial castration, he invited me and Alexis to the first game of the play-offs. The Pistons were going to be in Los Angeles playing the Lakers. He said he needed us to be on the sidelines to inspire him. I had been spending a lot of time in Sacramento and Los Angeles, and Dennis and I hadn't seen much of each other lately. I did miss him and thought maybe there was a chance we could work things out.

I agreed to fly down and attend the game. Dennis wanted me to come to his hotel the night before. Marvin had told me to stay away from Dennis, but I just couldn't. I flew to L.A. with Alexis, checked us into a hotel, and called Marvin. I told him I was in town to watch Dennis in the play-offs and wanted to work things out with Dennis if I could. I asked him to hold off on serving the papers. I wanted to give Dennis one more chance. Marvin didn't think it was such a hot idea but deferred to me, saying it was my money and my future. I thanked him and told him I'd call after the game.

The Pistons were shacked up at a nice hotel near the airport. The team was on an early curfew, so we couldn't spend the night. He was as warm as he could be when we arrived. He played with Alexis for a little while, then turned to me.

We started talking and pretty soon he had me up against the wall and was kissing me passionately. He told me everything was going to be different between us from now on. "This is the most important time of my life, and I need you and the baby," he said. "Let's start over. We'll buy a home, get married, and have another baby."

He looked deep into my eyes with a sincerity I hadn't seen since he proposed to me on the hood of his Mustang in Oklahoma. "I'm ready, Annie," he continued. "I've had a lot of time to think." Then he told me all of the women he'd been playing around with meant nothing to him, and they only made him realize how much he loved me. Then he promised, right there, to drop them all and be with me and our daughter 100 percent.

Wow.

The whole palimony mess was now just an unpleasant memory. I decided at that moment that I would drop it and it would never come up again. Dennis then reiterated that he wanted Alexis and me to be at the game, cheering him on. Nothing in the world was more important to him than that, he insisted. He said he'd leave us the tickets at Will Call. I told him we'd be there.

We kissed good night, and I wished him luck in the game. As I walked down the hall, Alexis cradled in my arms, Dennis leaned out the door to say he was already missing me. I was floating. It was such an intense, romantic encounter that I was almost dizzy. All my fears were gone, and I knew, without a doubt, that we were going to be fine.

Sucker.

The next day I gathered Alexis up and went down to the lobby. We caught a cab to the Forum in Inglewood, a few miles from our hotel. The place was a total zoo, and the cabbie didn't want to go into the parking lot and get stuck. We got out of the cab on the outer edge of the parking area. We must have walked half a mile, dodging cars, to get to the Will-Call window. I went up and asked for our tickets. Nothing under Rodman. Hmm. "Try Bakes," I said. It was still my name at that point. No, ma'am. It all became crystal clear. Again. "How 'bout under Miss Incredibly Fucking Gullible?" I asked. "No? Not under that name either, huh?"

I asked whether there were any regular tickets available, and the ticket guy laughed. I hiked across the parking lot again and hailed another cab. We went back to the hotel and I started packing. I was so hurt I just wanted to go home. I thought maybe there had been some foul-up, but I didn't hold out much hope.

Then Dennis called. He apologized and said the tickets had been given to someone else. A thought flashed through my mind: Who could be more important? Elvis? "Who was it?" I asked. "Who was more important than me and Alexis, the 'two most important people on earth' to you, Dennis?" For once I actually wished he'd lied and said it had been some handicapped kid or maybe a 102-year-old lady who wanted to see a play-off game before she died. Instead, he told me the truth.

Mike Gold. I think the two syllables "fuck you" would have been far less offensive than hearing that man's name at that time. It was as if Dennis had punched me again. I couldn't believe it. Apparently Dennis had been given only six tickets, and Mike Fucking Gold had shown up with two extra friends. Presto, Alexis and I were off the guest list. Screwed again. That did it. I said, "I'll see you in court." I hung up. Then I thought, *I hope he didn't think I meant the basketball court.* Just to make sure there was no misunderstanding, I made a quick phone call.

To Marvin Mitchelson.

I told Marvin I wanted Dennis to pay through the nose and every other orifice. I told him to serve the papers during the next play-off game. Right on the court. I figured if Alexis and I couldn't get into the game, maybe a process server would enjoy it. That would really hurt him. And embarrass him.

Marvin called me back and told me they couldn't serve Dennis during either warm-ups or the game. Too much security. I settled for a service at his hotel. I had told Dennis at various times during our fights that I could be his best friend or his worst enemy. It was his choice.

The incident with the tickets was the last nail in the coffin for me. I went back to Sacramento, hurt and angry. I started planning to move Alexis and myself to L.A. The next day a process server knocked on Dennis's hotel room door, the same one behind which he said he'd miss me. Dennis probably opened that door thinking it was either room service bringing him his bacon or an on-call hooker. I guess he was pretty surprised.

It was in all of the newspapers the next day. I was characterized as a major witch for kicking a guy at the moment of the greatest triumph of his life. Well, the greatest triumph of his life was and always will be the birth of his daughter, no matter what happens on that basketball court. Dennis would probably agree. But at that moment I was the "mean girlfriend" who was trying to derail "the Great Rodman." Little did they know that this all could have been avoided had "the Great Rodman" come through with the two chickenshit tickets he had promised.

Mom and Dad drove me and Alexis down to L.A. and got us settled into an apartment. It was a small place in West Hollywood on Poinsettia, about two blocks south of Sunset. When the last box had been set down and we had said our good-byes, I went back inside our little apartment, put Alexis to bed, and went into the living room. I looked around that sparse room that contained only a high chair, a TV, and a dining table. I had no furniture. I was scared, worried, and most of all, lonely. I sat down on the carpet in the dark and cried.

Marvin Mitchelson wasted no time in opening up a vintage bottle of whip-ass on Dennis. First he filed a restraining order based on Dennis's smashing my leg in the car door. Dennis could still see Alexis, but the order legally controlled his access to us. This helped hammer home the idea that I was serious. Then Marvin went after his wallet. He forced Dennis to show what he earned. He *claimed* he had a monthly disposable income of $27,850, and soon Marvin had forced Dennis to pony up some money for child support. A measly $750 a month. That was all he claimed he could afford for the time being. I took it.

Meanwhile Dennis was calling me and telling me how much he missed me and how sorry he was for the ticket screwup. I hadn't lived in L.A. for years and really didn't know anyone, so I welcomed any phone calls from people I knew, even him.

Dennis would tell me he wanted us back, and then he'd complain about the lawsuit and what a waste it was for him to spend all that money on lawyers. I responded that if he hadn't cheated on me every time I turned around, and then tossed me around like a goddamn rag doll when I complained, we wouldn't be in this situation. It was the same old circular discussion: "Come back." "Then don't cheat."

Dennis made all sorts of promises to get me back. He promised me we'd get married and share everything in life. He said he'd quit chasing women and settle down. He claimed he was a family man at heart and he'd just lost his way. He promised to get psychotherapy to help end his lying and cheating. He said he'd pay for my college education as well as a new modeling portfolio, even though he really didn't want me modeling. He promised to get me a nanny to help out with Alexis. All of it was a lot to lay on a girl like me who had been through so much and still wanted to have a life with the man she loved. I told him over and over that I'd think about it.

That summer in L.A. was hot, and I barely knew anyone. The combination of the two made life there harder to take. When

Dennis asked me to bring Alexis out to Dallas, where he was spending the off-season, I agreed. All the things he was telling me— the promises about getting married, going back to school, the therapy—all sounded so good. It was exactly what I wanted to hear. And Dennis was just the salesman to pull it off.

In Dallas he went to work on me again about our future and dropping the lawsuit. When I returned to L.A. I was softened up. Marvin counseled me to be strong, and we didn't back off on the suit. Eventually my deposition was taken, and in it I told the whole story of our relationship. Apparently Dennis's lawyers, after hearing my tale, decided I probably had something to my case. Plus, having Marvin Mitchelson in my corner added a huge amount of credibility and horsepower.

During this time I needed a car. Through the lawyers I asked for the '88 Mustang Dennis had bought me for my birthday. Dennis and his lawyers argued that the car was *never* a gift and that I was not entitled to it. They also said my claims were inflated and Dennis could never afford to pay me what I wanted. I just wanted to take care of our daughter. In my deposition I said that I met Dennis at a time when I made more than he did and that I left modeling to start a family with him. His lawyers implied that I had no chance of getting modeling work and that my claims of not pursuing it because he didn't want me to were overblown. Modeling actually sort of left me after the accident, and I never pursued it again, so who knows what could have been? Besides, Dennis had encouraged my becoming a homemaker.

Then Marvin called me and asked if I'd like to be on *Geraldo.* Marvin had been asked by Geraldo's producers to appear on a show dealing with palimony lawyers and their clients. Marvin thought I should appear with him because Dennis was getting exposure and he thought I had an interesting story. Looking back, I realize it was a publicity shot for Marvin, but I still respect what he tried to do for me.

I agreed to do it and the taping date was arranged. At the taping I was introduced to the other show guests and their attorneys, who were also going to be on stage with us and Geraldo. There was

William Hurt's ex-girlfriend and Johnny Carson's son's girlfriend, who happened to be black and had their child with her. During the show we talked about common-law marriages. It was kind of interesting, but I could have done without it.

About this time Dennis did an interview with *Detroit Monthly* magazine. He told them we were going to be married in 1990 right after the season ended. I read that and shook my head. That's good, Dennis, I'm glad I found out when we were getting married. Maybe I should get a subscription to *Detroit Monthly* so I can find out the next time I'm going to get pregnant. Later he called me and promised he'd never hit me again. Things were gettin' good: I found out my wedding date in a periodical, and my intended was offering not to beat the shit out of me anymore. Believe me, he was the master at pitching woo. Problem was, I was buying it.

When the basketball season got under way for the 1989–90 season, the Pistons were scheduled to play the Clippers. Dennis called and said he would be in town and wanted to see me and Alexis. I never prevented Dennis from seeing his daughter. I also missed him. I went to the game (this time we had tickets), and afterward he told me he missed us and wanted us back.

By the time fall came around, I hadn't gone back to Dennis, but I'd weakened enough that I agreed to listen to a proposal from his lawyers. They asked me to drop everything against him. In return, he would give me and Alexis twenty-five hundred dollars a month in support. That solved two problems I had. The first was the lawsuit. I didn't want to hurt Dennis as much as I wanted to get his attention. The second was the money. Living on $750 a month just wasn't cutting it. So, starting that November, I took the money, but in the back of my mind I held out hope we could be a family once again.

Soon we were.

■ ■ ■

I have a tremendous amount of guilt about the four abortions I had. Even though it was Dennis who either talked me or outright pressured me into having them, I know it was ultimately my decision. The ironic thing was that my Catholic upbringing may have had something to do with my decisions to have them.

I was raised believing that the wife is supposed to honor and obey her husband. Though Dennis and I weren't yet legally married, he had proposed, and we were living as husband and wife (albeit a dysfunctional husband and wife). The fact that we had had Alexis together made me feel even more strongly that we were married. Despite everything that had happened between us, I loved him so much that I was willing to do almost anything to make him happy. Of course, I did these things at great personal cost. When Dennis *said* he wanted to have another child, I was overjoyed. And when he changed his mind about it, well, I was willing to honor and obey him.

I wondered why he was so eager to have a son. I mean, lots of men want to have a son, but Dennis *really* wanted one. During the years that have passed since this happened, I've come up with some possible explanations.

First of all, I think Dennis was jealous of my relationship with Alexis. She and I were and still are as close as a parent and a child can be. She shares her thoughts with me without reservation and we laugh a lot together. I think Dennis wanted a son so he could have the same sort of relationship. If only he had realized that if he spent some time with Alexis, maybe the two of them could have been close, too.

Perhaps Dennis's obsessive desire to have a son is related to whatever it was about him that led having young boys around our house all the time—and I don't mean that in a Michael Jackson kind of way. Dennis may think a son would be like a permanent play-mate, someone who would always be there to do guy stuff with him. A permanent video game opponent.

I sometimes got the feeling that he thought he couldn't do that with Alexis because she is a girl. Dennis has always had serious problems with people of the female persuasion. Or, as they like to say in psychological circles, he has "issues" about women. If I were a shrink, I'd be inclined to think that it goes back, as they say so many things do, to his perception of how his mother treated (or mis-treated) him. As a result, he simply seems to hate women. He certainly doesn't show them any respect. To Dennis, women are here for no other reason than to serve him. They stand up on stages and take their clothes off and shake their firm titties for him. They seek him out after basketball games and offer to have sex with him and do whatever he wants. And I mean whatever. Fans constantly tell him how wonderful he is. And the media, which require "personalities" like Dennis to feed their machine, glorify him constantly.

All of this simply feeds Dennis's childlike need for attention and reinforces the public behavior that keeps the media coming back for more. It's another ugly cycle. He got so little attention as a child that he's making up for it now.

Dennis is the single most self-centered person to walk this earth. In his mind, everyone is here to do his bidding. He does not put up with people who tell him no. One of the perks of having lots of money and being a celebrity is that he doesn't have to put up with people who tell him no—at least as long as the money and the celebrity lasts.

The pregnancy–abortion cycle worked like this: Dennis and I would fight about something (nine times out of ten it was about sleeping with other women; the tenth time would be because he beat me up). After the fight I would leave him and return to Sacramento. After a while Dennis would start asking me to come back. He promised he would change. He would swear he would get psychotherapy to help him deal with his problems. He'd even cry, just like he would do for Oprah.

If none of that convinced me to come back, he would use the one thing that always worked. He would say we should have another baby. He would talk about how having a bigger family would finally make him settle down and be a good father and husband. I was so desperate to have this mythical family with Dennis that I bought his lies every time, because that's all I ever wanted in the first place.

I would go back to him, and soon I would be pregnant. He'd act all excited when I gave him the news and repeat all the bullshit about his settling down and becoming a family man. I thought my dream was finally coming true. But as the weeks progressed he'd drift away from that sort of talk, and before I knew it he was saying things like, "Hey, do whatever you want, but you just got your body back into shape. Do you really want to keep this baby?"

That was the depth of his thought process. When it came down to a choice of having either my body appeal to him or my body being pregnant (and my poor tits sagging even more), Dennis felt the tight body was the clear moral choice.

As my pregnancy advanced, Dennis would become more vocal about his opposition to it. He'd say he wanted to be more financially stable before we had any more kids. Or he'd start manipulating the situation by picking a fight about something. Once the fight was in full swing, he'd say something like, "Hey, look, we're not exactly getting along here, are we? Maybe you shouldn't have that baby. You know what I'm saying?"

I think what really worried Dennis was that another child would mean more responsibility. Another child might also mean an end to his footloose and fancy-free days (even though Alexis's existence had never stopped him). Maybe he knew he wasn't going to stay with me, and another child would simply mean more child support when he dumped me down the road.

Of course, I wasn't thinking about any of that. All I was thinking was that he would resent me if I kept the baby. And if he resented me, that would make a bad situation even worse. I should have been thinking about the baby, but I was so screwed up emotionally I wasn't thinking at all.

So I'd have an abortion.

Then the cycle would begin again. Dennis would start talking about having more children and he'd swear this time it would be different. And I'd fall into the trap and get pregnant again. I got pregnant three more times after the first abortion in 1989. It was completely irresponsible on my part, and I will suffer the guilt for the rest of my life. Guilty of being so weak that I didn't stand up to Dennis and that those children didn't survive.

I remember Dennis accompanying me to the fourth abortion. He repeatedly asked the doctor to leave the room because he needed to talk to me. He seemed to be feeling unsure about what he had talked me into, and now he wanted me to tell him, to reassure him, that it was the right thing to do.

I was living in Sacramento, having recently left Dennis. We weren't exactly getting along. As the abortion started, I remember him holding my hand, his head next to mine. I started to cry and turned my head away. For all I know, he was probably smiling as the doctor relieved him of his latest potential responsibility.

— — —

By 1989 Dennis's fooling around was in full swing. He was on his way to leading the league in field goal percentage—and probably infidelity as well. I was going nuts trying to keep track of all of his women, all of his affairs. His cheating was like those trick birthday candles that keep lighting back up after you think you've blown them out. I kept finding all sorts of evidence of his conquests, from scribbled phone numbers to stray pieces of clothing to nude photos. It was all heading toward a single climax: Annie was going to go insane.

The capper came the day I returned to the West Bloomfield condo and found our video camera set up on the tripod in an odd place. My radar was activated. I found a pile of tapes and started plugging them into the video deck, scanning each one. Finally I found what I was hoping for. Or rather, not what I was hoping for, but what I was expecting.

If Dennis ever lost his basketball career, the one job he will *never* have is as a cameraman. On the video, which was badly lit and shaky, I saw a woman undressing. I couldn't see her face because of the shadows and the shaking camera. As soon as she was naked, she turned around and bent over the stairs. Our stairs, in the condo.

As I watched this woman's backside as she struggled to get into position, I remember thinking, *Man, she sure has a fat ass.* Then I heard Dennis directing her off camera. There was a lot of laughing and joking. When he entered the frame and started doing his back-door business, I went nuts. I yanked the tape out and got an aluminum bat out of the closet. First I smashed the holy dog shit out of the tape, then the VCR, then the rest of his audio gear. When Dennis got home and saw the trashed equipment he simply went out and replaced it with more expensive stuff.

In the days that followed, I'd think about that incident, and all I could see was that moony white fanny and how it looked like a huge pear. I decided I'd better make light of it or it would drive me nuts. I came up with a name for that prominent part of that naked mystery woman's anatomy. Every time I thought of that creamy, bulbous butt, I'd call it the Pear. I often wonder how the Pear is doing. I hope it's met a good Stairmaster and settled down.

— — —

After finding an info card from a car dealership in Novi, Michigan, with the year, make, and mileage of a piece-of-shit Volkswagen owned by Karen Stewart, I decided to call the dealership and ask some questions. I asked for the salesman who had sent the card to Dennis, and he came on the phone. "Hello?"

"Hi," I began. "This is Alice, John Salley's girlfriend." I actually don't remember John's girlfriend's name, but I don't think it was Alice.

"Hi, Alice," the salesman replied pleasantly. "What can I do for you today?"

"I was wondering, are you the guy who sold that cool-looking Cabriolet to Dennis Rodman for his girlfriend Karen?"

"As a matter of fact, I did," he replied.

"Well, Johnny said he wants to buy me a car, and he told me to pick one out. When I saw Karen's car, well, I just knew it was exactly what I want. I just love it."

"Well," the happy salesman said, "I'm just the guy to sell it to you, Alice. Do you want to make an appointment and come down to test-drive one?"

"Actually, I wanted to talk to Karen first and see how she likes hers, but I lost her number. Could you give it to me?"

"Sure!" he chirped. "Hang on." A minute later he was back with the phone number.

"Is she still living at the Colbath Street address?" I asked.

"Nope, she's at 349 Hawkins Avenue," he said.

"Thanks a million. Oh, you know what? Could you do me a favor and call her to see if she minds if I call her? I'd really appreciate it."

"No problem. That's probably a good idea," he agreed.

"Great. If it's okay with her, I'll give her a call, then I'll come down and take that test drive. What's your name again?"

He gave me his name and I pretended to write it down. I waited a bit, then dialed Karen's number. "Hello?"

"Hi, Karen," I said. "It's Alice. John Salley's girlfriend."

"Oh yeah, the guy at the dealership said you would be calling. You wanted to ask about the Cabriolet Dennis bought me. I can tell you, it is a *great* car. I just love it."

"I bet you were so excited when he gave it to you," I said, trying to sound happy. "Did he surprise you, or did you already know about it?"

"It was so funny! Dennis calls and tells me to meet him at Mountain Jacks for dinner, right? So I go there and Dennis is standing next to the car and it's got a big red ribbon on top of it! I was, like, so freaked out! I couldn't believe it!"

"Wow! I bet you were surprised," I said. I knew she was going to be a lot more surprised in a minute. "Gosh, did Annie know about it?"

"Heck no, she was home with the baby," Karen answered. "And she would absolutely kill me if she ever found out." She started laughing.

"Boy, you're not kidding," I continued. "Listen. Do you think it would be possible for me to, maybe, I don't know, test-drive your car?"

"No, I don't mind. Let me tell you where I live." She proceeded to give me directions.

"I know exactly where that is," I said. "Oh, just one more thing. You really are a stupid bitch, aren't you?"

"What?"

"I'm not John Salley's girlfriend, you idiot. This is Annie, Dennis's fiancée, in case you forgot!"

Dead silence. I knew she was still there. I just wish I could have seen her face. "I am going to do everything I can to make your life as hellish as you've made mine," I said in a low voice. "And somehow, some way, I am going to get that car from you!" I slammed the phone down and felt much better.

About two weeks later, Karen crashed and totaled the car. Unfortunately, she was all right. Her only problem was that she didn't have insurance. I was nowhere in the vicinity when the crash occurred. I guess voodoo dolls really do work.

# CHAPTER 7
## I'm Goin' to Dennisland!

IN LATE 1989 AND EARLY 1990, AFTER ALL THE CRAZINESS OF MOVING to L.A. and filing the palimony suit, I was more of an emotional wreck than ever. At the ripe old age of twenty-five, I was becoming farther removed from my prime modeling years and was having a difficult time finding both representation and work. One of the problems was that my portfolio was so outdated. Of course, that was because I had stopped working based on Dennis's promises that he would support me financially if I stopped modeling and became his homemaker and future wife. Two sad realizations were making me more emotionally vulnerable. My modeling days were coming to an end and I had lost most of my opportunities based on the lies Dennis had told me. Also, my relationship with him was looking more and more like a train wreck.

Dennis was calling me constantly or having others call me on his behalf, trying to pull his ass out of the fire. He resorted to his usual method of swearing he was sorry and that he was going to change. He told me that he had *finally* seen the light, not like before, when he only *thought* he'd seen the light. This time, Dennis said, prompted by the reopening of all those old wounds via the declarations and interrogatories and depositions, he meant it. He would change. We would share everything. We would get married. He would get help. We would be a family.

Given that, one, my own career had gone down the toilet while Dennis was using me as a punching bag; two, I didn't have any other professional experience; three, the only thing I'd wanted all along was to make things work for Alexis, Dennis, and myself; and four, I was an emotional disaster, I wanted to believe his promises. I agreed to drop the palimony suit if Dennis agreed to pay child support.

But that wasn't good enough for him. He kept making promises about how he was going to change and how things were finally going to be right between us—if only I'd move back in with him. So I did. This meant that Dennis paid that twenty-five hundred dollars a month in child support for a grand total of one or two months. Once I moved back in, he was off the hook. I wasn't back for a month before I caught him cheating again. In February 1990 I confronted him about it. And he got pissed when I did.

At that time Dennis was coming into his own with the Pistons. He wasn't a full-time starter yet—that would come at the end of the season—but he had been named to the East All-Star team, so he was full of himself.

When I demanded that Dennis keep his promise and stop fucking around on me, he hit me so hard he dislocated my jaw. I was laid out on the floor and couldn't believe how hard he'd hit me. The next day I still had the imprint of Dennis's hand on my face. I also had a bad headache and a new bite; that is, my upper and lower teeth no longer came together the way they were supposed to. I needed to see a doctor. Dennis said I was overreacting. He told me I didn't need to see a doctor for every little ache and pain I had. Later I called his agent and told him I was going to the police. The agent told me that would only make matters worse. He suggested I refrain from going to a doctor in Detroit, much less to the police, as it would cause his client trouble.

The agent talked to Dennis. Again, Dennis said I was blowing the whole thing out of proportion, that it was just an accident and my jaw was fine.

I thought it wise to seek a second opinion, that of a person who had actually attended medical school. I returned to Sacramento and made an appointment. The X rays indicated that the blow to my face had resulted in TMJ, temporomandibular joint syndrome. The doctor sent me to a dentist, who made a mold of my teeth and created a mouth guard-like device designed to relieve the pressure on the joint and realign the whole thing.

I stayed in Sacramento for the next two months. I thought that was it. I'd had it with Dennis's shit, and my dislocated jaw was the last straw. Then one day, just after Easter 1990, Dennis called to talk to my mom. She told him that Alexis and I were the reason he was playing so well and that we would give him the incentive to continue doing so. She told him he needed us back, and since he was getting older, it was time for him to settle down.

I couldn't believe what I was hearing. She may as well have said, "Dennis, just take her back and stop beating her so much." Mom was doing to me what she used to do to herself. She was forgiving Dennis, just like she used to forgive Dad after he treated her badly.

Mom gave me the phone. Dennis launched into a virtuoso performance of how sorry he was. He said he was *so* sorry he hit me. He knew he needed help, and he swore he was going to get it if I came back. He said this was the thing that was finally going to turn him around. He said we would get married and he would stop seeing other women. He said all the things he knew I needed to hear. He sounded as sincere as he ever had in his life. Just like every other time he made those promises.

I moved back to Michigan a few days later. It was the stretch run of the season, when the Pistons went on to win the 1989–90 NBA championship. I got to go to the parade, too.

■ ■ ■

In June 1990 the Pistons nailed their second NBA championship in a row. Dennis had received a lot of accolades by then and was suddenly a very visible player in the NBA. He was a hero in Detroit, and as a hero, he wanted the public to see a certain image of him. He hadn't yet cultivated the bad-boy image, and he was still concerned about the fans in Detroit and their perception of their monster rebounder.

Dennis had a problem. He needed me and Alexis, and we weren't there.

We had had a whopper of a fight about Karen. I was sick and tired of his attentions to this woman, and I put my foot down. Slinking around with her in the shadows might have been one thing, but giving her a car, furniture, lavish gifts, tickets to games, and spending the occasional night out on the town with her was too much.

So I left.

I took my baby, who was a little over a year and a half, and went to stay with Monique. No sooner had we walked in the door than the phone started ringing. It was Dennis. "You and the baby gotta come home. The championship parade is tomorrow and I want you with me."

I thought, *This is interesting. He* needs *me*?

Detroit was going bonkers over its team and wanted to throw a big party. All of the team members were going to be paraded through town, and they'd get the key to the city. Dennis wanted his family at his side in his moment of triumph. When the Pistons had taken the championship the previous year, Dennis and I were locked in a legal battle, and at that time the only appearance I was planning to make on his behalf was in court. This year was different: We were merely separated.

I told him I'd get back to him. After the first championship, the Pistons each received a championship ring. Anyone who gets a ring like that is terribly proud of it and wants to share it with their loved ones, so most of the team went out and had copies of their rings made into smaller rings or pendants for their wives or girlfriends. (Or wives *and* girlfriends.) Well, I didn't get squat. I saw the other women wearing their championship jewelry, but I did without. Do you think it was because I sued Dennis for $1 million? I was really hurt by it but never said anything. I wanted him to do it because *he* wanted to.

That was one of the thoughts that went through my head as I tried to decide whether to go to the parade. I talked to Monique and eventually we decided I should go, but she'd come along. I called Dennis back and told him the terms and he jumped on it.

Monique and Alexis and I drove to the Palace early the next morning. We were a little tired, but there was a lot of excitement in

In Italy with my friends Heather and Dana. (1985)

I dream of Annie. (1986)

Anorexic in Los Angeles. (1986)

The car wreck that ruined my career. (1987)

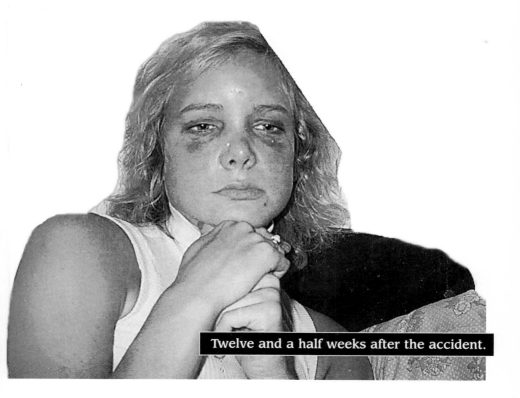

Twelve and a half weeks after the accident.

Proud daddy with his new daughter.

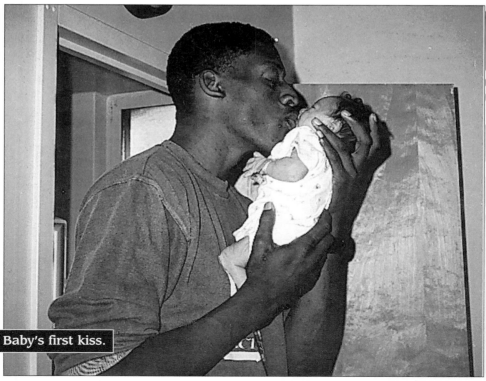

Baby's first kiss.

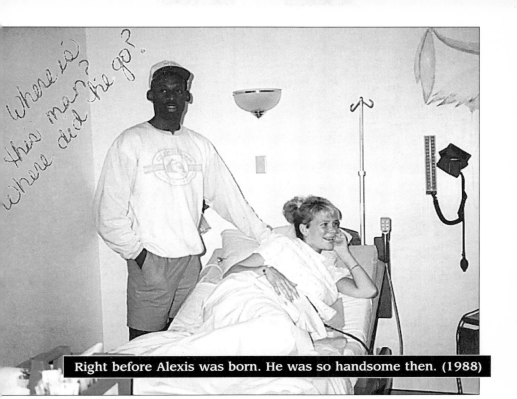

Where is this man? Where did he go?

Right before Alexis was born. He was so handsome then. (1988)

Alexis in front of Dennis's trophy collection. (circa 1992)

The three of us, happy again after the divorce. (1994)

Another no show: Alexis's seventh birthday. (1995)

Alexis's first holy communion. Dennis was at his book signing that day. (Spring 1996)

Daddy acts his age. (Summer 1996)

Dennis and Monique. In times of friendship.

At the video arcade, one of Daddy's favorite places. (Summer 1996)

Me and my dog Cleo and skinned knees.

Mom and Dad with Chris. Notice the way Mom is looking at Dad.

Alexis with her uncles Matt and Chris in France. (circa 1990)

"Our" Bloomfield Hills house.

Grandma comes to visit. (1991)

Kym and Debra at an exciting All Star game. We seemed to get along then.

Alexis, Monique and me at Planet Hollywood in Miami. (circa 1994)

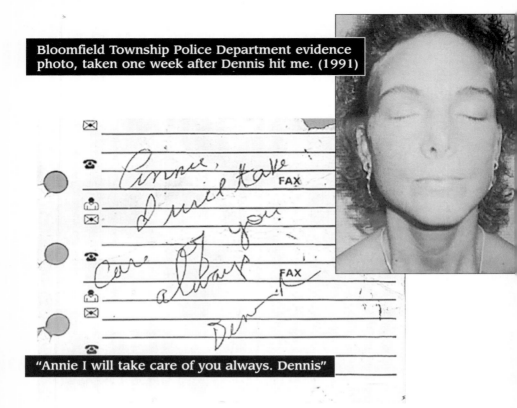

"Annie I will take care of you always. Dennis"

*A couple of Dennis's notes and promises to me.*

"I no [sic] in my heart you were the reason for where I am today. Love, Dennis"

Annie,

I wish I could rewind the past days, I would have followed thru with what I promised you. I promised the world to you and # all I gave you was SHIT. No matter what ever happen I will always love you and no in my heart that you were the reason for where I am today for

Me and Vinnie Johnson. (circa 1991)

Clubbing it with Dennis. (1992)

I had this photo taken for Dennis before Kym Lee was exposed. (1994)

To Amine

Love M

Dennis was so cruel to send me this photocopied "greeting" from his new girlfriend.

the air, so we rose to the occasion. The first event was a big rally at the Palace, followed by a parade and a drive through the streets of Detroit, with the finale being a ceremony downtown.

The whole thing was obviously very important to Dennis, but I was beginning to feel that my charity and goodwill toward him was wearing thin. Here was the guy who had verbally abused and beaten me and left his daughter for weeks or even months at a time, and now he needed us to show the world what a great husband and father he was. Forgive me if I was a little underwhelmed.

I still loved him deeply, but what the public saw and what was real were so different, I had to be somewhat cynical. As we got seated in the Palace and watched the Pistons assemble for the rally, I watched Dennis take his place among his teammates and thought about the old saying, "Behind every great man, there's a great woman." I wouldn't say he was a great man by any stretch, but he was damn sure a great basketball player. So where did that leave me? Maybe just a good woman with too much patience.

The rally got going and eventually it came time for everyone to give speeches. As the speeches droned on, what struck me most was how much each player thanked his family, and if he was married, his wife and kids, if he had any. I thought Dennis was really going to lay it on because we were sitting right there, just as he wanted. I knew he would thank me and Alexis for being his inspiration. He had told me that many times, and I thought it would be nice to hear a proclamation by Dennis Rodman in front of God and everybody: "Yes, sir, that's my woman and that's my little girl, and that's who I play and I live for."

Finally it came time for Dennis to take the stage. He approached the podium. First he thanked the Pistons organization. That was a good start. Then he thanked Chuck Daly. That was expected; Daly was like a mentor. Then he thanked William Bedford. Then he sat down. William Fucking Bedford? Give me that again?

I was absolutely, completely crushed.

William Bedford was a guy that got traded to the Pistons. Dennis hardly ever mentioned him. Now he's the guy Dennis owes it all to? Give me a fucking break. I was humiliated. Monique knew how hurt I was and held my hand. Tears came to my eyes. I didn't want Alexis to think something was wrong—that poor little girl saw so much insanity—so I squinted hard and took a few deep breaths. What the hell was wrong with me? I should be used to this by now!

After the rally Dennis herded me and Alexis over to the bus for the players and wives, and Monique took the bus reserved for the families. As the buses made their way downtown, the fans thronged the streets. At one point a young black woman ran alongside the bus to shake Dennis's hand. Then she looked at me and said breathlessly, "You're the luckiest woman in the whole world. I'd give anything to be in your shoes!" I smiled. When she turned away I muttered, "Honey, you can have my fuckin' shoes. If you wear a size 10, I'll trade you right now." I don't think Dennis heard me. If he did, he didn't let on.

We arrived downtown, and Monique told me that when she got on the bus the only seat available was next to Isiah Thomas's mom. How ironic! In a whisper, I asked Monique if she had told Mama Thomas that she was sleeping with her son. We giggled. I think Mrs. Thomas's respect for her son might have dropped a notch or two had she known Isiah was dippin' his quill in a lot more than just his wife's inkwell.

The ceremony was a handing over of the keys to the city and all the other happy horseshit that the politicians cooked up. Monique, Alexis, and I sat down in the stands. I ended up next to Angela Aguirre, Mark Aguirre's wife. I liked Angela. She struck me as a straight shooter, not like most of the other NBA wives I'd met. While some politician was babbling away about the team, Angela turned to me and said, "I heard Dennis bought some girl a car."

She wasn't trying to start trouble; she was just looking out for one of the team wives. I replied, "Yeah, he bought this bitch named Karen a Volkswagen Cabriolet."

Angela paused, then said, "I heard it was a Saab."

This was new. "No. I'm sure it was a Cabriolet," I repeated. "You either heard wrong or there's more than one proud owner of a new car, compliments of Dennis Rodman."

**116**

Angela leaned in close. "Girl, why you put up with that?"

I shook my head. "I don't know, Angela. I guess I love him. He's my daughter's daddy and he belongs to me. For better or for worse."

Then I learned something else. Mike Gold was in attendance at the festivities with some bimbo. She was pretty good-looking—nice teeth and big tits. I wondered what the hell she was doing with that oil slick that passes for a man. Anyway, I found out that Dennis hadn't mentioned me or Alexis in his speech because the bimbo with Gold was *really* with Dennis, and he didn't want to confuse her with all sorts of messy information about his perpetual fiancée and little girl and his life outside the hotel rooms and strip joints. The guy had us come out to be with him but didn't dare mention us because it might hurt his chances with some chick he met in a strip joint.

On the ride home I turned to Dennis and said softly, "You get that fuckin' car back. I don't give a shit if it's a Cabriolet or a Saab, I want that fucker in the driveway tomorrow."

Dennis looked around nervously. "I can't just get it back like that," he said.

I lowered my voice. "Tell that bitch her Cabriolet's turning into a fucking pumpkin at midnight. I want it back." I unleashed my anger on him. "How fuckin' stupid can you be? Don't you know a professional athlete's supposed to get a piece of ass for free?" He looked queasy.

Dennis kept stalling, telling me Karen would bring it back. Two weeks later she totaled it. By then we had settled back into the condo and life was back to its normal abnormalcy.

I left him after he persuaded me to have the second abortion and returned to Sacramento hoping to get my life back together and gain my independence.

I always wanted to be a cop when I was a kid. That dream got sidetracked when I was whisked off to Tokyo to become a model. If your dream is going to be sidetracked, I guess that's not a bad way for it to happen. But now, with my modeling career over, I decided I would once again pursue my dream of being in law enforcement. I wanted to become a motorcycle cop for the city of Sacramento. I began doing volunteer work for the police department's vice squad.

I had taken some classes at Oakland Community College outside Detroit, and I've been riding Harleys for a while, so I figured that would help me get a foot in the door and earn some of the units to become one of the girls in blue.

My first day there I was fingerprinted, then shown to a desk in a room with three detectives. On the wall directly in front of my desk were about fifty photos of murdered women. The pictures were horrifying. The women had been prostitutes, but I couldn't help but think they had also been little girls at some point, with mothers and fathers. Or maybe not. Maybe their fathers were Philander Rodmans. Most of the girls were runaways who got caught up in drugs and alcohol, got hooked up with a pimp, and got killed. I stared at the photos until one of the detectives asked if I wanted to sit somewhere else. I told him no.

My job was to remove the names of the dead women from a database on the computer. I also had to capture and input information on the prostitutes' arrests, convictions, and probations. When I wasn't working on the computer I was organizing the photo book of all the prostitutes. If there were recent arrest photos, I replaced the old ones with the new.

I loved the work despite the fact that it was sometimes depressing to think about how lives can go so wrong. Still, I couldn't wait to become one of the rank and file. The work gave me a sense of belonging and accomplishment, and on top of that, it was flat-out fun. The other cops would tell me what they were doing each day, from investigating massage parlors to busting johns. I really wanted to be a hooker decoy. I'd stand on a street corner, looking cheap and flashy, and wait for some hapless man to come along and talk about the cost of service before we swooped in and busted his ass!

I was working to better myself, and I was in complete control. Dennis wasn't around to screw anything up. My plan was to earn the necessary sixty units and become a cop. I had a new direction, a new career, and a new life in front of me. Or so I thought.

This was in the fall of 1990. Alexis was almost two, and I was flat broke. Dennis was on the championship Pistons team and was earning nearly a million dollars a year, but he wasn't sending child support consistently. I had to depend on my mother to help me keep my head above water. As always, the one person in the entire world I could count on was Mom.

Unbelievable (and stupid and demented) as it sounds, I was still seeing Dennis. In spite of everything, I held out some hope that we could work things out. I thought his separation from Alexis and me would finally snap him out of his fantasy world and make him realize his responsibilities. Then again, since all of the groupies and sluts were a reality, *not* a fantasy, maybe I should have known it would take more than that to bring him around.

I think the fact that I was on my way toward financial independence put a pretty big scare into Dennis. He knew I was enjoying the work and the camaraderie. If I actually became a police officer and started drawing a regular paycheck, he would no longer be in control—and Dennis prefers to be in control, even though he doesn't do it very well.

He did not appreciate the fact that I was enjoying myself. He preferred to see me fail, because that proved to him that I was nothing without him. He didn't seem to remember that I was a professional model long before our paths ever crossed. Whenever I talked to Dennis about my becoming a cop, he would say I didn't have what it took. He told me I was too crazy for the job. He said if I ever went on a domestic disturbance call, I'd probably blow the guy away if it looked like he had been beating his wife or his children. There might be some truth to that. I think the police officers who see that sort of thing all the time must have tremendous self-control not to kill some of the scumbags they run across.

After I'd been away from Dennis for a while, he started pleading with me to give up the police work and go back to him. I'm sorry to say that I did exactly that. Looking back, it's embarrassing to realize how I let him control me.

Soon afterward I caught him again breaking his latest promise to change his ways. I moved back to Sacramento. One day my dad told me that the California Highway Patrol test was coming up. Even though I hadn't been in school for a while and I didn't prepare at all, I took the test. I passed! There were about 20 women taking the test out of about 250 total applicants. I got one of the highest scores. If I could pass the agility test and the oral exams, I was in business. I'd finally be able to say to Dennis, "Ha! I did it. And you said I'd never make it." I was pumped.

I arrived at the CHP academy ready to face whatever would be thrown at me. After a series of lectures it was time for the physical tests. We had to run something like a five hundred meter in less than three minutes, then do a hundred-meter sprint in under twenty seconds—all in the 110-degree summer sun. I passed, no problem.

About a month or so later, it was time for the oral exams. I arrived early. Everyone told me to dress conservatively and to make sure I covered my tattoos. I thought, *They can't judge me based on my tattoos.* So I wore a sleeveless pantsuit and made sure they could see exactly what they were getting. I wasn't going to hide anything. Maybe I should have. There were three proctors in the room, a man and two women. The man was a classic. He had chauvinist written in big block letters across his face. I got the immediate impression that he didn't care for my looks, and I didn't much care for his either. Bad start. The two female proctors deferred to the man like their lives depended on it.

The man as much as told me I shouldn't be a cop, since I hadn't worked a real job in the last six or seven years. (He's obviously never tried to raise a child and run a household, or he'd know better than to say something that pig-ignorant.) He noted that I was engaged to Dennis Rodman. He more or less wanted to know why the fiancée of someone famous would want to be a cop. I wanted to know what one had to do with the other. He asked if I realized I was up against people with college degrees and others with military experience. That's about all I could take of this nitwit's nonsense. Of course I knew some of the other people had been in the military. The man glared at me. I glared back. The two women just sat there, quiet and pointless.

"We've done a background check on you," the nitwit said. "We also know you're on an antidepressant. What is it? Zoloft?"

I knew I was being washed out at that moment, and I really didn't care. If I was going to have to deal with boneheads like this guy,

I'd rather work elsewhere. On my way out I thought about dropping my pants and telling the old fart to kiss my ass. I also wanted to see if the two women were actually alive and thought such a gesture might cause one of them to at least blink or something. But I refrained.

In the end I decided I wasn't cut out to be a cop. Alexis told me she was scared of me getting shot—and that prospect never appealed to me either.

During my time with Dennis I had plenty of run-ins with officers from different police agencies. Once they found out I was Dennis's fiancée or, later, ex-wife, they treated me differently. They put extra heat on me! I got the distinct impression that they did not approve of a white woman being with a black man.

I've also been pulled over by the CHP several times, mostly after I got vanity plates that read 2RODMAN. Of course I might have been going a little over the speed limit, too, but there were other cars that were passing me as well. I wasn't sure if they pulled me over in hopes of meeting Dennis, or if they were out to intimidate me because I was white and married to a black man.

After being in the public eye with Dennis, I started to get recognized on the street. Even today I get hustled to the front of the line at clubs. I get special attention at department stores. When I pull my car up to a self-serve island at the gas station, I still get full service. And quite frankly, I don't like it. It's not right to treat me any better than someone else simply because I'm Dennis Rodman's anything. It's just not my cup of tea. That's another reason I like being in Sacramento. There I'm Annie Bakes more than I'm Annie Rodman. After all, I don't consider myself Dennis Rodman's ex-wife. I think of myself as Alexis's mom.

Not that I think I'm a real badass, but after everything I've been through I just feel like I need to stick up for myself and not take any shit, whether it's coming from a prejudiced cop or my husband. If you don't have at least a little attitude, the world will chew you up and spit you out. Maybe my attitude comes from a fear of defeat. I saw my dad try to defeat my mom, and Dennis tried to defeat me. Mom came from a generation that was taught to put up with that kind of shit from husbands. I wasn't willing to, not after a certain point. And I don't want Alexis to think for a second that she ever has to put up with it. I want to teach her to stand up for herself, and I want to give her the tools to do it: education and self-confidence. With those two weapons you're in pretty good shape. I didn't get as much of an education as I wish I had, but I got the self-confidence.

It's not that I want her to distrust everyone. I don't. But I want her to be wary. People need to earn your trust before you give it to them, not just because they wear a uniform or drive an expensive car or think they're important. I want Alexis to be strong, not a bully. I want her to be cautious with people, but at the same time I want her to be kind. Most of all, I don't want her to be taken advantage of. I don't want her to take shit from anyone. Not surprisingly, she's already got a lot of this. She has a lot of respect for herself and for others. She's compassionate and never does anything to hurt anyone's feelings. Yes, she's a little stubborn, something she may have picked up from me. But I think that stubbornness will soon be tempered with reason.

When the time comes I can only hope that I've given her the right tools for forging a good relationship. She will know that a man has to treat her with respect, and if he doesn't, she'll say good-bye as she's walking away. Alexis is my little princess, and one day she's going to deserve a prince. She deserves the best the world has to offer. God help anyone who offers her less.

— — —

I met Vinnie Johnson in the fall of 1987, when I met the rest of Dennis's Pistons teammates. Vinnie wasn't like a lot of the other players. He was quiet and humble. He never played the showboat, just took care of business. When he came in off the bench he could shoot the lights out. He didn't even need to warm up. That's why they called him the Microwave. He came into a game and got hot immediately. It was unbelievable. Vinnie would sub into the game, and the opposition knew exactly what he was going to do: shoot the ball. There was nothing his defender could do to stop him. Vinnie would get the ball and *bam!* Count it.

Vinnie was kind and gentlemanly, and I enjoyed his company. After Dennis started to treat me so badly—something Vinnie knew about and disapproved of—I found myself turning to him, and he let me cry on his shoulder. He never tried to take advantage of my vulnerability. He just had a good soul and treated me with the respect Dennis rarely did.

My attraction to Vinnie grew the longer I knew him. Next to Dennis, Vinnie was the pope. I got to know Vinnie during all the time I spent at various Pistons functions. Initially he was just a friend, and it never occurred to me that anything would ever happen between us. Alexis also liked Vinnie. It was during a Pistons game that I realized I was watching Vinnie, not that other guy.

One day I made an offhand remark to William Bedford that I thought Vinnie was extremely sexy. I had spent time with William and his wife, Pamela, and I felt comfortable enough with them to banter like that. I never thought Bedford would pass the comment on to Vinnie. Or maybe I was hoping he would.

Right after a game one night, Vinnie walked by me and pressed a piece of paper into my hand. I must have turned beet red. On the paper was his number and a note to call him.

My head was spinning.

First of all, the idea that William Bedford, who idolized Dennis, would try to set me up with someone else, let alone one of their fellow teammates, was a total mindblower. The second, more difficult concept was so huge I couldn't grasp it: cheating on Dennis.

I had been in countless fights with Dennis, left him on numerous occasions, and even come to blows with him over the very thing I was now considering. I liked Vinnie. Maybe even a lot. But the idea of breaking the faith with Dennis was just not possible.

Or was it?

I wrestled with the idea for a while, rolling that piece of paper around in my hands until it felt like fabric. At that point in my life, the idea that someone, anyone, found me attractive was like a blessing. What gave me the biggest glow was one simple, little thing: Someone found me sexy. My head won out, though, and I decided I just couldn't do it. I put Vinnie's proposition out of my mind and into a drawer. At least for a few days.

It wasn't long before I was sitting home one night, waiting for Dennis to come home, and something snapped in my brain. I knew he was with one of his ho's, and I decided I wasn't going to take this shit any longer. He had tortured me and stroked me, tortured me and stroked me, and repeated this cycle so many times I was punchy and fed up.

I looked in my drawer for that particular piece of paper. Then I picked up the phone.

Vinnie was excited to get my call, and I told him I wanted to see him. I didn't play coy or giggle or mince around—I took control. I knew exactly what I wanted. I got off the phone and found myself breathing hard. I felt *alive* again.

I called the baby-sitter, then Monique. I told her, "I'm at your house in case Dennis calls." She squealed with delight and knew exactly what I was talking about. Monique didn't like Dennis, mostly because of how he treated me. She was always supportive of anything that would piss him off or give him his comeuppance. Like I said, she was sort of my Mike Gold. When the baby-sitter arrived I told her I'd be at Monique's.

At the time I think I rationalized that I was doing this to hurt Dennis, but I realize now that I was doing it for myself. I was also trying not to worry about Dennis finding out. I had no idea what he would do, and *that* scared me.

Both Vinnie and I felt the electricity in the air, and it was absolutely exciting. After the battles with Dennis I welcomed Vinnie's relaxed vibe. We were soon swept away with passion and were making love. Then the phone rang. Vinnie caught his breath and answered it. He handed the phone to me. It was Monique. Dennis had called her from home wondering where I was. I asked Monique, "Where am I?" She replied, "You're on your way home from my place." I hated to do it, but I had to get home.

We got dressed and Vinnie walked me out to my car. "Dennis is one lucky man," he said. "If you were my girl, Annie, I'd never let you out of my sight." That was the problem: I wasn't his girl. In spite of all of Vinnie's great qualities, my heart still belonged to Dennis.

All the way home, and even after I got there, I was waiting for one thing to kick in: guilt. It never did. I think women are genetically more faithful than men. Once they get one guy, they usually don't cheat. But with all his psychological torture, Dennis had caused me, at least temporarily, to go against my natural inclinations.

As time went by, I would have my secret rendezvous with Vinnie. I yearned for someone to hold me and tell me I was beautiful, both inside and out, and just care about me, and Vinnie gave me all of that. We never went out in public. We'd just hang out at his place and enjoy being together. If he needed to conduct some business at home, I would occupy myself by using his Stairmaster, or we'd just go out in his backyard and play with his dog. It felt normal and right.

Vinnie and I saw each other off and on for the next six months or so. He was a great guy and I'll always consider him my friend.

— — —

In the meantime I discovered something that sent chills down my spine: I was pregnant again. Dennis and I had been having problems, to say the least. So when I missed my period and felt a change come over me, I suspected a pregnancy. I had already suffered through two abortions and had no reason to believe Dennis would react otherwise to this news.

I told him.

He reacted in the way I expected and feared: No question about it, you're gonna get an abortion. I went numb. After the first one it was supposed to get easier. It didn't. I started to get angry with myself and with Dennis, but then I just let it go. By now my will to resist and my good judgment and all that I had believed in went out the window.

I just threw up my hands in resignation. Okay, fine, I'll call the doctor and have him warm up his siphon. Just like that.

The day I was scheduled to have the procedure, our plan was fairly simple. Early that morning he would drop me off in Farmington at Dr. Migdal's office, go to practice, and pick me up on the way home. He was only going to be at practice a couple of hours, as usual. We'd be home by lunchtime.

As we drove to the doctor's office, I didn't say a word. Dennis talked a little, trying to lighten things up, but I couldn't even look him in the eye. He dropped me off like I was going in to have my hair done. I grabbed Alexis and slogged through the snow toward Dr. Migdal's office.

Once inside, I checked in and the receptionist immediately offered to keep Alexis company for me while I was "busy." I sat down and slowly looked around the room at the smiling faces of all of the expectant mothers—probably there for their weekly exams— and I suddenly felt like I had "here for an abortion" written all over my face. I focused on Alexis to take my mind off it.

When they escorted me into the abortion chamber and handed me a gown, I saw that now-familiar glass jar with the hose attached. I cringed. I lay down, and my thoughts turned to Dennis. What was he doing right now? Was he thinking about me? My imagination went wild. Would someone rush into the room just as they were hooking up the equipment, like in the movies, and say, "Stop! Your fiancé just called and said he's changed his mind"? Nope. No call ever came. The doctor entered the room, as usual, stuck in the hose, as usual, and got to work.

As usual.

While the doctor calmly vacuumed away another life, I thought of my mother and how this scene would have broken her heart. This girl on the table wasn't the Annie she knew; this was an impostor. I desperately needed my mother to be with me, but I knew I could never share this part of my life with her. The shame I felt was based on how much I knew she would disapprove. My secret, painful life with Dennis—the abuse, the other women, the games we played, the affairs to punish him, the abortions—would have pushed my mother over the edge. I know she felt my pain whenever we talked on the phone. No matter how hard I tried, I couldn't mask my sadness.

I stared at the ceiling tiles and tried to think of something else, but the drone of the suction pump kept pulling me back. I never had an abortion any later than six weeks because I thought that if I waited longer, whatever got sucked into that jar was going to look too much like a human being. That gave me nightmares. The doctors warned me that having an abortion at four to six weeks might result in a "missed abortion"; in other words, the abortion wouldn't be successful, and you'd have to do it all over again.

When the doctor was done he said I could stay and rest a while. I couldn't stand looking at that glass jar anymore, so I jumped up and got dressed. When I got to the lobby I half expected to find Dennis—it had been long enough for him to have finished practice—but he wasn't there. I used the office phone and called home. No answer. I called the Pistons. Practice was long over. I figured he was on his way and sat down to wait. I played with Alexis and glanced through some of the magazines, but the clock was ticking. Having an abortion is an emotional experience, and I wanted to go back to the comfort of my home and be alone with my thoughts. I didn't want to sit in a waiting room with pregnant women as a constant reminder of what I had just done.

As lunchtime approached, the office began to clear out. I had made excuses to the staff, but now they were beginning to ask if Dennis was actually coming. They knew about Dennis, and their concerns were valid. I said he was probably on his way. I felt their pity, and my anger flashed inside me. I felt I didn't deserve any sympathy because of what I had just done. As they closed up the office for lunch, I grabbed Alexis and told them I would wait downstairs.

When I got to the lobby I thought about walking home. It was bitter cold outside, and I had to think twice. I had this image in my mind, right out of a nineteenth-century English novel, of a young woman, a baby in her arms, staggering through the snow and biting wind after having just had an abortion.

Just as I was picturing myself in an Emily Brontë novel, one of the receptionists came downstairs on her way to lunch and asked if I would like a ride home. She knew as well as I did that Dennis wasn't coming. She said I should be home in bed resting. A moment later Alexis and I were in her car and on our way home. I didn't say much on the way, but I think she sensed my feelings and had nothing but kind words to say. I was at a very low point and just needed someone to care, so her gesture touched me deeply.

Dennis was not at home. I put Alexis down for her nap and then lay down. I was emotionally and physically exhausted, but I couldn't sleep. I just lay there, tortured by his cruelty. How in the name of God could he have left me at the doctor's office after an abortion? I began thinking that something had happened to him, then found myself hoping that something had. Finally I got a blessing: I fell asleep.

I awoke later to the sound of Dennis arriving home. I just lay there, too tired to get up, and certainly too tired to fight with him. He felt really guilty and couldn't do enough for me. He took care of Alexis, got dinner going, and even came upstairs and lay down with me for a while. I didn't say anything to him. What could I say? It tore me up inside that it took such horrible things to cause him to be kind to me. I don't know what I expected from him at that point.

Later, when the pain eased and we were talking again, he tried to console me. "The next one we'll keep, okay? I'll be more stable, we can get married and buy a home, okay?" I had heard it all before. Ever since I had anorexia as a young model, my period was no longer regular. As a result, I never knew when I was ovulating. I couldn't take the pill because of a heart murmur, so I started using the contraceptive sponge religiously. I hated it. I'll tell you, those things are a bitch to get out, but I felt that anything was better than having another abortion. Despite Dennis's soothing words about "keeping the next one," like it was a stray puppy, I didn't trust him. "Fool me once, shame on you. Fool me twice, shame on me." Fool me five times, definitely shame on me.

I was learning.

Whenever Dennis would get in the mood for another baby, he would always talk like it was *going* to be a boy. Sometimes he sounded like he wanted to create his own basketball team. He'd say, "Man, with your long legs and height, we'd have a superstar." I'd tell him we already had one: Alexis. He used to say I was what men refer to as a breeder. Charming. I like being reduced to the level of livestock at an auction. I wanted to say, "If I'm so hot, why do you choose all these short, dark-haired bimbos?" I guess they weren't breeders. Just recreation for Stud King Dennis.

# CH**AP T E R** 8

## *Your Cheatin' Part*

ONE OF DENNIS'S THINGS-ON-THE-SIDE BETWEEN 1989 AND 1991 was Kathi the Stripper. A 5'5", twenty-two-year-old "exotic" dancer, Kathi was a tad rough around the edges. By that I mean she was cheap-looking, with massive makeup and too-short, baby-shit-brown hair.

Dennis had a lot of side dishes, but it was women like Kathi the Stripper, the ones he allowed to play a big role in his life, who caused so much trouble. Dennis had the nerve to move Kathi into a condominium about a mile and a half from where we lived. As you might expect, she had absolutely no respect for me or the fact that Dennis, Alexis, and I were a family. For a long time I couldn't understand how one woman could do this to another, but I've seen it happen so many times now that I guess I'm used to it.

Kathi flaunted her relationship with Dennis in a way that made me feel like the butt of a bad joke. This was when I had finally admitted to myself that my modeling career was finished, and had aspirations to become a cop. Dennis would have preferred that I stay at home and take care of Alexis while he paid the bills and ran around with Kathi and the others. Nevertheless he made good use of the opportunity I gave him. He spent all his time at Kathi's apartment after practice while I was attending classes toward a degree in criminology.

Before she came along, Dennis's side dish was a waitress named Tracy. As much as I hated Tracy, she was probably the only one of his sluts who had at least a little sympathy, if not respect, for me, although she did record my threats and call the cops on me. Dennis was lying to her about me so she'd stay with him. He apparently lied to the others, too, and he got so mixed up trying to keep the lies straight that it's no wonder he got so crazy.

Dennis bought gifts for me and all these other women. Sometimes he bought us all the same thing, other times he didn't. I sometimes wonder if having Tracy and Kathi just made gift giving easier for Dennis since they were both 5'5" and apparently the same size.

During the 1989–90 season Dennis got Tracy seats at a Pistons game just a few rows behind me. This proved to be an especially bad idea, because once I knew who Tracy was, the fact that she was sitting back there—literally and symbolically *behind my back*— drove me crazy. The way it always worked, Dennis's other women knew who I was, but I never knew who they were unless I caught them. And how did I catch Tracy? I actually found a nude photo of the bitch among some of Dennis's stuff at the house. God, he was stupid. Now I knew who to look for.

Monique was with me that night I saw Tracy at the game. I had already shown Monique the photo, and she thought she recognized Tracy a few rows behind us. I kept turning around, trying to make eye contact, and Tracy knew it. Monique was telling me to let it slide, that there was nothing to be gained by doing something crazy. She was right, but I was way past acting on logic at that point. Tracy was doing everything she could to avoid meeting my eye. Finally I couldn't stand it anymore. I stormed up to where she was and grabbed her by the shirt. "You're fucking my boyfriend!" I said. Even though she should have been scared shitless, she copped an attitude with me. Big mistake. One thing led to another, and before I knew it, I had snapped the necklace off her skinny little neck.

I wanted to tear her apart, but fortunately Monique grabbed me and kept me from doing any real damage. The fans in the neighboring seats seemed to find my assault on Tracy more interesting than whatever was going on down on the court. And they weren't the only ones. Dennis was standing on the court watching, his jaw resting on his high-tops. During the rest of the game he kept looking up into the stands to see if the catfight was still going on. But Tracy had the good sense to leave early.

Not surprisingly, she broke off with Dennis soon after that. At first I thought it was a case of the guilts, or maybe she was worried that this "psycho" (as she called me) would hunt her down and finish what Monique had stopped me from doing. I later found out Tracy dumped him because she caught him with Karen Stewart.

Tracy herself told me the story. One night when I was in Sacramento, after Dennis and I had had another fight, Dennis and Tracy were on the phone. He told Tracy he wasn't feeling well and was just going to stay home and rest. She offered to come by and make him soup or something, but he said, "No, no need for that. I'll be fine." Minutes later he had an amazing recovery. He showered, dressed, and went straight over to Karen Stewart's. The two of them then went to Club Land in Detroit. Unfortunately, Tracy was there, too. When she saw them she marched over and gave Dennis a piece of her mind. Then she turned to Karen and said, "For your information, I was fucking him last night!"

An argument ensued. After they traded barbs one of them finally had a realization and said, "Hey, we can argue all we want, but the real problem is Annie. We're fighting over nothing. He's never going to belong to either one of us. He loves her."

Dennis had walked off, leaving his lovers to scream at one another. I don't know if he was proud or embarrassed. Probably proud. Because right there, for all the world to see, two white women were actually fighting over him. That's not the sort of thing he would have even allowed himself to *fantasize* about while growing up.

Tracy didn't have much to do with Dennis after that. But I'm the one who ended up being known by Dennis's pals and girlfriends as "the psycho." Why? Because I wasn't like most of the other NBA wives who knew their husbands and boyfriends were fucking around but kept their mouths shut. I refused to be silent about it. Fat lot of good it did me, but that's the way I am. I think if I had put on the blinders like the other wives did, I think our marriage would have worked. But is that a marriage? It's not my idea of one. I was damned if I was going to let him treat me like that. It became my hobby—no, more like my mission to catch Dennis in every one of his affairs. In time I was obsessed with it, pushing the redial button on our phone to see who he had called last, calling numbers I found on hotel phone bills to see who answered, over and over again.

The thing I had the hardest time understanding was why he was cheating. I gave him anything he wanted. Sex on demand, 24-7. I made sure I always looked good. I took good care of him and our daughter. The only explanation I could come up with was that there was something wrong with *me*.

Dennis took full advantage of my insecurity. The physical abuse was bad, but sooner or later bruises heal. It was his emotional terrorism that stuck with me longer. After so many years of his verbal abuse I had the self-esteem of a slug. He used to tell me, "You're a loser, Annie. You never made it far in sports, your modeling career is washed up, your tits sag, your family doesn't love you 'cause you're with me, your dad's an alcoholic, you're fucking worthless!" After hearing that over and over, I began to think it was true.

▬ ▬ ▬

Karen Stewart was working as a tanning technician when she began seeing Dennis. When I started going to her salon, she stopped working there and became a cashier at Arbor Drugs. Karen was my complete opposite, not only in size, but in temperament as well. She was thoroughly gullible and conservative. But she wasn't stupid. She got Dennis to buy her that Volkswagen Cabriolet. He also bought her a nice Gucci and Louis Vuitton wardrobe and some jewelry. I think Dennis really cared for her, and knowing that just made me hurt more. After he was through with her, he came crawling back, and like the fool I was, I left the door open.

Sometimes I'd get another rude awakening: I'd find panties in the laundry that didn't belong to me (or to Dennis)! The other players' wives would confide to me that Dennis had some girl in the back after the game. And many of his floozies were so brazen they'd just phone the house looking for him.

I became so obsessed with rooting out the many women in Dennis's life that I sometimes crossed legal lines. When I found out that Karen was working at Arbor Drugs I called her and told her to stay away from Dennis. She hung up and phoned Dennis, who in turn called me on his cellular. "Leave that girl alone! Quit fuckin' with her, Annie. I'm not messin' around with her. There ain't anything goin' on. We're just friends!"

I hung up and called Arbor Drugs again, but they wouldn't put Karen on the line. I said, "Tell the bitch I'm on my way." I was there in about ten minutes, and so were the cops. Two patrol cars were parked in front of the store. I didn't bother getting out of my car. I just went back home and stewed.

Karen later got a restraining order against me. That's rich. I couldn't get an order to stop her from fucking my husband, but she could keep me from telling her not to.

What bothered Dennis the most about my going after these women was not that he'd been caught but that it clued them in to the fact that he was lying to them about his relationship with me. He had told the others that we were no longer together, so you can imagine their surprise when I showed up saying things like, "Stop fucking my boyfriend!"

I came to realize that the best way to ruin his other relationships was to pull out all the stops. Confronting the girls themselves was a hit-and-miss proposition. But when I went to these young girls' mothers—yes, many of them were still living with Mommy and Daddy—and told them their lily-white daughters were getting boned by a large, very attached black man who already had at least one child, well, my success rate soared. The Atlanta Hawks cheerleader was a perfect example. The look on the face of that Southern girl's mother was priceless. You'd have thought I was General William Tecumseh Sherman standing on her front step with a lighted torch.

Not surprisingly, Dennis would get irate. But because he wouldn't admit he was messing around on me, he could hardly confront me about it. So he kept it inside until I confronted him.

Most of the time I would call the women and tell them to back off, though sometimes I'd run into them at bars. There were even incidents long after I'd left Dennis for good. He had moved a girl named Linda into the big house, where we had lived together. Their relationship had to be hidden from Linda's Armenian family. One day she called me in Sacramento to tell me Dennis had given her herpes. "Congratulations," was all I could say.

Even after Dennis and I were legally separated, I had encounters with his girlfriend Kym. Dennis was still playing in San Antonio and had met her in Las Vegas on one of his gambling binges. She introduced herself as Kym Hunt, as in the J. B. Hunt trucking empire—owned, I believe, by a respected old family in Arkansas. He swallowed it hook, line, and sinker. Kym told Dennis that she was used to only the best, and thus he showered her with expensive gifts.

*Hard Copy* was doing a story on Dennis around that time, and it somehow came to light that he was going out with Kym Hunt. Below Kym's photo onscreen was the caption "Kym Hunt—Daughter of Millionaire Trucking Magnate J. B. Hunt." When members of the real Hunt family heard about her relationship with Dennis, they were not exactly pleased. It turned out that Kym Hunt was actually Kym Lee, a grifter who had taken Dennis for a short, expensive ride. The Hunt family contacted Dennis or *Hard Copy* and demanded retractions or they would sue.

After Kym Lee, Dennis hooked up with a stripper named Staci Yarbrough. She's a little trash bucket hanging around, waiting to see what gets thrown her way.

— — —

On January 2, 1991, the Pistons played the Denver Nuggets, and Dennis did something rare: He scored points. Lots of them. In fact, he had the highest point total of his career: 34. Pretty damn good for a guy who claimed scoring was not important to him. He also could lay claim to another title: Person with the Highest Level of Chlamydia Living in Our Household. I did not know this until it was too late. One day I noticed a burning sensation in my urinary tract. I went to the doctor and soon learned I had chlamydia. I knew I could have gotten it only from Dennis. I *had* slept with Vinnie Johnson in 1990, but that was six months ago. And we had used a condom.

I became Sherlock Holmes. I looked through the dirty clothes and found some of Dennis's underwear. Sure enough, I found the tell-tale evidence: ugly yellow stains. I was furious. I wanted to give Dennis a second circumcision with one of my kitchen knives. I decided I would examine the source.

One night Dennis and I began to get intimate and I reached for his "member," if you get my drift. I thought I'd warm him up as usual with some oral stimulation. As I opened my mouth and leaned in close, I noticed his Oscar Mayer had some mustard on it. Yuck.

I suddenly lost my interest. I pointed out to Dennis that the yellow discharge at the end of his penis was the result of chlamydia. I added he had given it to me. He was extremely defensive and denied that he had it. He also refused to take the tetracycline the doctor had given me.

— — —

By early 1991 Dennis and I had already seen more conflict than most couples do by their golden anniversary. For months we fought constantly, and I would move out and go back to Sacramento, only to be lured back by his promises of fidelity. Now I'm not one to talk, what with my affair with Vinnie, but to me that was like an insurance policy that I could cancel anytime Dennis decided to be truly faithful to me. So I went back to Vinnie partly to escape Dennis, partly to hurt him. I'm sorry it all happened, because Vinnie was a nice guy and a gentleman. I think he felt sorry for me and wanted to give me some comfort in all of the chaos. Sure, we had good sex, but our connection went much deeper. I felt a peace with Vinnie that I never felt with Dennis. But bad boys were my vice, and when Dennis called, I came.

During the time I was bouncing between Detroit and Sacramento, I was keeping an apartment in Sacramento at a complex called River Terrace. My folks had a neighbor named Ray, who told my mom that he had noticed a Lincoln Continental parked near their house. After two days he had gotten suspicious and had kept his eye on it. There were two men inside, and they appeared to be watching the house. Ray spoke with the men, and they told him they were private detectives from Michigan. Dennis had hired them to watch *me*, but they ended up watching my folks. Dennis was trying to catch me at something.

I called the police and asked them what I could do. They told me if the detectives were just watching me, they had the right to do so. I called Dennis. At first he said he didn't know what I was talking about, but I pushed. Finally he came clean. I tore a strip off him over the phone and hung up. The detectives disappeared.

At that point I had spent some time off and on with Vinnie, but it had been during the previous year and in Detroit. And most important, *Dennis didn't know about it.* He was having a great season with the Pistons, making Defensive Player of the Year for the second year, but his personal life was a mess. He had been suspicious of me long before I ever thought about cheating on him. My fooling around with Vinnie had been pretty limited, so I thought it was extremely paranoid to hire PIs to watch me. It was also illogical. I was in Sacramento for *one* reason: we'd had an argument about another of his tramps. All Dennis had to do was be faithful, and we wouldn't have had any of these problems.

Whenever Dennis would go for his women, I'd retaliate by going back to Vinnie. You could probably say it was hypocritical of me to date him on the sly, yet kick Dennis's ass when he strayed, but I would have dropped Vinnie in a second (no offense, Vinnie, but Dennis was first) had Dennis gotten with the program.

A few months after the detective incident, Vinnie called and invited me to fly out to Detroit to spend a little time with him. I didn't want Dennis to know, so when I arrived at Wayne County Airport the last thing I planned on was someone watching my every move. And reporting to Dennis. Later I found out Dennis had a guy on me all the way from Sacramento. The report from his PI probably went something like this: "Yeah, Mr. Rodman, we observed the subject arriving from Sacramento Airport. She retrieved her luggage and met a black man in a black Porsche Carrera at the curbside pickup. The subject and the man loaded her luggage and left. Our DMV check reveals the car is owned by a Vincent Johnson."

Busted.

The Pistons had a game that night, so before the game Vinnie and I just spent a quiet afternoon at his place. It was nice to be back in his arms and his bed. It was also nice to get attention from *someone.*

Later on we were enjoying an early dinner when we heard a knock at the door. I didn't see who it was, but Vinnie came back after answering the door and said it was somebody looking for directions. He said the guy seemed suspicious, so of course we suspected Dennis may have something to do with it. I cleaned up while Vinnie got ready for the game. A little while after he left I turned on the TV and found the pregame show. I figure I'd watch the game and keep an eye on *both* my men. At some point I went out to walk Vinnie's dog. When I came back into the house I got the shock of my life.

Dennis was standing in the kitchen.

Vinnie's kitchen was large, with a huge island in the center. I was on one side of the island and Dennis was on the other. He had an expression on his face I had never seen before. He looked completely stunned.

Trust me, it takes a lot to stun Dennis Rodman, and he was shocked out of his size 13 shoes. "How could you do this to me?" he asked. I said turnabout was fair play. He had screwed me over so many times I was angry enough to let him have it right back.

He started circling around the island. I kept moving, never letting him get close. I wasn't sure how he might react, since I'd suffered his wrath on more than a few occasions. Then I got another shock.

Dennis started crying. Like a baby.

He crumpled to the floor and cried so hard I thought he was going to have a seizure. I went to him and he kept crying. I remember feeling sorry for having hurt him, despite his having hurt me countless times. The TV was still on, and I glanced at it. I couldn't help but be struck by the surreal nature of what I was seeing: The announcers were wondering why Dennis wasn't in the pregame warm-up. I knew. Now they'll know.

He finally picked himself up, staggered out to his car, and drove off. A few minutes later, as I watched the game begin on TV, I wondered where he was. When the game got to half-time and he hadn't shown, I started worrying that he might have done something crazy. Then the phone rang. It was one of Vinnie's friends. He was on his way over to come and get me per Vinnie's instructions. Apparently Dennis had stirred up a real hornet's nest in the Pistons locker room. Vinnie thought I should get out of his house and promised he'd see me after the game.

Dennis did go to the Palace, but before he took to the court he had a heart-to-heart talk with coach Chuck Daly and Isiah Thomas and told them all about his faithless bitch and back-stabbing teammate.

As I waited for Vinnie's friend to arrive, I watched the team take to the court after the half-time break. Dennis was now with them. I worried about Vinnie, and I'd be lying if I said I wasn't worried about Dennis. I didn't know how this situation would play itself out. I called Monique and told her what was going on. Right then Vinnie's friend showed up.

Vinnie's friend took me to his place, and Monique joined me there. We watched the rest of the game. The phone rang shortly after the team went to the locker room. I answered it. It was Vinnie. I asked him where he was, and he said he was out front. I thought that was strange until I looked out the window. He was sitting there, in his Porsche, the phone to his ear. Parked next to him was Dennis's Mercedes.

I watched them for a few minutes. They had their windows down and talked without getting out of their cars. Then Vinnie came in and got me. "I'm so sorry, Vinnie," I said.

He was calm. "I'm a big boy. I can take care of myself. You just do the same, all right? If you don't want to go with him, then don't."

I knew I had to go with Dennis and said so. I walked outside and Dennis came over to me. "Let's go," he said. I was pretty concerned about his state of mind, especially after seeing him break down earlier, and asked where we were going. He wouldn't say. I decided not to get into the car. We went back and forth. Finally Dennis got tired of the sparring and pushed me into the car.

As we drove, Dennis was quieter than usual. We were supposedly driving back to the condo, but when he turned down a different street I got nervous. He said he wanted to show me something. Pretty soon we were entering the very exclusive suburb of Bloomfield Hills. I thought if we were going to end it all, he had picked a nice area. We reached a private drive and Dennis steered the car down it. We approached a huge, beautiful home that looked deserted. There was a For Sale sign on the lawn. I saw a beautiful lake and realized it was Gilbert Lake. I thought Dennis was going to kill me and throw my body into the lake. I looked at the moonlight shimmering on the water, and it hit me that there were worse places to die.

We got out of his car. Dennis can be theatrical, and he made a sweeping gesture. "I'm buying this for us. For you, me, and Alexis. And you treat me like this."

I was floored. It wasn't the first time Dennis had substituted a purchase for emotional support, but this was, I must say, pretty damn impressive. I looked at that sprawling three-level mansion and started to think maybe the three of us *could* have a good life inside.

Dennis is a master at pulling things out of the fire. Himself. His career. Our relationship. We drove back to the condo and he let me know, through his actions and expressions, how hurt he was. I was leaving for California the next day, so he made sure he pleased me. We made love like we hadn't done for a long time.

The next day he took me to the airport. When we arrived he did something he had never done before: He actually parked and walked me in. He had always dropped me off and left me to fend for myself with my bags and getting checked in. Not only did he walk me to the gate, he even got permission—because of who he was— to walk me down the gangway right to the door of the plane! All the way, from the car to the plane's doorway, he was kissing me and wouldn't take his hands off me—and he didn't care who watched us.

At the door to the plane, he held me close. "I love you so fucking much, Annie, it kills me," he said. "You belong to me. We belong together." I walked to my seat in a blur. As I flew west, I wondered just how long the glow would last.

Two months later we moved into our dream home.

— — —

We had been in our new home a little more than six months, a beautiful estate on Gilbert Lake in Bloomfield Hills. Bloomfield Hills is an area of rolling green hills and magnificent manors fifteen miles or so northwest of downtown Detroit, just south of the Palace. Our house was the former home of one of the right-hand men of Chrysler chairman Lee Iacocca.

It was a far cry from that first tiny apartment Dennis and I had together. But in a lot of ways I missed the times we had in that humble $620-a-month one-bedroom with the rented furniture, because we were happy then. Now, in this huge palace, we were miserable.

The home was beautiful, though. Every day when I got up and started my chores, my thoughts went back nearly twenty years to seven-year-old Anicka, who would fantasize about big homes and her life to come. But never in my wildest of dreams did I imagine anything like that house. It was not only enormous but also breathtakingly designed. The living room had an Italian marble floor and a sunken bar in the center. The windows went from floor to towering ceiling. I'd always decorated and done a good job in our homes, but for this house Dennis went overboard. Rather than let me do it on a budget, he spent sixty-five thousand dollars on everything from high-end Indian carpets to fabulous artwork to top-of-the-line black leather furniture.

The kitchen, down a long hallway from the entry, was humongous, with hardwood floors and every built-in appliance you could want. The greenhouse window over the sink area faced a courtyard, and the windows opposite that overlooked our lush backyard, which sloped down to the lake.

Dennis and I shared the bedroom, not far from the kitchen. That bedroom was filled with super-high-tech, all-steel furniture. The two his and hers walk-in closets were each as big as normal-sized bedrooms. Dennis was very clean and particular about where his clothes went. His closet was arranged by color, and things like his underwear and socks had to be folded and placed in their own drawers—dress socks in one, tube socks in another.

Our master bath was a sight to behold. On one side was a long marble counter with two gold sinks and matching fixtures. The solid marble Jacuzzi would easily fit four, and it was surrounded by hanging and potted plants. The shower next to it was a huge enclosure of glass and marble and gorgeous black tile.

On the next floor up from the main level that contained our bedroom, the living room, and the kitchen were two bedrooms, each with its own large bathroom. One of the rooms was for Alexis and the other was a guest room. Below the main level was the entertainment room with a big-screen TV, stereo, Stairmaster, pool table, Ping-Pong table, and of course, Dennis's drums. The maid's quarters was a few steps away from the entertainment room. When we first moved in we had a full-time housekeeper. I eventually let her go after deciding I could do the job she was doing and save Dennis the twenty-five hundred dollars a month he was paying her. I know it sounds crazy that I wanted to save him that money, especially since he was making in the neighborhood of several hundred thousand a month, but I just wanted to make him happy. I did all the cleaning, laundry, shopping, and meal preparation. I took the cars in for oil changes and maintenance, paid bills, and supervised the gardeners. I worked my butt off keeping that house spotless while taking care of my man and our three-and-a-half-year-old daughter.

Unbeknownst to Dennis, I let Monique stay in the maid's quarters after I let the housekeeper go. She was there off and on for quite a while, almost as long as I lived there. We would park her car down the road so Dennis wouldn't see it. In all that time I don't think he had a clue his archenemy Monique was living under his roof.

I waited on Dennis hand and foot. Whenever he needed something, I was there. I'd even run out to the store in the middle of the night to get heating rub after a game. Sometimes he'd come home after a particularly tough game, and his legs would be sore and cramped. He'd sit in front of the TV while I massaged the pain away. Even though I was doing all the work, I treasured those times, because we were together and for the moment he was appreciating me.

I also made sure dinner was ready to go every night, whether he was home for it or not. I never knew if he would come home, but I damn well knew the grub had better be ready or I'd catch it. Alexis and I would often end up eating alone at the fourteen-place table in our formal dining room. She used to get a big kick out of that; I guess it was sort of like playing dress-up to her. I just wish Dennis had been home more often, but I went out of my way not to bitch about his absences. I knew a man like Dennis couldn't be controlled because the minute I tried, I'd be in trouble.

If he did come home for dinner, he'd come into the kitchen and say, "Serve me up a plate." I'd hand him a plate of food, and he'd head down to the entertainment room and shut the door, leaving us to eat by ourselves. A little while later I'd go down and ask if he'd like some more. Without looking away from the TV, he'd say something like, "Yeah, get me some more slices of bread, but don't put so much fuckin' butter on it." Whether he wanted more bread or iced tea or pork chops, I'd cheerfully get it. Anything to make him happy.

When he was done he'd bring the plate into the kitchen and announce he was going out with the boys. As much as I wanted him to stay home with us, I never said anything.

I had an opportunity for a social life with the other NBA wives, but I chose not to participate. They had bowling nights and dinners and tea times. After going to a few, I decided I was better off by myself. All they did was sit around and compare the size of their rocks or their husband's salaries. It got boring real fast.

I didn't really fit in either. I wore what I wanted and said what I wanted, and I think I freaked most of them out. They talked about me behind my back, but I couldn't have cared less. I even started doing little things that would give them something to talk about. I also think a lot of them were posing big-time, and the idea of having someone real and down-to-earth in their midst was too much. Most of the wives who had children never brought them to the games because they had nannies back home watching them. Then I'd show up at a game with Alexis on one arm, a baby bag on the other, and Cheerios stuck to the back of my shirt. That didn't sit well with the wives who covered themselves in diamonds and mink-collared jackets.

The only Pistons wives I liked were Lowanda Moore, Pamela Bedford, and Angela Aguirre. Bill Laimbeer's wife, Chris, and Isiah

Thomas's wife, Lynn, were two I absolutely couldn't stand. They were spoiled, arrogant women who looked down on anyone they perceived to be lower in status than themselves. They both thought they were Queen Shit and pushed around ushers and security and anyone else they felt was beneath them. I always went out of my way to be nice to the service people and made it a point to freeze out the wives who thought they were better than everybody else. Most of the other NBA wives and I were from different universes. I didn't wear makeup, cleaned my own house, washed my own cars, picked up my own dog's shit, and occasionally ran through the sprinklers with my little girl. To this day I even push my own lawn-mower. The only thing I can imagine Lynn Thomas pushing would be the door into a bank.

I finally got sick of the socialites and asked Dennis to have me moved away from the players' section in the Palace. I was beginning to see in those women the girls from high school who tortured me as a teenager, and I wanted to get as far away from them as possible.

When Dennis requested a new seating arrangement for me, Chuck Daly asked Dennis why I couldn't start acting like an NBA wife. The NBA sees itself as having a perfect image and anything "unseemly" is not acceptable. In truth, the NBA has as many potential scandals going on at any given moment as any organization that size with that much money and power circulating. They publicly spank Dennis for his behavior, but behind closed doors they wring their hands with glee over the piles of money he makes them.

To me Daly represented what was corrupt in the NBA, and I despised that egotistical old fart in the cheap suit, partly because he messed around on his wife and partly because he represented a force that threatened to separate me from my man. Daly was always giving Dennis advice, and Dennis would usually listen, so why couldn't he have said, "Dennis, don't cheat on your wife"? Then I might have had some respect for Daly. I think he and Dennis got together to trade the lies they told their women. As far as the rest of the Pistons organization, I liked Dick Versace and Brendan Malone, but that was about it. Daly was definitely on my shit list. And I was certainly on his.

As far as the seating problem went, Dennis did actually have the guts to stand up for me, and soon I had a new seat, albeit on the third deck. Up there I could eat popcorn, scream my head off, and do the wave with the rest of the real fans.

I hardly knew anyone in Bloomfield Hills, so I pretty much kept to myself in that big house, cleaning, taking care of Alexis, and working out. I was pretty lonely.

And Dennis didn't help.

If Dennis wasn't hangin' with his boy-cronies at home, he was either napping, sleeping, eating, or watching *Robocop* or *Naked Gun* over and over. Sometimes he'd spend an hour with Alexis so I could have a little time to myself, but that was about his tolerance threshold: an hour. Then he'd hand her back to me, take a shower with U2 blaring in the background, and go out for the evening. I often felt like the parent of a teenage son who'd taken over the house. I was powerless to stop him. Only Dennis wasn't a teenager; he was the father of my child, and I loved him with all my heart.

So, whenever he'd drive off into the night I would not only worry about where he was going and who he was going to see, but I would also miss his company. As much as I love my daughter, a three-year-old isn't the most sterling conversationalist. I really missed adult contact during that period in my life. I'd call my mom a lot, but she was halfway across the country. As soon as I hung up, that warm, loving contact was broken, and I was suddenly back in that big house with no one to talk to, knowing Dennis wouldn't be home until 3 A.M. at the earliest.

If at all.

# CHAPTER 9

## Ozzie and Harriet From Hell

A T SOME POINT IN THE SECOND HALF OF 1991, AFTER DENNIS AND I moved into the house in Bloomfield Hills, my parents surprised us with an unannounced visit. The timing was bad. I had a black eye, and they knew Dennis had done it despite the fact that I told some lie about having banged my eye on the handle of the Jet-Ski.

And even though my parents were already in a pretty foul mood about things, those things were about to get even worse.

William Bedford came over to pick up Dennis and go God-knows-where. He left his truck in the driveway with some dog tied to the bumper. Now, this wasn't a toy poodle. This was a chow, and it was a mean son of a bitch. And Bedford failed to warn anyone about the dog.

My dad was taking Alexis outside for a walk when he saw this poor dog tied up without any water to drink. Being fond of animals, he decided to bring the dog a bowl of water. When he got close, the dog attacked my dad and bit his leg bad enough to require medical attention.

I couldn't believe it! This dog could have just as easily attacked Alexis. It was typical Dennis, not thinking about anyone but himself. With my dad's leg bleeding like crazy, we rushed him to the hospital to get him stitched up and get a tetanus shot, and then the doctors started asking about rabies. Well, since it wasn't our dog, we had to find out whose it was. It turned out the dog wasn't Bedford's. He was dog-sitting for some drug dealer friend who was not available at the time to answer questions regarding the dog's vaccination status. We had to call the animal control people to come out and sedate the dog so it could be tested for rabies. The animal control guys said that chow was the most vicious animal they'd ever dealt with. Great.

After finding out that the dog did not have rabies, the animal control department was going to hold it for two weeks until the owner came and picked it up. They sent the owner several notices, but he never bothered to pick up his dog, so they had to put the dog to sleep.

Even though the dog had bitten my dad, I felt sorry for it. I identified with its being tied up and abused and knowing nothing but meanness. The poor dog had probably been treated horribly, and now it was put to sleep because—through no fault of its own—it had been raised to be such a monster.

But that's not even the end of the story.

After my dad returned to Sacramento he started feeling like he deserved to be reimbursed for his medical expenses. Unfortunately, the dog's owner was nowhere to be found. Dad turned to the next set of pockets he could think of—Dennis's. Or more precisely, the insurance company that had the homeowner's policy.

My dad never told me he was doing this. I only found out when his attorney contacted us. I couldn't believe my dad was suing us. Granted, Dennis was stupid to leave the dog outside without warning us, and my dad was justified in wanting to get reimbursed, but a lawsuit?

I think Dad was pissed at Dennis for giving me a black eye. Maybe it made him realize what a shit he'd been to Mom all those years. I hated him for doing this. I called him up and gave him both barrels. I told him that if he went ahead with the lawsuit, he would never see me or Alexis again. What a turn of events. I was now defending the guy who had given me the black eye. It was me and Dennis against my family, my only support group next to Monique. Dennis couldn't have asked for more.

The lawsuit pushed me even further away from my dad than I already was. I had not yet forgiven him for what he had put my brothers and me through when we were kids. Eventually my mom told me they had dropped the suit, but Dennis told me otherwise. I was going crazy not knowing who to believe. Was Dennis lying to keep me set against my family so I'd have nowhere to run the next time he blackened my eyes? Were my parents lying so I'd forgive them? To this day I don't know the truth. So many traumatic events lay in my future that this one just got filed away as unresolved.

■ ■ ■

August 1991 was the beginning of the most insane period of my relationship with Dennis. We had moved into the house on Gilbert Lake the previous month, and I was still completely overwhelmed not only by its size and opulence, but by what it symbolized to me. I wanted to believe that the purchase of the house was a sign that Dennis was finally ready to settle down and become the family man Alexis and I needed so badly.

We actually set a wedding date. We didn't plan anything elaborate; in fact, we were simply going to go to a justice of the peace for a quick civil ceremony. It wasn't exactly what I had in mind, but I was willing to settle for it, as long as we'd be married.

It had been four years—four crazy years of manic love–hate cycles—since that day in Oklahoma, when he first asked me to marry him on the hood of the car. After all the crap I'd put up with, I still said I'd marry him. What does that tell you about my state of mind? What it tells me is that whatever good sense I may have once had was long gone. I was living in a delusional world where I believed Dennis's pattern of behavior could change 180 degrees overnight.

However, once again I was rudely awakened from my dream of domesticity. I soon caught Dennis in another lie, and all evidence pointed to Kathi the Stripper. I confronted him about it, and we got into a fight. He reminded me we were about to get married. I told him to think again—the wedding was off.

I decided to go to Monique's. I had my car keys and my purse, and I think I was on my way to get Alexis from her bedroom when it happened. Here's how the Bloomfield Township Police Report put it:

> *On listed date (8-12-91) AR* (Annie Rodman) *came to this department to make an assault and battery report. AR stated that the A&B* (assault and battery) *occurred one week ago (8-5-91) but she did not report it then as she thought "things would get better between her and listed suspect." AR reported that there has been a history of A&B in the past, in which listed suspect* (Dennis) *batters AR. AR has made several reports with West Bloomfield P.D. (where they used to live). AR stated that on this occasion (8-5-91) she and listed suspect were having an argument, AR wanted to leave the residence at 5635 Shadow Lane (where argument was ensuing); however suspect took AR's purse and would not give it back. AR reached for her purse that the suspect was holding, and in doing so, she grabbed his shirt. As AR did that, suspect struck AR's right eye with the back of his hand. AR reported that just after listed suspect struck her, her nose began to bleed and she felt light-headed. AR then left residence. AR did not see a doctor. She stated that the right side of her face bruised and swelled. Writer observed a bruise above AR's right eye and under the right eye. AR states that she does wish prosecution in this matter. The address she gave for herself is her parent's home in CA. She stated she would be returning there shortly as she has moved out of suspect's home. AR will be staying with a friend for the next few days. Writer took two Polaroids of victim's face—attached.*

The fact that a week had passed between Dennis's assault and the point where I finally mustered up the courage to report him—and when the police took the photograph of my face—is evidence of how hard he hit me. Even after seven days my face was still a bruised mess.

I'm just glad Alexis was so young when this happened. I suspect that Dennis's emotions (and mine) were so out of control that even a three-year-old could sense that things were bad between her parents. But precisely because our emotions were so out of control, and I was so focused on trying to get my keys back from Dennis, and we were fighting, and he backhanded me, and the whole episode was just violent in general, I can't even remember if Alexis was in the room or not. I hope she didn't witness it.

After the assault Alexis and I finally got to Monique's house, where we were safe for a while. The day after I made the report, one of the police officers requested copies of all the other A&B reports I filed against Dennis with the West Bloomfield Township Police Department. They noted that I had never followed up (I never prosecuted) on any of those complaints.

I think it was on August 14, two days after I filed the report, that Dennis and his "agents/attorneys" called me and talked me out of pressing charges. I agreed to do so only if Dennis agreed to some counseling, which he did. Same old promise. I started having second thoughts the way I always did. Then I started rationalizing. Hadn't he just bought this house for us? For our family? Was it realistic for me to expect him to change overnight? Should I prosecute my daughter's father? This is the cycle. It's nothing new. I called the police and told them I didn't want to prosecute. They told me I'd have to come to the station and tell them in person.

I went to the police station on August 15. They asked if I had been intimidated by the "agents/attorneys," and I said no. They asked if I had received monetary goods or favors for not prosecuting, and I said no. Then I wrote the following:

> *I Anicka Bakes have decided not to press charges against Dennis Rodman with the understanding that he seeks help. I do not wish in any way to prosecute. I have indeed dropped the case against Dennis Rodman. Anicka Bakes, Aug 15-91.*

With that, the case was closed.

— — —

We hadn't been in the house on Gilbert Lake more than a month when Dennis and I got in another huge fight over another woman.

I had had my fling with Vinnie Johnson, but once Dennis and I moved into that house, we were starting anew. That meant I would give up Vinnie, and Dennis would give up all the women from the strip joints, the women on the road, the women after the home games, even the women he met at stoplights. It was a whole new ball game, if you'll excuse the pun.

I was happy to make a home with my daughter and my man, and all I asked of him was respect. Apparently it was too much to ask.

When I found out he was still seeing the ho deluxe, Kathi the Stripper, I went nuts. But I waited until he got home to do so. I'd had enough practice going nuts that I actually began to plan when I'd come unglued.

I waited until Dennis came into the kitchen, and then I lit into him. I accused him of still hanging on to Kathi the Stripper, and we got into a shouting match. When he lost that, he attacked me. Dennis had a habit of grabbing me by the neck until I shut up, and that was his tactic that night. He grabbed me and we thrashed around until we tumbled to the floor. He finally got on top of me and wrapped his hands around my neck. I fought him hard, and he kept telling me to shut up. Actually I think a more accurate quote would be, "Shut the fuck up, bitch."

I broke loose and jumped to my feet. I was madder than shit, and I needed to do some damage. I was a she-cat fighting with, and for, my man, and my claws were out.

Okay, figuratively.

Since I didn't *really* have claws, I went for the next best thing: scissors. Sharp enough to get a person's attention, but you'd be hard pressed to kill someone with them unless you were considerably stronger and more motivated. I didn't want to kill Dennis—at least not *that* night—I just wanted to make him think. I figured stabbing him somewhere would do the trick.

I grabbed a pair of scissors from a drawer and, assuming the classic *Psycho* pose with scissors raised high, I went after him. Like a true professional, I went for a particular body part. In this case, I went for his leg. I figured he needed both of them operational to do his job. If he were out of commission for a while, he could recuperate while he discussed his wayward behavior.

We circled around the kitchen's center island. Dennis was wary but calm. "Put 'em down, Annie. Put the scissors down," he said evenly. He was good at recognizing my anger and then speaking softly to me like he was a SWAT negotiator trying to disarm a crazed postal worker. I think he thought it would defuse the situation and get me to stand down from my red alert.

Finally I gave in. I guess I got bored circling that island like a shark, and my rage vanished. At some point I handed the weapon over to him and walked away. It was the same old thing: He'd cheat, I'd get mad, we'd fight, and I'd either give up or walk away. That night I was just tired out, and I caved.

Dennis maintained his cool, and we both went on about our normal routines. I did notice that he kept those scissors in his back pocket the rest of the evening.

A couple of weeks later, around September 5, it was clear that the professional help wasn't doing much to alter Dennis's behavior, because once again I caught Dennis in a lie. He was still seeing Kathi the Stripper. I decided to leave. But this time I had the sense not to do it in front of Dennis.

I stole his brand-new black Mustang Saleen and headed toward Sacramento with Alexis and Monique.

He reported it stolen the day after we left, making us fugitives. Monique and I felt like Thelma and Louise as we drove across the country. We drove at night, always going the speed limit so the cops would have less of a reason to pull us over. When we finally got to Sacramento I hid the car in the garage of one of my friends and started driving the other Mustang Saleen that Dennis and I kept in Sacramento.

About four days later, Dennis, Mike Gold, and the cops showed up at my mom's house. Dennis knew Mom was my Achilles' heel, so he went straight to her, knowing I'd respond. I despised him for that act of cowardice. My mom, detached from my crazed emotional state, told me I'd better give the car back. Having cooled off a bit, I agreed. Dennis, Mike, and the cops followed me to my friend's garage. After I handed over the keys I said, "Take your car and get the fuck out of my face forever!"

The next day Dennis was hiding outside my apartment complex in Sacramento. When I came out he said, "Annie, why are we doing this to each other? We love each other, man. I promise it will change. I promise I will give up Kathi. I promise. I promise."

I just looked at him. "I am not going back as your girlfriend anymore. If you won't marry me, Dennis, then take your sorry ass back to Detroit and leave me be!"

Then, out of the blue, he said, "Marry me today."

I was stunned. "What?"

"Let's go. Today."

We grabbed Alexis and, with nothing more than the clothes on our backs, we jumped into the car, hopped on I-50, and headed east for the wedding chapels of South Lake Tahoe.

As far back as I can remember, I always dreamed of a big wedding. I would be wearing a beautiful gown. My man would be in his tuxedo, standing at the altar as my father walked me down the aisle. After I fell in love with Dennis I had fantasies of him lifting up my veil to kiss me. I was so in love with him that I would have married him in a barn. All that mattered was that I was marrying the man I truly loved with all my heart and soul. This was my dream wedding. It turns out dreams don't always come true.

The ceremony was a comedy, and not a very funny one. We were at the beautiful and romantic Chapel of the Bells. Dennis wore his sunglasses throughout the service and looked like a two-bit gangster. Did I care? Hardly. I cried all through the ceremony, and not because of the sunglasses. I was so happy. I was finally marrying the man I wanted to grow old with. Other than the day Alexis was born, this was the happiest day of my life. I absolutely believed that from that point on, everything was going to be different. We would be faithful till death do us part, in sickness and in health. He would love and honor me!

Dennis was probably wondering how he was going to explain this to all his sluts. He was going to have to come up with a good lie for Kathi the Stripper.

After the ceremony we were both in a state of shock. For our lavish reception we drove to a McDonald's drive-up window. "Would you like fries with that cheating husband?" We ate, and Dennis fell asleep. I ended up driving all the way back home.

Is that romantic or what?

I can't tell you how surprised I was at Dennis's telling of the story in his brilliant autobiography. First of all, he got the year wrong. He said it was September 1992. The wedding license I have says it was September 10, 1991. But I suppose it's easy to add or subtract a year when you're talking about an event that really didn't matter to you. What I don't understand is how he got the rest of it so wrong.

In his book he says we were at a hotel in Tahoe with Alexis— we always stayed at Caesar's when we visited Tahoe—and Alexis, the inquisitive four-year-old, kept asking, "Daddy, when are you going to marry Mommy?" Well, according to his story, poor Dennis hated to keep putting her off, so he suggested we get married as long as we were there. "Eighty-two days later it was over," he writes. Well, I'm nit-picking here, but the divorce wasn't official until August 1993. And even after that we continued to see one another off and on.

I called Caesars and they told me they had no record of Dennis and me staying there on September 8, 9, 10, 11, or 12. Funny, Dennis was so sure about that. Well, maybe he's thinking about some other marriage he was involved in.

After we were married I found out Dennis was still carrying on with Kathi the Stripper. I had hoped against hope that wedding vows, those promises to honor and obey, would finally stop Dennis from cheating. When I found out he considered our vows about as important as an illegal defense call, I knew there was no hope.

I must comment on a couple of other things he wrote in his book. "If I get a new contract, the first thing I'm going to do is take $250,000 and put it in an account for Alexis. She won't be able to touch it until she's 18, and then it can be used for college. By the time she's 25, she can have it all." First, I don't know if that comment includes endorsement contracts, or if he means just basketball contracts. Second, I don't know if he's received a new basketball contract, but I think he's had some endorsement contracts come and go since then. And third, while Dennis certainly isn't required to tell me if he's actually set this account up for Alexis, it would be nice if he told her.

Finally, while it's touching to read about how important Alexis is to Dennis, I can't help but wonder why he missed her baptism, her first Communion, five of her eight birthdays, her first day of school, her basketball games, her ice-skating competitons, Christmases and her Christmas plays, Halloweens, Easters, Thanksgivings, and on and on. Granted, some of these are in the middle of his basketball season, but her birthday, for example, isn't.

Most likely he'll claim that I won't allow him to see her, but that's nonsense. I went through hell trying to keep us together so Alexis would have a father. Dennis simply prefers strip bars and firm titties.

A few days after the wedding, Dennis was off to Spain. He left his new bride and his daughter behind and flew off to some Reebok function. He said Reebok hadn't bought tickets for Alexis and me and, after spending so much money on our reception, I can understand that he certainly couldn't afford to buy them. Cheap bastard.

Later that month, in a show of his love for me, he started seeing a stripper from Dallas who he had known since the previous summer. I found out about her when she called to talk to Dennis. She actually answered all my questions, like, "When was the last time you were with Dennis?" She was quite cooperative in that regard.

From the time he first asked me to marry him in 1987 to the time he said "I do," more than four years had passed. If you've read this far, you know what I had been through. After a few blissful days of marriage, it was obvious that Dennis was spending his honeymoon with someone other than me. I was completely and utterly crushed. What I needed was for Dennis to finally start treating me with love and respect. What I got instead was a phone call from that stripper. I was emotionally numb.

— — —

By Thanksgiving Dennis and I were back to our old rocky relationship, and I missed my mom. Whenever I would leave Dennis and flee to Sacramento, he would cut me and Alexis off financially. I never got involved with him for the money—when I met him I made more than he did—but now I was accustomed to certain things, and it would have been very hard to go back. Dennis and I had also brought a life into this world, and she had requirements that cost money. Mom would take care of us, but I couldn't use up her resources. After a while I would miss Dennis, then he'd call, and we'd go back.

This back-and-forth was taking its toll, and at the time I didn't see any other way out. I was starting to change my approach, though. Like I said, my relationship with Dennis was not based on money, but as time went by and I realized how important I had been in helping him become the player he was, I felt some entitlement. The next time we had a fight and I left, I got smart.

It was a few weeks before Christmas, and Dennis and I had another fight that was significant enough to warrant my leaving. As soon as Dennis left, I told Monique to get Alexis ready because we were about to do a road trip. I told her I'd be right back. I jumped in my 4-Runner and, having decided we should have a little traveling money, headed to our bank.

In the bank I was relaxed and charming as I sat down with a lady bank officer. I explained I didn't have a check with me, but I wanted to withdraw a small amount of money from our entertainment account. I said I wanted to buy Dennis a little something for Christmas and wanted it to be a surprise. "Oh, really? That's nice," said the banker. "What are you going to get him?"

I thought fast. "A boat. Yeah, that's right, a speedboat."

She nodded. "That's lovely. How much will you be needing?"

I had a vague number in my head, but then I thought, *Oh, this is too easy.* I doubled the number, then added five thousand dollars. "I think, uh, thirty-five thousand?"

The banker smiled and went away. A few minutes later she returned with a cashier's check. "I'm sure he'll be surprised," she smiled.

"I'm sure he will be," I smiled back. I got in my 4-Runner and stuffed the check into my bra. I went home, grabbed Alexis and Monique, and hit the road. When we got to Sacramento I went to the local American Savings and opened an account with the check. I should have spent the whole thing, but I'm just too frugal. I ended up buying Alexis an electric car for Christmas and some miscellaneous stuff. In the end, I had blown about a thousand dollars. That's it. Call me crazy.

Mom was sad about the whole situation and didn't approve of Dennis's behavior or the way I was dealing with it. She cared for him, but she really had no idea what my world was *truly* like. And I couldn't tell her because she just would not have understood.

# CH APTER 10

## *Annie's Inferno*

B Y FEBRUARY 1992 DENNIS'S CAREER WAS IN OVERDRIVE. HE'D BEEN the league's leading offensive rebounder of the year and ranked second overall as a rebounder behind David Robinson. That helped him nail a position on the All-Star Team. He'd been named NBA Defensive Player of the Year in 1990 and 1991 and would make the All-Star Team again in 1992. He was also becoming a regular fixture on the NBA All-Defensive Team, having made that every year since 1989. Of course, all this made the Pistons pretty happy. Consequently they pumped up his contract to $3.1 million a year. Dennis was also becoming popular with advertisers and had just signed a fat deal with Nike. On top of all that, the fans loved him. And, though he had only one real friend on the team, John Salley, even his other teammates were getting along with him. As time went by, he and John drifted apart. John turned more toward the world of business, and Dennis turned more toward the world of...whatever.

All in all, Dennis should have been a very, very happy man for a lot of reasons. But he wasn't. Despite his incredible performances on the court, off court he seemed to have lost a lot of the enthusiasm he had for the game back in 1987. I see Dennis as someone who is blessed with incredible talent and luck yet cursed with the inability to be satisfied for very long. He is like a man who sacrifices everything to climb Mount Everest, but once he accomplishes that, he is instantly bored, and so he sets his sights on the moon. Once he gets there, he becomes bored again. I look back to that time and see what he's now become, and I can't help but feel Dennis is one of the unfortunate few for whom everything is just not enough.

As the benchwarmer he'd been so positive, not only about the game, but also about me and life in general. But money and fame don't come with a set of instructions. I think, to some extent, he felt a little lost and totally overwhelmed. Once he worked his way off the bench into the starting lineup and then onto the All-Star Team, what else was there? He started stewing about who in the NBA made more money than he did and who in the NBA wasn't as good as he was. It was pretty much the same list. He let it drive him crazy.

The funny thing was, it really wasn't about the money. Don't get me wrong, Dennis loves the money. But the idea that someone he regarded as lower on the skill scale and crowd-drawing scale should make more irked him. It was a matter of principle. I think it was the same old pattern of never being satisfied. They make him an offer. He says, "$3.1 million? Great!" A month after signing the deal he says, "Shit, look what so-and-so makes. $3.1 million? It ain't shit."

Despite being a multimillionaire, he couldn't forget he had once been poor. Some people move on, some don't. Beneath all the showmanship and tough talk, Dennis is still, in his mind, the poor kid from the Dallas ghetto. But he's going to show them, he tells himself, and that means doing what he can to literally shock the shit out of people by behaving in a way that's completely counter to what he thinks society wants. The trouble is—and I think Dennis may have figured this out by now—the world has and always will love a freakshow.

One of his biggest problems was knowing when something was good in his life, when he had something of real worth. He was always a bad judge of character and relationships. So it was with us. Once he had wooed and then won me over, what else was there? Now that he had a woman who loved him unconditionally, he came to see me as a drag. He was at a point where he could have just about any woman he laid his eyes on, and it was too much for him to handle.

Dennis never really came to terms with his looks. His fairy godmother had waved her magic wand and turned him into a total babe magnet, yet underneath he was still the short, geeky, shy high school kid. And it drove him nuts. He was like a starving man let loose at an all-you-can-eat buffet: I was offering him filet mignon, but all he wanted to do was stuff his face with chicken salad, pizza, and home fries.

As his life became more complicated and his responsibilities increased, he retreated more and more into a world of his own creation. It was a world populated by people he really didn't know, full of hangers-on like strippers and the stream of sixteen-year-old white boys who seemed to be a constant presence in our game room or in my kitchen.

What Dennis didn't understand was that, unlike his groupies, Alexis and I only wanted Dennis the Husband and Father, not Dennis the Rich Celebrity. He became extremely short-tempered with Alexis and me as the pressures built, pressures he wasn't equipped to deal with.

Although there are athletes who are good family men, I've seen too many of them so caught up in being worshipped that they ignore the simple and important things like family and commitment. I think one of the reasons is because many of these guys didn't have strong relationship role models as kids. Dennis certainly didn't.

Another reason is that since these athletes were stars from the time they could dribble a basketball, no one ever told them no. At one end of the spectrum you've got Dennis (and a lot of others) out slutting around, satisfying their urges like two-year-olds. At the other end of the spectrum you've got Shaquille O'Neal, who I heard asked his mother if it was okay for him to get a tattoo. Not a big thing, but it shows respect.

As for Dennis's mom, Shirley, she just wanted a handout. At least that's how Dennis felt. Now, his mom didn't like me for several reasons. First of all, she didn't like the fact that I was white.

Second, she didn't like the fact that I was the mother of Dennis's child. But I think the main reason was that she saw me as a financial threat. I think she felt I was taking her cut of the pie.

I had other problems with Shirley, not the least of which was I wouldn't kiss her ass. She liked to keep people under her thumb, and if you didn't do what she wanted, you were history. Dennis always resented the fact that Shirley fawned over his sisters, Debra and Kym, while he got hind tit. I think he was made to feel inferior at an early age, and he's never let go of it. He had to grow up in the shadow of two sisters who were better at everything than he was. They were star basketball players in high school and college, whereas Dennis got cut from his high school basketball squad for being too short.

Shirley was another story. She had to raise the kids on her own, and I'm sure that wasn't easy, but she was too hard on Dennis. She's one of the main reasons he has had such trouble coming to terms with his self-worth. To put it bluntly, I think Shirley really fucked him up.

When she thought Dennis was showing signs of shiftlessness in his late teens she responded by throwing him out. Given her track record with men, she probably figured, hey, he's a man, he's probably worthless, too, so *boom,* out on your ass. But years later she came back—after he'd made it big, of course—and felt entitled to dip her beak into his success. Once Shirley learned how much Dennis made (somebody probably read a *Sports Illustrated* and told her) she was all over him. She called constantly to hit him up for dough. Dennis even changed the number a few times to throw her off.

She came out to visit us for the first time in 1989. Alexis was in her first year and would wake up in the middle of the night crying. Babies wake up for one or all of the following reasons: They are wet, they are hungry, or they need love. The next day Shirley was all over me. "You spoilin' that child. Let her cry." She was constantly criticizing me about how I was raising Alexis. I was tempted to say, "Hey, you should talk. Look at *your* son." It was a good thing I didn't because Dennis finally had enough of her one day and told

160

her off. "Leave her alone, Mom. She knows what she's doing," he said. "She's a good mama." Shirley left me alone after that, but she didn't leave Dennis alone.

For a couple of years Shirley and her sister, Dennis's aunt, put pressure on Dennis to help them get out of the ghetto. They wanted him to pay their bills or buy them cars or whatever, and Dennis's attitude was they could go fuck themselves. Shirley was always complaining about her arthritis and her heart and having to work for a living, but it fell on deaf ears. When she realized she was getting nowhere fast she threatened to go to the *Enquirer* and tell what a shit Dennis was, making his ol' mama live in the ghetto and all.

Dennis caved.

In 1991 he paid Shirley's credit card bills and moved her out of the projects and into an apartment. Then he bought her a car, a Ford Tempo. She shut up. Until she decided the Tempo was a piece of junk. Which it was. Dennis had to think fast and decided that rather than go out and buy her another car, he'd give her one of ours. My car.

Shirley became the proud owner of my beautiful black Mercedes 420 SEL. She was happy until she decided she didn't like the Mercedes. Didn't like the *Mercedes*. Hello? Earth to Shirley? So she traded down to a Lexus.

There was even a time, before he got her the apartment, that Shirley kept suggesting, strongly, that she should pack up and move to Detroit to live with us. Great. I think everyone should respect his or her mother within reason, but I had to put my foot down. Dennis agreed with me. I think the thought of having *two* mothers in the house at once scared the bejeezus out of him.

As far as I know, Shirley has stopped demanding stuff from Dennis. At that time, when Shirley threatened to expose her son in the tabloids, he actually cared what people thought of him.

— — —

The partygoers at Rodman's Clubhouse began to get out of hand. More and more people were constantly hanging around our home. Dennis called them friends, but they were only vague acquaintances, friends of friends of friends, just a bunch of moochers. They were mostly young white boys and their tramps slurping up the perks of being near a celebrity. Our house felt like a Chuck E. Cheese franchise, and I hated it.

Even though the house was huge, I had absolutely no privacy unless I went and hid in my walk-in closet. These kids leeched off us. They'd help themselves to whatever was in the kitchen. They spent all day and all night playing with Dennis's video games, and no one asked permission to do anything. They just came in like stray dogs and made themselves at home. The only thing I could hear over the sounds of the games and the music blasting from the entertainment room was the sound of women laughing and giggling that went on into the late hours of the night.

I came to be known as the "bitch of the house" because I disapproved of this atmosphere. I believed one's home was for one's family, not a pack of irresponsible little punks who were cleaning out our kitchen and fucking each other.

One night at about 1 A.M. I got hungry. I went into the kitchen for a snack and found some half-dressed, clueless floozy wandering around looking for a bathroom. She was stoned or drunk or maybe both. "Where's the bathroom?" she blurted. "I'm like totally lost in this place."

I grabbed her, marched her to the door, booted her ass out, and stormed down to the entertainment wing. Admittedly I was looking for trouble. I walked in, took a look around, and realized that I didn't know anybody in the room, that they were in my house, and that none of them had had the decency to at least introduce themselves to me. I eighty-sixed the whole gang.

When one of Dennis's boy groupies called me a fucking bitch on his way out, I turned to Dennis. He just looked at me, as if the guy had said "Have a nice day." I thought Dennis was a spineless weenie, but he probably agreed with the guy because I was beginning to act more like a disapproving mother than a lover.

After the all the parasites had left, Dennis packed a bag and left, too. I remember feeling completely alone and unhappy. I was so frustrated that Dennis couldn't see what he was doing to us and that I couldn't make him see. He wanted a family to show off like a trophy, but he didn't want any of the responsibility.

His problems were also magnified by his paranoia that everyone he came in contact with wanted something from him, and in a way it was true. His team and fans wanted him to play well, the girls he met in bars and strip joints and at games wanted his attention and then wanted to sleep with him, and his entourage of young white boys wanted to be near the great man while licking up the crumbs from his table and maybe even beating him at Sega.

Alexis and I just wanted to be loved.

On March 4, 1992, Dennis hit another milestone in his career. The man who wants to be remembered as the rebounding monster of the NBA pulled down an astounding *thirty-four rebounds* against the Indiana Pacers that night. To put it in perspective, fifteen rebounds in one game is really good. Twenty is phenomenal. Thirty is legendary.

He also hit another milestone at that time. He gave me chlamydia for the second time in our relationship.

— — —

Dennis had latched on to Kathi the Stripper during one his many expeditions to the various strip joints he frequented. He took a liking to her and set her up in a very nice condo only a mile from where we lived. It was conveniently located between our house and the Palace, and he would often go there after practice instead of coming home. I knew this and it hurt. Dennis was unwilling to fully commit to me, so Kathi the Stripper got a piece of him that I felt Alexis and I deserved. It was the cause of some of our worst fights.

Kathi played a major role in our problems during that time. With her in the picture, I started to get in Dennis's face about where he was going, what he was doing, and who he was doing it with. If he wasn't going to stop cheating on his own, I was going to do everything I could to stop him—kind of a one-woman intervention squad.

He didn't respond well to that approach.

This, combined with all the other pressures—pressures that other players in the league handled without all the drama we suffered—drove Dennis increasingly nuts. The press is demanding of professional athletes, always needing interviews and photos and comments. All of the corporations who pump money into the league feel entitled to have access to the players. The team organization also requires the players to do more than just practice and play. Charitable organizations are constantly trying to get players to donate money and attend functions.

Dennis wasn't equipped to deal with all those demands. He had enough on his mind as he constantly tried to juggle me and Kathi the Stripper.

He gave me a constant load of shit about where he was and what he was doing when he was out of my sight. My problem was that I tended to believe him. After the first lie I had to forgive him, after the second lie I had to forgive him, and so on. You'd think that sooner or later he would cross the line and tell too many lies and I'd crack, but I didn't know how much was too much. I just kept letting him off the hook and giving him another chance. With each lie I grew more determined to catch him in his next one. It became an ego thing with me, maybe even a twisted game to some extent. I wanted to outsmart him.

I would put my foot down about Kathi the Stripper, and Dennis would promise me he would cut her off, but he would end up right back in her bed. He not only paid for her condo, he even got her a membership at the same gym we went to. I also found out he had spent over two thousand dollars to install a mega–sound system in her Jeep. The Jeep he had bought her.

Dennis and I got into a fight about the sound system. I called Kathi every name in the book, and Dennis told me to let it go. I decided to take a slightly different approach this time.

When Dennis left the next day for a game, I quickly loaded everything of mine that I could lay my hands on into my 4-Runner. Then I bundled Alexis up, and off we went. It was cold and snowy as I drove to Birmingham and the home of a friend of the family. After she got off work, Monique met me and Alexis there to offer her moral support. The woman who owned the house gave us a room, and the three of us piled into one bed to sleep.

Early the next morning I awoke to find Dennis's face not three inches from my own. For a second or two I thought it was a nightmare; then I realized my life was a nightmare and I was awake. Before I could scream he put his hand over my mouth and dragged me out of the bed and out into the subfreezing morning air. I was dressed only in boxers and a T-shirt. I saw him grab my keys to the 4-Runner. All my stuff was in that car, and I wasn't about to let him take it.

The owner of the house, who I thought was my friend and who will remain nameless, had spilled the beans to Dennis earlier. Then, to add insult to injury, Dennis had Kathi the Stripper *drop him off* at the house.

So there we were: I'm barefoot, in my underwear, with Dennis dragging me, kicking and screaming, through the snow. Another storybook moment.

As we fought I noticed the neighbor across the street shoveling snow. He looked over, then slinked into his house. I began screaming, "Call the police! Call the police!" No one did a damn thing.

Except Monique.

She took Alexis upstairs and came running outside to help me. "Haven't you done enough? Leave her alone!" Monique screamed at Dennis. He had a solid grip on me and was dragging me to the truck. I didn't want to go with him, but I didn't want him to take the truck either. Finally I made a decision. I kicked loose, and he jumped in the truck and zoomed away.

I was desperate. He had all my stuff, my clothes, my wallet, my jewelry, personal effects, even my shoes. I had to get them back. Monique helped me up as we watched Dennis turn the corner at the end of the block. "He can't get away with this," I said. "Give me your keys, Monique. Please."

She said I was crazy and tried to talk me out of it. "What're you going to do? Chase him down? In the snow? You're not even dressed."

I just stared at her, fuming, the look in my eyes telling her all she needed to know. She handed me the keys.

I jumped into her Chrysler LeBaron and floored it. It must have looked like an episode of *Starsky and Hutch* with those two speeding vehicles sailing down the snowy streets of that quiet neighborhood. I felt like a cop on a call. The only thing I didn't have was a lightbar and a gun. And shoes.

I followed his tire tracks and found him parked by a school, tossing my belongings into a snowbank. I couldn't believe it. I slammed on the brakes and almost skidded into my 4-Runner. I jumped out and staggered through the snowdrifts toward him. "What the fuck are you doing?" I screamed. He didn't even look at me and kept tossing. "What's it look like, bitch?"

I fell to my hands and knees and started grabbing things: my wallet, some jewelry, whatever I could. He turned and saw me, then hauled off and kicked me hard in the ribs. I went down sobbing, my face in the snow.

That was it. I snapped. I looked up at him with such hatred and rage that he blinked. Immediately he stopped throwing things, jumped back into the 4-Runner and took off. All I had in my hand was my mother's watch, which she had given me, and my tennis bracelet. I got up and climbed back into the LeBaron. I started it up and jammed it into gear. Now I wanted blood. His.

I fishtailed away, the car sliding from side to side. I wanted to make him pay.

The LeBaron didn't handle that well in the snow, but I caught him through sheer force of will. I pulled alongside him, in the wrong lane, and honked for him to pull over. He looked over, eyes wide. Suddenly he yanked the wheel to the left and tried to knock me off the road. I responded by ramming my car into his car. Or should I say, I rammed *Monique's car* into *my car*.

We rammed each other all the way down the block, and the only thing that got hurt was the two vehicles. Our destruction derby came to a stop when we reached a red light at an intersection. Dennis decided retreat was the best solution. He made a Bat-turn to the right and went down a busy street. I calmed down and took what was left of Monique's car back to her. She was a pretty good sport, given the car had about twenty-five hundred dollars in damage.

Later, Dennis paid for Monique's bodywork.

▬ ▬ ▬

Kathi the Stripper was possessive of Dennis's time, and she eventually got confident enough to start calling him at home. At all hours. At least when I answered she had the brains to hang up.

Dennis loaned her one of our cars, a Corvette. Like my relationship with Dennis, she piled it up. The Corvette could be repaired, unlike our relationship. Normally I wouldn't have given a shit about the car, but the fact that it was totaled by the same tramp who was screwing Dennis enraged me.

The Kathi the Stripper problem smoldered inside me for several days. Every time I thought about her my blood pressure would shoot up. I'd do housework twice as fast and do extra time on the Stairmaster, but I couldn't get the thought of her and Dennis together out of my mind. I wanted to go over to her condo and confront them, but I didn't out of fear of what might happen—that is, what Dennis might do, or, mostly, what I might do.

The next to the last straw came a few days before Valentine's Day, 1991. I was four months pregnant. That afternoon I got a call from a local jeweler, who informed me that the diamond pendant Dennis had ordered had arrived. I was excited for a few hours, then I got suspicious and called the jeweler back. "Is there an inscription?" I asked. No. I got off the phone and started crazy-making in my mind. It was for me. It was for Kathi. For me. For Kathi. Me. Kathi.

Kathi the Stripper.

I was furious at her for existing. I should have been mad at Dennis, but I wasn't. Right then I wanted Kathi the Stripper to fall asleep at the wheel of some car, preferably one not provided by Dennis, and meet a semi head-on. I had worse thoughts, but I'm too ashamed to repeat them. I was a mess. I decided I'd give Dennis a chance and wait until Valentine's Day. After all, if the pendant was mine, what kind of bad karma was I creating by having all these unspeakable thoughts? I chilled.

Until three days after Valentine's Day.

▬ ▬ ▬ ▬

February 14 came and went. I got no pendant. As a matter of fact, I got nothing. I'm the mother of his child, I'm carrying his second child, and come Valentine's Day he gives me *nothing*. It started to eat at me.

A few days later, my morning started like most others. I was up at 6:30 to start my chores around the house and then fix Alexis breakfast before she went to school. When I got back from dropping Alexis off I noticed Dennis had left his car out, the one he took to practice. It was covered with snow. Despite having at least six other vehicles from which to choose, he was such a creature of habit I knew he'd have to drive that one to practice. I also knew I'd better allow enough time later to brush off the snow and get it warmed up or I'd catch hell. I made a mental note to take care of that, then went into the house and started making his favorite breakfast: cinnamon rolls, eight slices of bacon, and a glass of orange juice.

Dennis finally staggered into the kitchen and mumbled the only thing he would say to me that morning, and for that matter, most any morning: "Where are my practice shorts?" After this scintillating conversation, he ate while I went out and scraped off the windshield and warmed up his car.

All that morning the main question I had was: What happened to that damn pendant?

After he left for practice I finished up my cleaning, started the laundry, and did the Stairmaster. Even though I was pregnant I didn't dare gain an ounce of unneeded weight, or Dennis wouldn't let me hear the end of it. I picked up Alexis at 11:30 and came home to make lunch. Dennis got off practice at 2:30. Sometimes he would stay late and work out, but I would always look for him within an hour or two of that time. Usually I waited a lot longer than that for him to appear.

On game days his ritual would be to come directly home from practice and take a nap, usually with Alexis. Around 4 o'clock I would wake him, and he would shower while listening to U2. I'd make him the same dinner: fried chicken, rice blended with sugar and butter, three slices of white bread, and corn. But February 17 wasn't a game day, so after practice who knows where he went.

Actually I had a pretty good idea.

That evening we had the fight that I wrote about in chapter 1, where Dennis lunged for me, sending me tumbling down the stairs. It was the beginning of the end for us.

It was a little after 11 P.M. on that cold February night. I was lying at the foot of the stairs. Dennis had gone back down to his buddies in the game room. I tearfully picked myself up off the ice-cold marble and hobbled upstairs to calm Alexis. As she cried and I held her, I decided all I wanted to do was take her and escape. The fall had jarred me enough that I was in no shape to drive, particularly given the snow and cold, so I called a cab. I had no idea where I was going. My closest friend in the neighborhood was a mile away, but she was not home that evening. I knew another family about eight miles from our home. Despite the late hour, they told me to come over.

When Dennis realized I was not only leaving but taking Alexis, too, he went berserk. He screamed at me and threw what few clothes I was carrying into the snow in front of the house. Then he locked us out of the house. In a snowstorm.

While Alexis and I waited for the cab, I tried to keep us warm as I picked my clothes out of the snow. Every time I walked out on Dennis I promised myself I'd never come back. I always did come back. But that night he had gone too far.

After I arrived at my friends' home, I went into the bathroom. While urinating I passed something sizable. I called my friend in, and we stared at a bloody mass of tissue, perhaps three inches long, in the toilet bowl. I had no idea what it was, and it scared me. My friend reassured me and said it didn't look like the obvious subject of our fears: a small fetus. We flushed it. The next morning I called my gynecologist, Dr. Migdal. He told me it was probably a mucous plug, considered normal for some women during pregnancy. The following day I had an odd feeling I couldn't explain, a sort of strange, hollow sense of loss. With all the turmoil of the night before, I just blew it off as a depression brought on by a particularly bad fight with Dennis.

That day, with Alexis in tow, I flew back to Sacramento for the comfort and sympathy of Mom. As soon as I arrived I called the local obstetrician and made an appointment, for I starting to feel that something was seriously wrong. You see, I hadn't quite told Dr. Migdal the extent—and definitely not the circumstances—of my injuries, so he really hadn't had the chance to come up with an accurate evaluation of my symptoms. I decided to have another doctor check me over. I feared the fall might have harmed my baby. Since this doctor didn't have an ultrasound unit in his office, he first scheduled an appointment for me at an ultrasound clinic. Mom went with me.

When the ultrasound technician was all set up, the consulting doctor stopped in. He expressed his lack of worry and said he expected everything to be "perfectly normal." Then he left and the technician started her reading. I had had an ultrasound before, and I knew it didn't take long to get results. After a moment the technician lowered her eyes and turned the display screen so Mom and I couldn't see it. "What's wrong? Is my baby okay?" I asked. She got up. "I'll be right back," she said.

Mom tried to reassure me, but I feared the worst. A few minutes later the doctor entered with the ultrasound technician. They were noncommittal when Mom and I asked what was wrong. The doctor did another reading with the ultrasound, then quickly turned off the screen. "Tell me exactly what happened to you," he said. His words and concerned look sent a chill through me.

I calmly explained what had happened. *Exactly* what had happened. I felt that at this point the truth might somehow undo what damage might have occurred to my baby. I hadn't even told Mom the whole story, and her eyes widened as I went on. When I finished the doctor left the room to call Dr. Migdal back in Michigan.

I was going crazy with fear for my unborn baby and probably, in my heart, fear of hearing the truth. After a few minutes I cracked and ran into the hallway wearing only an examination gown. "Please, tell me what's wrong!" I screamed. My mom and a nurse calmed me down and got me back into the room.

Finally the doctor came back and gave me the worst. The "mucous plug" I passed had in fact been *my baby*. I have since heard that abusive relationships can cause diminished growth in the fetus and ultimately low birth weight. That may have been the reason the fetus was so small when I passed it.

It hit me like a sledgehammer. The baby that I had carried for four and a half months, the baby that was going to grow up with Alexis. The baby that never had a chance when it fell halfway down a staircase and was knocked loose from its warm cocoon and swept away into oblivion.

That night I cried for my lost baby, for my daughter, for myself. And I cried for what might have been.

# CHAPTER 11

## The Worm's Turn

BY 1992 DENNIS AND I HAD KNOWN EACH OTHER FOR FIVE YEARS. The bad outweighed the good about a hundred to one. I was tired, beaten, and rejected. I needed a time-out. A full time-out, a twenty wouldn't do. I needed to regroup.

Then I met Louis Riddick. Louis had graduated from Pitt and signed with the Forty-Niners. We met after he got cut by San Francisco and then signed with the Sacramento Surge of the Canadian Football League. At the end of the WFL season he signed with Atlanta, was released, then got picked up by Cleveland and then traded back to Atlanta.

Louis and I loved one another the way two people should. The only pain he ever caused me was when he left Sacramento to go back home. He loved me for me. He didn't need me to dress up like a whore the way Dennis did. (Dennis used to buy me lots of provocative clothes and lingerie. I think he was trying to do anything to keep me from looking motherly.) Louis showed me simple respect. He treated me with dignity. He expected the best out of me and demanded that I have respect for myself. I didn't have to win his approval the way I did with Dennis. I didn't have to show cleavage or wear short skirts with Louis. He never ogled other women, and he never belittled me. And he didn't expect any weirdness in bed in return for all his kindness. He also made me laugh, which wins me over every time. I love to laugh and joke around and I hadn't done that in a long time before I met Louis.

He did all the little things that are so important. When we went out he held my hand. He opened doors for me. He asked if there was anything I needed. In short, he was a gentleman. He was the exact opposite of Dennis, and most of the other men I've ever gone out with, for that matter. To this day I still regret leaving Louis and returning to Dennis. I'll never forget the kindness and love Louis brought into my life. I went so far as to have Louis tattooed on my hip at the same time I had Dennis covered over.

Dennis knew about Louis. Dennis was coming to California frequently because he knew he was losing me to Louis, and he couldn't control his anger about it. One time we had a fight, and he had me on the ground. He was sitting on my stomach and had his hands around my throat. He said through clenched teeth, "Why do you make me hurt you?" I couldn't answer because his hands were around my throat. When he released his grip and started hitting me I screamed, "Help me! Help me!" One of our neighbors banged on the door and said he was going to call the police. Dennis stopped and left before the police arrived.

Dennis was losing me to another man, and it was killing him. Another man was touching and caressing his wife. It made him so jealous that one time in particular he went off the deep end. He was in town for one of his visits with Alexis and was staying at the Residence Inn. I was dropping Alexis off when Dennis came out to my car and said, "What are you doing? Where are you going? Why don't you want me anymore? You're my wife, dammit!"

"Dennis," I replied, "I can't take the roller coaster anymore."

He went berserk. He reached into the 4-Runner, grabbed the gear shift, and pulled it out! I couldn't believe he did it. I thought, Damn! That could have been my head. It probably wasn't the smartest thing I've ever done, but I said, "It ain't fun having the tables turned, is it?" Another Dennis moment.

Why did I ever leave Mr. Perfect for Mr. Psycho? It had something to do with stability. I didn't want some other man raising Alexis. I wanted her to be raised by her mother and father despite the fact that Dennis was rarely there to be a father. That's how crazy I had become. I was in a lifeboat with Louis, and I decided to go back aboard the *Titanic* with Dennis because I thought it would be better for my daughter. Was I certifiable? You tell me.

Other than all the abortions I went through, the biggest regret in my life was leaving Louis. This may not sound overly romantic, but his tattoo will *never* get covered over. I walked away from the man of my dreams to return to my nightmare. As they say on the basketball court after making a turnover, "My bad."

I seemed unable to function without Dennis, no matter how much lunacy there was in our lives. I just kept going back to him. Or he kept coming after me, begging to get me back. A friend of mine told me I was like a gambling addict who kept playing even after I'd lost all my money. I felt like I'd put so much money into Dennis the Slot Machine that I had to get it back, and the odds were that the next pull on the lever was the one that would pay off.

Even though Louis showed me what I was missing, even though he showed me how true love worked, I returned to Dennis. It was like a sickness, and deep down I knew I was making the wrong choice, but still I made it.

And Dennis was as sick as I was. He knew how troubled our relationship was, but he didn't want to lose me. You should never, ever want to hurt the one you love, but we did it to one another over and over.

I think I made the mistake of applying the wrong lesson to the wrong situation. The lesson was one my mom taught me. She taught me never to quit on anything, never to give up. It's a fine lesson, but one best applied to situations other than dysfunctional relationships. The lesson I should have been applying was: Run like hell.

Louis knew how much pain there was in my relationship with Dennis, and he wanted to take me away from it. I just wouldn't let him. At the time I didn't think I deserved better. Well, Louis, if you're reading this, I just want to let you know that I'm happy now. I'm not in pain anymore. And thanks.

- - - -

I couldn't begin to explain my state of mind as I lived this insane life with Dennis. I was certainly miserable. And, depending on his behavior day to day, I was also fearful, angry, jealous, or deeply in love. I kept holding on to the hope that Dennis would wake up one day and realize how much he'd changed since we first met. I just kept thinking he could still be that shy, sweet, romantic young man he once was.

Each day was different. Some days our life was crazy, filled with screaming and violence; other days Dennis would be sweet and apologetic. I never knew what to expect.

One night during the summer of 1992, Dennis, Alexis, and I were in Dallas. He had some business to deal with regarding his excavation company. We were driving back to the hotel and, as usual, we were arguing. However, instead of arguing about one of Dennis's affairs, we were arguing about one of my tattoos. Specifically the tattoo of Louis on my hip. Not surprisingly, Dennis wasn't keen on it.

I had filed for divorce six or seven months earlier, so I didn't think Dennis had a lot of ground to stand on, bitching about my tattoos. But bitch he did. And when he was through bitching, he suddenly pulled the truck off an obscure exit, then to the side of a very dark road. "Get out," he ordered.

"What?"

"Out," he repeated. "Get out of the car, Annie. Now."

He didn't sound like he was in the mood to discuss it, so I took Alexis and got out. Then another car pulled up. The driver, a woman, asked if we needed help. Dennis said no, and before I could say anything, she pulled away. Dennis drove off right after her, leaving Alexis and me in the dark on the side of the road in a deserted industrial part of Dallas.

We walked even though I had no idea where we were going. There was no traffic, no one passing by for me to flag down, and no pay phones in sight. There was nothing but darkness. I was pissed at Dennis and scared of being out in the middle of nowhere, in the middle of the night, with my baby. We walked. And walked. I don't know how long we were walking down that dark road, but it was too damn long for my tastes. Finally a car approached from behind. I turned to flag it down and saw it was Dennis.

He pulled up next to us. "Get in the car, Annie."

I put Alexis back in her car seat, and we drove off to the hotel in silence. He never apologized for what he'd done. He probably blamed me for making him do it.

**- - -**

For Dennis, watching Alexis was always a chore. He'd play with her for an hour or so, and then, when he got tired of her, he'd give her back to me. I really believe there was a part of Dennis, in the beginning anyway, that wanted to be a good father. But as he earned more money and became surrounded by groupies and gained more notoriety, that part of Dennis got pushed out, and the only thing he was concerned with was running around with his sleazy pals. He found it was easier and a lot more fun to be the center of everyone else's attention than to be a good father. He knew I was a good wife and mother, but his attitude was, "You only live once, so do whatever you want, no matter how it affects others." The only person Dennis was worried about was himself.

Another example of how insane our relationship got is when Dennis and I started attacking one another's race.

There's something curious about Dennis and his racial relationships. All the people Dennis used to invite over to our house in Michigan were white. For that matter, they were mostly young white boys.

Dennis once told me he actually hated being black, though I'd bet my life that he'd deny it now. I told him, "Dennis, be proud of who and what you are! Our daughter is just as black as she is white, and I want her to be equally proud of both."

In all the years we were together I never knew him to date (much less fuck) a black woman. He once told me that he despised black women because "they smell and they bitch too much." When Dennis used to talk shit about black women I'd say, "The only reason you don't mess with black chicks is because they intimidate you. They'd be able to see right through you and kick your ass. Us white girls are so fucking clueless that if we walk in and see our black man with another ho, we believe it when you tell us there's nothing going on." Black women know that game better than white women do. I just wish it hadn't taken me so long to learn the rules. For better or worse, though, at the ripe old age of thirty-one, I can now play it with my eyes closed and both hands tied behind my back. After all, I learned from the best.

When Dennis would start talking shit about white-this and white-that I suddenly started defending whiteness. Maybe at the time the racist in me emerged. I was so distressed about the way he was treating me that I generalized to myself that all black men were the same. My experience with players in the NBA, which is dominated by black men, was that many of them (a disproportionate number relative to the population in general) cheated on their wives, except for perhaps David Robinson. I never heard about the white guys in the NBA doing that. I heard plenty of negative stuff about Laimbeer, Bird, McHale, Stockton, and Price, but none of it had to do with them being unfaithful.

Which brings me back to the point about Dennis and his curious racial relationships. On the one hand he only invited young white dudes to our house. He also only screwed white women (maybe that was symbolic?). He even said he hated being black. But on the other hand he sure hated white ball players, with the exception of his white buddy Jack Haley.

Dennis especially hated Larry Bird. He hated him because Bird was the real deal. The other players and the fans respected Bird because of his all-around skills, not because he dyed his hair and wore wedding dresses. Okay, so Dennis is a great rebounder, but don't count on seeing him in the Hall of Fame. It was after the Pistons lost to the Celtics in the Eastern Conference finals in Dennis's rookie season that Dennis opened his big rookie mouth and uttered his now famous words, "Larry Bird is overrated in a lot of areas. I don't think he's the greatest player. He's way overrated. Why does he get so much publicity? Because he's white. You never hear about a black player being the greatest." Oops.

I don't know what planet Dennis is on sometimes, especially when he says things like that. I think it's generally agreed (and said) that Michael Jordan is the greatest. Before Michael, Magic Johnson was the greatest. Or was it Kareem, or Wilt, or Oscar?

After reviewing the facts and being counseled by the league, his coach, his agent, and his PR people, Dennis recanted. "I shouldn't have said what I said. Larry Bird proved to me he's one of the best.... I made a mistake." Well, at least he admitted it, even if he had to be prodded a bit.

As a general rule I think Dennis tends to start shit on the court with white players. Sure, he gave Stacy King a nice head butt, and he once gave Scottie Pippen some stitches, but he's under the impression that the white guys are too scared or too mature to fight. He thinks the other black players would just beat the shit out of him if he tried some of his shit on them.

One of my reactions to all of Dennis's racial taunts was that I started doing very "white" things. I started getting tattoos, getting into Harleys, listening to Guns 'N Roses. What's more, Dennis started copying me. Go figure.

I remember the first time I called Dennis a nigger. He was talking shit about my family, and I slapped him and used the N-word.

I've probably dated as many black men as I have white men. I never pursued black men specifically. When I was back in Sacramento after I finally left Dennis, I was dating white guys, and when Dennis found out he got pissed. (Of course, he was already pissed, and I don't think it would have mattered who I was dating.)

As long as a guy can make me laugh, he's got a chance with me. But I must admit that I've always been inclined toward bad boys. The problem I've run into is that most of the white guys I've dated have been *too* good to me. I think that says something about my self-esteem. I was actually out there looking for someone to treat me badly—and boy, did I find what I was looking for.

I dated a cop by the name of Chris Cully. He didn't give a shit that I had been married to Dennis. He wasn't at all intimidated by that. Chris made me laugh all the time. I had some great times with him, but Dennis was always lurking in the back of my mind. It was like I was having Dennis withdrawal. In the end I wasn't able to give Chris the attention or time he deserved, so we broke it off.

I later dated Troy Wilkes, who played for the New England Patriots and later for the Sacramento Gold Miners. This is after I had left Dennis and he was constantly flying to Sacramento, trying to get me to come back to him. Troy was another great guy I let get away. Strangely enough, after all the emotional stimulation—bad as it was—with Dennis, it was almost boring to be with a "normal" guy. I threw away the men who treated me with respect and kindness. I knew deep down in my heart that I was fucking up royally by letting these guys go. If a relationship was too easy, I was outta there. The badder the dude, the better. I was clearly in serious need of professional help. Fortunately I'm getting it now.

Just so you don't get the wrong impression (though it may be too late for me to start worrying about that), my house didn't have a revolving door. Alexis was not exposed to dozens of men coming and going all the time. She met very few of the men I dated, only the ones I knew were really good guys, the kind I couldn't sustain a relationship with.

Here's how screwed up I was: I thought the way to a man's heart was through his dick. I thought the only thing that could make a man like me was my pussy. Looking back, I see that Louis and Troy and Cully and some of the others actually liked *me.*

My mom had a lot of friends who were black, but she didn't think blacks and whites would ever "come together." She knew how much hatred some whites instilled in their kids and how much some blacks instilled in theirs, and she knew that didn't bode well for racial harmony. Mom also knew that an interracial relationship, let alone a marriage, would be difficult even if the two parties involved were psychologically sound. So she probably didn't hold out much hope for Dennis and me from the start, but bless her heart, she never came right out and said it.

My dad was against my relationship with Dennis from the start. It was clear that he did not want his daughter to be with a black man. But then fate threw my dad a curve, and he was befuddled as to how to handle it. As Dennis became increasingly famous, Dad became more enamored of the idea that his son-in-law was a star. So, apparently, it's okay to have a black man as a boyfriend or husband, as long as he's famous or maybe just rich. But if he's both, it's a slam dunk. Even after Dad learned that Dennis was abusing me, his advice ran along these lines: "You should just keep your mouth shut about whatever he does and just go back to him." Dad wasn't one to be casting stones in the spousal abuse department.

The fact that Dad was starstruck made me sick. My brothers Matt and Bill couldn't give a shit one way or the other, but Chris despised Dennis. He couldn't figure out why someone would hurt his little sister. After one of our big breakups, my brothers felt I was basically choosing Dennis over them. Dennis wanted to cut me off from my family, lest my brothers give me any ideas about leaving him for good.

After my mom found out about Dennis's abuse, my relationship with her was damaged somewhat. I think she may have lost some of her respect for me. She may have been ashamed knowing that I had learned from her to put up with the abuse. From then on I decided not to tell any of my family what went on between Dennis and me. I started keeping everything inside.

# CHAPTER 12

## Annie Get Your Gun

THE THOUGHTS OF DENNIS AND HIS OTHER WOMEN WERE POISONING my mind. The pain he was causing me was unbearable, so I decided to strike back. I'd hit him where it counted, the one thing in the world he cared most about.

His custom Jeep.

A brand-spanking-new Jeep Wrangler with gigantic tires that was high enough off the ground to make it illegal for street use, it sat in a place of honor in our garage. It had a superexpensive stereo setup encased in a Plexiglas box, and on its side, painted in huge letters, was the lifestyle expression WILD THING. This was Dennis's baby. He had about fifty thousand dollars invested in this toy, and its welfare was now in jeopardy.

I went out into the parking area behind our house, past all of the other cars, right to the Jeep. I had decided to poison it. Armed with anything sweet I could lay my hands on—white sugar, brown sugar, chocolate candies—I unscrewed the gas cap, stuck a funnel in, and started pouring. I was so scared he would drive up at any moment that I spilled sugar all around the filler neck and on the ground. When I figured the damage was done I went back into the house.

Later Dennis got home, and as he was getting out of his car, he noticed sugar on the ground. I looked out the window and saw him investigating. Right then I knew I was in deep shit. I went out to try and explain, and he blew his top. "Goddamn it, I can't believe you did that!" Then he punched me in the back, right between the shoulder blades.

A couple of days passed and then a flatbed truck showed up and hauled the Jeep away to be repaired. Three days later it was back again, better than new. That Jeep was my new enemy, and I knew we'd meet again.

Dennis's exploits with other women inspired me to craziness as well. I was driving along in one of our cars one day and the cell phone rang. I picked it up. It was one of his ho's. I screamed into the phone, then tore it loose and threw it out the window. I can still see that phone hitting the roadway and spinning into the ditch. I only wish Dennis's bitches had been that easy to dispose of.

Another time I was at home and one of his pagers went off. I called the number. What did I get? Another bitch. I calmly picked up the pager, walked out the back door, and went down to the lake. Then I threw that pager, and the ho attached, as far as I could. It made a satisfying little *plink* when it hit the water. I went back in the house. That became my new pastime: pager tossing. Every time one would go off and it was a ho, it was down to the lake, day or night, rain or shine. Problem is, he'd replace them just as fast.

I couldn't win.

I used to find all sorts of receipts for various items: Louis Vuitton bags, jewelry, hotel bills (for occupant *and guest*), pagers and cellular phones for his sluts, and clothes. Lots of clothes. In sizes to fit the shrimpy sluts he was shagging. One time I came back from Sacramento a day earlier than expected and found seven shoe boxes in my closet. I opened them up. They were all brand-new, all the same style, but in different sizes. Since most of them were more like children's sizes (I wear a 10—at least he bought *one* pair that fit me), I bundled them up, went down to the shoe store, and exchanged them all for size 10s in a variety of colors.

Another time we got into a fight over some tart, and when he left the house I went on a rampage. I gathered all of his leather jackets and pants, sliced them up with a knife, then turned the shower on full hot and chucked them in. When he came back he was pissed but didn't want to give me the pleasure of seeing him angry, so he went right down to the store and replaced everything.

The next time I varied the theme of destruction by piling his clothes in the yard, dousing them with lighter fluid, and *whoosh,* a nice, toasty little bonfire. I love the smell of burning leather in the morning.

Were we nuts or what?

Finally the day came when we had a huge blowout over some chick, and Dennis bailed and went to the residence of the ho in question. As he pulled out of the carport, my eyes came to rest on my old foe, Mr. Jeep. I thought, *Okay buddy, this is war.* I bided my time. I knew that if I was going to hurt Dennis, it would be through the Jeep. I had to come up with a fitting end for that thing.

It hit me. I put on my jacket and went outside. There were four cars in the carport and a few others, including the Jeep, in the garage. I opened the door of the Jeep, climbed in, and took it out of gear. Then I got out, grabbed the door and window frame, and heaved. It was heavier than I thought. But soon I had the thing rolling. When the Jeep and I cleared the garage, I saw we had a straight shot to our destination: The lake.

Just like in *The Godfather,* this baby was gonna sleep with the fishes.

As I was pushing, I thought, *God, give me a sign I shouldn't do this.* No sign. Good. I kept pushing. I got it to the edge of the pavement and had it on the grass, and then gravity took over. As I watched that Jeep bump and roll down the hill toward a watery death, I suddenly was hit with a sickening feeling: regret.

Just then Dennis drove up. He saw what was happening and jumped out just in time to see...the dock stop the Jeep. I couldn't believe it. But I really didn't have time to think about the luck or philosophy or karma thing, 'cause Dennis was coming toward me, and he had murder in his eyes. "You fuckin' bitch! I'm gonna fuckin' kill you!"

Well, at least I got his attention.

He chased me around and around our huge yard, and amazingly I managed to stay away from him. Had he caught me, he was mad enough to wreak some serious havoc. He finally got tired and went in the house. I wonder if the neighbors looked out their windows, shook their heads, and said, "Well, there they go again."

Dennis had another tow truck come out. This time the damaged item turned out to be an axle. He had it fixed. When the Jeep returned I decided, having tried twice to kill it, it was a worthy adversary and I'd call a truce.

— — —

When I was going to college, Dennis would usually watch Alexis if he didn't have practice, which wasn't very often. On a day he didn't have practice, I came home expecting to find him with Alexis, but they were gone. There was no note telling me where they were or when they'd be back.

My intuition—and paranoia—kicked into gear. I went to the telephone to do something I'd had success with in the past. I felt like Inspector Gadget when I hit the redial button.

Dennis answered. "Where are you?" I demanded. Click. The chickenshit bastard hung up on me. I redialed again.

This time Kathi the Stripper answered.

Now at least I knew where he was. "Let me talk to Dennis!" I said. There was silence on the line for a minute, then either Kathi the Stripper or Dennis gave the phone to Alexis. I was about to go ballistic. He was with one of his little sluts, and he had our daughter with him. "I'm eating ice cream at one of Daddy's friend's house," Alexis said just before the line went dead.

I hit redial one more time, but this time Dennis had the sense to take the phone off the hook. I got a busy signal. My heart was pounding. I was unbelievably pissed off. I had to do something. I knew which apartment complex Kathi lived in, but I didn't know the apartment number. After so many years of Dennis's bullshit, though, I'd become pretty resourceful. I called the apartment manager's office and manipulated the information out of whoever answered the phone. Armed with Kathi the Stripper's apartment number, I jumped in my car and squealed out of the driveway in a rage. The entire way over I fumed and had one thing on my mind.

I was gonna kick some ass.

I spotted Dennis's truck parked right in front of the apartment. I don't think he ever considered the possibility that I would find Kathi's place, let alone actually show up. I think he believed Martians would take over the NBA before I did what I was about to do.

My blood pressure was probably 150 over 120. I was hyperventilating, and I felt like I was going to explode. I went to the door and knocked hard. When there was no answer, I started to pound on the door and yelled for them to open up. Looking inside, I could see Alexis in her car seat, but I couldn't see Kathi the Stripper or Dennis. I freaked! I didn't know if they were hiding or if they were in the bedroom fucking.

I was not about to let a locked door keep me from confronting Dennis and his whore. I kicked the door hard. Nothing. That really pissed me off, so I kicked again, a lot harder, and the door came right off its hinges.

I couldn't believe I had done that—it was like something in the movies. I went in. By now Kathi the Stripper was more like Kathi the Scared Shitless, hiding behind the locked bathroom door, screaming like a lunatic, terrified that I had Ramboed my way into her apartment. A stunned Dennis started stuffing Alexis's clothes and toys into her bag, suddenly becoming the cooperative father I always knew he could be. He just needed the proper motivation.

I honestly think if I'd had a hammer, I'd have gotten a great deal of satisfaction just pounding in his head and then going for that squealing little bitch in the bathroom. It's definitely a good thing I didn't have a gun.

"You better get the fuck out of here," Kathi shouted from the safety of her locked bathroom. "I called the cops!"

I couldn't believe Dennis. He didn't have the balls to defend me *or* Kathi the Stripper. He just watched and listened, his mouth hanging open like an idiot. I picked up Alexis and turned to him. "If you want your little whore Kathi, then don't ever bring your sorry ass home, unless it's to pick up your shit!"

He ended up coming home late that night. He told me he would stop seeing Kathi the Stripper. Another lie. The police eventually showed up at Kathi's apartment that night, but Dennis made sure the charges were dropped.

And he paid for the door.

— — —

In February 1993 Dennis was on his way to winning his second straight rebounding title. He would be the first forward ever to accomplish this feat. Unfortunately he was also on his way to getting more out of control than I'd ever seen him. Our divorce had been in the works for fourteen months, and Chuck Daly, one of the few people in the world who seemed to understand Dennis, was no longer coaching the Pistons.

Dennis hated how his life was shaping up at that point.

On February 11, the police were notified that Dennis had left a friend's house with a gun. His mood was not good. The police later found him asleep in his truck at the Palace. That was the famous episode Dennis chose for the opening of his book, *Bad As I Wanna Be.*

A month later he was suspended from the Pistons for one game for missing a practice. Three days after that, he was fined five hundred dollars for leaving the bench during a fight in a game against some of his future teammates, the Chicago Bulls.

On March 24, we had a deposition in Sacramento for our divorce proceedings. We both left pretty angry at each other. The next day I was away from my apartment from about 7:30 P.M. to around 11:15 P.M. After I got home Dennis called several times to apologize for what had happened at the deposition. He called so many times I finally took the phone off the hook. It sounded like he was calling from a bar and had been drinking.

The next morning when I woke up I felt a draft. I looked into Alexis's room and saw the door to the outside patio had been forced open and then pulled shut. I called the cops. According to the police reports, I said, "Dennis did this to harass me. I'm afraid of him and will get a restraining order against him. He has no right to be inside my apartment. He has never lived here and is not on the lease. He is on medication for depression (Prozac) and has been acting strange. I think he might have been snooping around to see if I have a boyfriend."

Here is what the responding officer said in the Sacramento Police Department Report Supplement:

*Scene description: 2808 Grassland #313 is a two bedroom, two bathroom downstairs apartment located on the east side of Grassland, facing west. A small patio is on the west side with a glass single swing door to the spare bedroom.*

*Entry: The culprit(s) used body force to open the bedroom door. The dead bolt lock was completely broken off and the frame was splintered.*

*Actions: The culprit(s) actions are unknown. Nothing inside the apartment appeared disturbed.*

*Exit: The culprit(s) exited out the bedroom door (P.O.E.) Pulling it closed behind them.*

A million thoughts raced though my mind. I couldn't believe I hadn't heard the door being forced open. Maybe he had done it while I was out, and I just didn't notice it when I came in. But what if he *did* do it when Alexis and I were here? Was he standing at the side of my bed, looking down at me? Did he have a weapon? As big as he is, could he kill me with his bare hands? Would he hurt Alexis? Would a restraining order make any difference to someone this out of control? I was afraid of what might happen next.

— — —

Despite the ongoing divorce proceedings and my fears of what Dennis might do next, by June 1993, the end of his last season with the Pistons, he and I were friendly again. I wanted him back and he wanted to be with me, and we made plans to reconcile, but he had one small request. Actually, more like two not-so-small requests.

He wanted me to get a boob job.

After all of this, the insanity of the last six years, I said, sure, what the hell, let's pump those babies up, if that's all it will take.

I had had a lift more than four years earlier, after Alexis was born, but I wanted to please him. I knew he'd been staring at countless firm tits in an endless number of strip joints, not to mention the hands-on sampling of roadkill he'd had all over the country, and I felt a strong need to compete to keep his interest. I didn't stop to think why on earth I was in a contest with this army of anonymous hooters. To borrow the slogan from one of Dennis's products, I just did it.

I made the appointment for the surgery. Dennis flew in to be with me, not only for the operation, but for my recovery as well. I was doing this for him, so I figured he should pitch in and help me around the house with chores and Alexis and whatnot. It was also part of the process of getting accustomed to each other again. And Dennis actually volunteered to lend a hand.

On the day of the procedure I went to the hospital. During the standard preoperative exam, they heard my heart murmur and were concerned. I told them about the problem, but my doctor wasn't so sure it was just a simple murmur and sent me right over to a cardiologist. An echo cardiogram was performed. It was discovered I had mitral valve prolapse, which can be a serious condition. Knowing what the problem was, the doctors took precautions before the surgery.

Prior to the operation, Dennis and I had consulted with the doctor, and one of the decisions was over the size of the implant. The doctor showed us several sizes ranging from modest to bodacious. Dennis had a very strong opinion and expressed it in a variation on that old Zen philosophy: More is more. He pointed out that since I was a tall, big-boned woman, small implants would be a waste of a good operation. To liken this to his Jones for cars, the whole procedure, for him, was like putting oversized tires on his Jeep.

After the operation I was pretty groggy for a while. Dennis came in to see how I was doing. I remember having on an oxygen mask to bring me out of the effects of the anesthesia. He came in and started talking to me, and it took me a moment to figure out what he was saying. I finally answered him, but he couldn't understand me with the mask on, so he pulled it off. Typical Dennis.

He asked me how I felt. All I could say was one thing: "My tits are killing me." Dennis said he'd take care of me.

And he did.

I went home later that day and had a recovery period of a few days to look forward to. Dennis was good on his word and kept the house in order, seeing to Alexis and generally pampering me. I loved it. To actually have him pay attention to me, let alone be downright loving, was wonderful. Admittedly I was not in the best of moods, given the pain and drugged-up recovery period as well as the temporary loss of my workout routine. I was a little testy. Okay, I was a bitch. But Dennis hung in there.

I was bedridden for about two days. By the third I was up and around, but Dennis was still doing the chores. Mom was baby-sitting Alexis for a few days to take some of the load off Dennis, at least until I was back up to speed. That evening I decided I'd get up, move around a little, and take a shower. Afterward, I reached into a drawer and pulled out a clean, crisply folded pair of underwear. I thought it was sweet of Dennis to go to so much trouble.

Then I looked at the underwear.

They were women's underwear all right, but they sure as hell weren't mine. And they wouldn't fit Dennis. I took them in to him. "What the fuck is this?" I demanded.

Dennis looked puzzled. "Uh, underwear?" he said, like it was a trick question.

"You're fuckin' right it is, but it isn't mine!"

The war was on. Again.

We yelled a lot, and my emotions were enhanced by a combination of the painkillers, the actual pain itself, and the anger of betrayal for the billionth time. I was furious at him and furious at myself for trusting him.

I then did what I should have done long before that. I went into the bedroom, reached in my closet, unlocked a box, and took out a visual aid to help get my point across.

My gun. A neat little .32-caliber automatic. I had purchased it for peace of mind when Alexis and I moved out on our own.

I slammed the clip home and found the cold steel of the trigger with my index finger. It wasn't loaded, but he didn't know that. I was really angry and didn't have immediate plans for trying to beat a murder rap. Of course, after I told my story, any jury would have considered it justifiable homicide.

I'd be lying if I said I'd never thought about unloading a few rounds into Dennis. Back at the Gilbert Lake house, if I had a firearm, I swear I would have rendered Dennis a legend. But God was watching out for me and never put my hand near a gun when it would have been too great a temptation.

As I walked down the long hall toward the living room, gun in hand, I thought I'd at least put on a good show. I yelled for him, and he appeared at the other end of the hall. I pointed the gun at him. His eyes widened for a split second, then he got that old Dennis bravado. "Go ahead," he said. "Shoot me. Put me out of my misery."

I leveled the gun at the center of his chest and thought, *If this thing were really loaded, it'd be a good lesson to show you the pain of having a hole in your heart.* His cockiness was based on the certainty that I wouldn't shoot. He talks about death now in various articles and in interviews. He goes on about it at the start of his book, where he writes about how he was going to kill himself but decided to take the hard road and live instead. Yeah, right.

I'm here to tell you: Dennis Rodman does not want to die. Never has. The stuff in his book about wrestling with the gun and the thoughts of suicide is pure theatrics. The closest he has ever come to suicide was in carelessly taunting the people around him.

Staring down my gun was a calculated risk on his part. He knew I wasn't going to shoot him. He could sense my moods like an attack dog senses fear, and I know he felt completely safe.

Once that split second of terror had worn off.

— — —

Despite the fact that I had pulled a gun on Dennis after he had pulled that underwear stunt on me, the two of us were lovebirds again. All right, it was more like a cockfight, but for us that was business as usual.

He liked to buy things for me—he was bad around the normal gift-giving days like birthdays and Christmas—but once in a while, out of the blue, he'd knock me out. He had bought me furs and jewelry and clothing, but in the summer of 1993 he flew out to Sacramento and told me we were going for a drive.

The drive turned out to be to the local Porsche dealer.

He knew I was a huge fan of Porsches. I'd ridden in many but I'd never owned or even driven one. When we pulled up in front I was dazzled. I was even more blown away when he told me to pick one out.

We went into the showroom. I saw my dream car. It was a Porsche 911 turbo with all the trimmings: tricked-out bodywork, reworked engine, custom interior, the whole nine yards. Dennis saw my eyes go right to it—of course it was the most expensive car they had—and he told them to get the keys, as I was going to drive it right out of the showroom. Holy shit!

A salesman pulled the car out to the street. Dennis handed me the keys and said, "Go on, drive your new car." I got behind the wheel. As I put it in gear and drove away, I felt completely exhilarated. But as fabulous as the car was, I began to think about Dennis and the problems we had and realized all of the Porsches in the world couldn't fix the dysfunction we had going.

One time in 1992 I took Alexis out to Dallas to visit Dennis. He was in a great mood, happy to see us, and told me he had a surprise for me. We got into his truck and went for a drive. At one point he pulled over and asked me to close my eyes. As we continued down the street, he kept looking at me and saying, "Keep 'em closed. Don't cheat!" He was as excited as a little kid. Finally we stopped. I kept my eyes closed, and Dennis helped me out of the truck and through a door. Then he told me to open my eyes.

We were in a Harley-Davidson dealership.

Right in front of me was a stunning, sparkling Harley fat boy, jet black. Painted on the tank was L.A. WOMAN. I was touched. I loved the bike, but I was struck by how much Dennis really cared and what odd ways he had of showing his affection. He used to write me these lengthy notes and talk about our problems and how much he loved me and how much pain he was in about his life and our life together. Dennis is not an evil man, just mixed up.

**■ ■ ■**

After I had the miscarriage and the abortions I was plagued by guilt and feelings of inadequacy. Dennis had stripped me of whatever feelings of self-worth I may have had and made me believe no one but him would want me. Making matters worse was the fact that there was something in me telling me not to give up on the relationship, no matter how awful it was. Since Dennis was spending most of his nonbasketball time at strip joints, I set about trying to get his attention.

Nothing got his attention faster than when I dated other guys. It was my way of saying, "Hey, Dennis, look at me. I want to hurt you the way you hurt me. Feel the pain? It doesn't feel good, does it?" That's when he started going loony. He missed the entire Pistons training camp at the start of the 1992–93 season, and even after rejoining the team he started missing practices. And in his most famous incident, he wrote a letter to a friend of his in which he talked about how screwed up things had become in his life. He left the note at his pal's house and then drove out to the Palace. It was three or four in the morning when the cops found him, asleep in the truck with a rifle in his lap.

In his book, Dennis claims he was contemplating suicide because he "couldn't be what society wanted an athlete to be. I couldn't be the good soldier and the happy teammate and the good man off the court." Apparently he wanted NBA approval to beat his wife, cheat on her, and wear makeup and dresses.

He continues, "I tried, and I failed. I tried marriage for the good of my child and had it blow up in my face." It blew up in his face? Well, I remember when *he* blew up in *my* face, but before we examine that any further, let's see what else he had to say. "I tried to be loyal to my team and my teammates.... I tried to do all those things, all the right things, and I got nothing but pain and suffering in return." Well, at least he had the decency not to claim that he tried to be loyal to his wife and his daughter.

With his emotional stunts in Detroit, Dennis had begun his transformation from confused ragamuffin to media darling. But it wasn't until he started modeling himself after me that he began to get everyone's attention the way he wanted to.

The first time I cut and bleached my hair must have been around 1989, several years before Dennis seized on the idea as a marketing gimmick for himself. In another vain attempt to get his attention, I went out and got a tattoo—again, years before he got up the courage to do the same thing. My first tattoo was a little rose with a heart that had DENNIS written in it. I had it done on my ankle as a surprise for Dennis. When I showed it to him he was less than thrilled. He said it made me look like a biker chick. I was surprised to find out he meant that as an insult, given the trailer trash I'd caught him with in the past. But he finally came around and got one on his ankle. It was AA for Alexis and Annie.

After I got a sun tattoo, Dennis got one. After Monique and I got matching shark tattoos, Dennis got a shark on his arm. Later, when I got my LOUIS tattoo, Dennis responded by getting one of his girlfriend's initials, L.G. After L.G. dumped him Dennis said it stood for "Long Gone." I got a tribal band around my wrist. Dennis did the same. In a variation on our body mutilation ballet, I got my belly button pierced, and Dennis followed suit. I was with him when he had it done. Then I got a tattoo on the back of my neck, and not long after, Dennis got one there, too. I have a cross on my arm that says IN MEMORY OF MY MOTHER. Dennis got the same cross, but without the dedication. I then got a tribal design on my lower back; he did the same. I later got a panther on my ankle. Rumor has it Dennis has something similar, but I can't confirm that one. He copied me tattoo for tattoo, except for the names. In fact, there's a *Sports Illustrated* article quoting Dennis as saying, "I do everything my wife does."

After Dennis was traded to San Antonio he started doing the hair thing. The first color? Bleached blond. Gee, where do you think he got that idea? Everyone started calling him Demolition Man, after the Wesley Snipes character in the movie of that name. From there Dennis went through all the colors of the rainbow. I saw somewhere that the Spurs were 35–14 when Dennis was blond, 9–2 when his hair was purple, and 3–2 when he went with the blue.

— — —

In 1993 Alexis and I were living in Sacramento in the house on Forty-second Street. Dennis and I were still on again, off again. Despite the fact that I had filed for divorce in December 1992, he was still calling, asking me to get back together with him.

Louis was playing in L.A., so Monique and I decided to fly down to see him. Dennis was coming to Sacramento, and I told him we would be gone, that we were flying to San Diego to visit Monique's mom. I lied. So sue me. I thought it was high time to turn the tables on Dennis, and frankly I didn't give a shit if he found out. We had been back and forth so many times that I didn't care anymore.

When Dennis got to Sacramento he found Monique's address book in the house. He called Monique's mom and asked to speak to me. Oops. Shoulda told her the "story." Dennis flipped out and drove over to Mom's to find out where I was. She wasn't too worried about saving his feelings at that point and told him so.

He must have gotten right on the phone with his private eyes, because when Monique and I left Burbank Airport and landed at Sacramento Airport, it seems we had a "friend" with us. As we rolled out of short-term parking, I couldn't help but notice a Honda Civic that had been cruising the lot and was now pulling through the parking toll booth. After the driver paid, he pulled over and waited for us to pay. I'm pretty street smart and keep my eyes open. I smelled a rat.

We passed that pip-squeak Honda and headed home. I told Monique to keep an eye on it. Sure enough, it followed us all the way home—and in plain sight! What a bonehead! We concluded it was either a rapist or one of Dennis's private dipshits. Dennis had left my house so we went there and soon forgot about the Honda.

The next day I looked out the window and saw the Honda drive down the street. I yelled for Monique. A couple of minutes later we weren't disappointed. The Honda appeared again and drove down a cross street.

"That's it," I said. "This dude's following me!"

I told Monique it was time to kick some ass. We ran out like F-16 pilots on scramble. I jumped into my Corvette, Monique into the 4-Runner. We burned rubber outta there.

I spied the Honda almost immediately. The driver was pulling up to a stoplight. I roared up next to him, slammed on the brakes, leaped out, and ran around to his window. This little Poindexter-lookin' motherfucker was so scared, I thought he'd have a heart attack! I screamed, "LEAVE ME THE FUCK ALONE!"

Just then the light turned green and he shot away from me.

Monique continued the chase, and I got back into the 'Vette and gunned it. I caught up with them quickly. Monique was right on the guy. That little Honda was no match for Salt and Pepper! We finally pinned him between our cars and were going to cut him off when we got to a stop sign. He went right through it. We'd had enough fun by then and went home. I'm sure Dennis got a call from that breathless little twerp saying, "Mr. Rodman, those chicks are *crazy*!" And we were.

# CHAPTER 13

## Bye, Bye, Bad Boy

THE FIRST TIME I SAW DENNIS OUT OF CONTROL WITH ALCOHOL WAS when I was living in Sacramento on Forty-second Street. This was in 1993, just before we were officially divorced. It was summer, and Dennis was at an all-time low despite winning his second consecutive rebounding title and being named to the NBA All-Defensive Team at the end of the previous season.

I remember coming home and finding Dennis in the gutter. Literally. It was around one or two in the morning, and there were two onlookers standing over Dennis, watching him vomit. The couple had driven him, in his rental car, from the bar where they had met him. At least that's the story they told me. They said Dennis kept saying "4201 Forty-second Street, 4201 Forty-second Street, 4201 Forty-second Street." So here he was, in the gutter at 4201 Forty-second Street.

They helped me drag Dennis up some stairs and into the living room. I suppose they then drove his rental back to the bar.

Dennis went in and out of consciousness. His breathing was erratic and, since he has asthma, I felt around his pockets for his inhaler, but he didn't have it. I got a warm washcloth and washed his face, then put a pillow under his head in the hopes that if he threw up again, at least he wouldn't choke on his own vomit. All the while he kept muttering, "Annie...I need you...Annie, I love you...Annie...Annie...Annie."

He rarely drank when we were together, so I was shocked to see what had happened since Alexis and I had left him in Detroit. A little while later I noticed he was having difficulty breathing. I called 911. That brought out every emergency vehicle you can imagine: police, ambulance, fire department vehicles. It was an impressive turnout.

Dennis was in the back of the ambulance being attended by paramedics. I was in the front seat looking back. "Dennis, you're going to be all right. I'm right here. Don't worry."

When we got to the hospital one of the nurses asked if Dennis took drugs. I told her he had never taken any as long as I had known him. The nurse asked if I had been with him all night. I said I hadn't been. She said, "Well, then, you don't know if he's taken any drugs tonight, do you?" She had me there. They decided they needed a urine sample to test for drugs. Unfortunately Dennis couldn't have peed even if you offered him a dozen strippers for his troubles, so the nurse fetched a catheter and gave it to the doctor.

When the doctor first tried inserting the catheter you'd have thought someone had run over a sack of cats. Dennis let out the most bloodcurdling scream anyone has ever heard. I remember holding him down and talking in his ear, telling him he was going to be all right. "Hold still, Mr. Rodman," the doctor said. "You've got to hold still."

After Dennis screamed again I turned to the doctor. "Have you ever had this done to you?"

He looked rather surprised and shook his head no. "Then shut the fuck up and hurry up with it. And be careful!" I said.

As far as I know, the only drug they found in Dennis's system was alcohol. And they found plenty of that. They kept him overnight at the hospital, passed out in his bed. I went to the hospital's chapel and prayed very, very hard. I then went to the lobby and fell asleep curled up on a chair. Someone woke me at about seven the next morning and told me Dennis was ready to go home. From the few times I remember Dennis being drunk, he never had hangovers. He'd pop some aspirin and be good to go. That morning I figured he'd have a doozy. I was wrong.

I went into his room and helped him get dressed. He was moving a little slower than usual, but when he opened his mouth to speak I knew he was back to normal. Did he ask what had happened? Did he thank me for all my help? Did he apologize for what he had done? Nope. He said, "I'm hungrier than fuck. Let's go eat."

▬ ▬ ▬

Dennis didn't start drinking until I left him for the last time in Michigan. After that night I found him in the gutter, drinking become something of a habit for him.

The next time I saw him really toasted was at America Live, a bar in Sacramento. He and I were there with friends, and Dennis was getting schnockered on Jagermeister. On our way out of the bar at the end of the night, he decided he needed to tackle me. We crashed to the ground and laughed for a minute before I got up. But Dennis didn't. He couldn't. He was too drunk. Fortunately another player, Olden Polynice, was there to help. He helped Monique and me get Dennis to the car. Unfortunately Olden didn't follow us home to help unload him.

Monique and I aren't small, but dragging 6'8" and 220 pounds of dead weight is a task. I had Dennis by his big feet, Monique had him by the head. I think I suggested that she could use his ears as handles.

In the course of dragging Dennis's big ass into the apartment, I kicked over the cat's litter box. We didn't stop to clean it up. We had momentum and we didn't want to lose it, so we just dragged him straight through the cat shit, laughing all the way. We were laughing so hard that we had to stop and catch our breath. We dropped Dennis for just a minute. *Wham!* His head made a big noise when it hit. "Sorry," Monique said. When I finally stopped laughing I stood there looking down at Dennis. "God, Monique," I said, "to think of all the shit this man has put me through, and now look at him. He's completely helpless."

Monique flashed a devilish smile. "What are you thinking, Annie?"

We joked about taking him to a city park and dumping him on

**198**

a bench, but we thought two white girls dragging a big black man through a park might look a little suspicious. "Besides," I reasoned, "he weighs too damn much. Let's just get him to bed."

We got him into the bedroom, undressed him, and put a wastebasket near his head. When he threw up he managed to get some of it into the basket. I'd say he shot about 50 percent that night. No rebounds, no blocks, one turnover. As usual, the next day I had to do all the cleaning. The house stunk of vomit and Jagermeister.

After Dennis came to, he never bothered to thank us for helping him out. He just woke up and said, "Let's go eat." Typical Dennis.

— — —

August 1993. The day had finally come to bring an official, legal end to my marriage. According to Dennis's book, our marriage had lasted only eighty-two days. According to legal documents, it lasted nearly two years. According to the amount of time we were "together," it was more like six years.

I remember Dennis not being in the best of moods that day. Neither was I. After all I had been through, after everything I had done to try to keep us together, the whole thing was about to end in a brief legal ceremony—a ceremony with a bit more stuffiness and dignity than the wedding itself.

I was there with my attorney and my therapist. Dennis was there with his attorney as well. At least he had the decency not to bring Tracy or Karen or some other such slut.

I had put the whole thing in motion in December 1992, after the accumulation of events had finally pushed me over the edge. And even though it was obviously the right thing to do, it didn't make it any easier for me and Alexis.

We were in the courthouse waiting for our case to come up when Dennis came over to me. "Annie, we have to talk," he said. "But not here. Away from everybody, away from the lawyers."

When our attorneys saw us talking they started toward us. They wanted to keep us away from one another. And for good reason. But I was willing to give Dennis a chance to say whatever he wanted without interference from the lawyers. We got out the door before they could stop us and took the elevator up to the next floor. We wandered around until we found an empty hallway. Dennis put me up against a wall and himself right next to me, side by side, the way we should have been all along. "Are you sure you want to do this?" he asked. "We can walk right out of here. Just fuck 'em, Annie. This is you and me. I don't want this, Annie, and neither do you. I know you don't."

The lawyers had sounded a red alert, and everyone had fanned out trying to find us. My mom and Monique. My therapist. Dennis's lawyer. My lawyer.

But they hadn't found us yet. We were still alone in the secluded hallway when Dennis started kissing me. I didn't resist. If my therapist hadn't found us, I might have walked out of the building with Dennis that day.

My therapist pulled me aside and, as tears rolled down my cheeks, she said, "Annie, Dennis has manipulated you so many times in the past, you have to recognize that he's trying to do it again. You have to be strong. You have to follow through with what you set out to do. I know you still love Dennis, but he's never going to change."

Dennis was standing a few yards away, calling my name. I felt like the rope in a tug-of-war contest. My heart—the thing that had gotten me into this mess in the first place—was telling me to run off again with Dennis. But my mind—the thing that had finally learned its lesson—told me to stay strong. I had to get free of Dennis for Alexis's sake.

Then, like the hapless cavalry from *F-Troop*, the lawyers, all scowling, came running around the corner, too late to save the day. They told us to get downstairs immediately. I remember my therapist hugging me and saying, "You know, Annie, a lot of couples who divorce, remarry. Right now you cannot stay in this marriage. Maybe a few years down the road, you two might get back together, but now you and Alexis don't fit in Dennis's world. He doesn't want you there, no matter what he says. It's what he *does* that matters."

Oh yeah, actions speak louder than words. I seem to remember hearing that somewhere. As I walked down the hall to return to the courtroom, I turned back to Dennis and said, "I'm sorry I have to do this, but I can't go on believing your lies anymore. I love you with all my heart, but I know you'll never change. I'm sorry."

When we were back in the courtroom I was so emotionally screwed up I couldn't even follow the proceedings. Suddenly the judge slammed the gavel down and mumbled something that may as well have been in Latin. In fact, it probably was in Latin, since judges and lawyers are so fond of obscure language. I turned to my attorney and asked what was going on. He looked at me and said, "Your divorce is final."

As my attorney started packing up his papers, I slumped in my chair. "Fuck," I muttered. "What have I done?" I noticed Dennis standing by the table, and I looked up with tears in my eyes.

"Are you happy now?" he said. "Remember, this is what you wanted, not me."

I managed to say something like, "I never wanted this. You pushed me into this, Dennis. All I ever wanted from you was your love."

He didn't respond. He just turned and walked out of the courtroom. That was, perhaps, the second worst day of my life.

That night I was back at my mom and dad's house, alone. I think my mom and Alexis were out somewhere. I don't know where Dad or my brothers were. There was a knock at the door. It was Dennis. It wasn't a surprise. He was coming over to see Alexis. I let him in and we went into the kitchen. My emotions were in check, and even though I was a little drained from the day's events, I was under control. We were standing in the kitchen making small talk when out of the blue Dennis said, "Annie, would you marry me again?"

"What?" I was pretty sure I had heard him correctly. I just couldn't believe it. "Are you nuts?"

"No. I mean it, Annie. Would you marry me again someday?"

The question was so absurd I don't think I answered verbally. I think my expression answered instead; it said something like, "I'd rather stick needles in my eyes."

— — — —

The following month brought the single worst day of my life. It was September 29, 1993, the day after Alexis's fifth birthday. I was at the gym working out when I got a page to call Alexis's school. When I reached them, they told me to go to the emergency room at Mercy Hospital. Panicking, I asked if Alexis was all right. They said she was, that it was my mother.

When my mom was a young girl living in the orphanage, she contracted scarlet fever or something. As a result she ended up with a heart murmur. (I ended up with a murmur as well, having been born with a hole in my heart. Fortunately, mine healed without surgery.) The medical term for my mom's condition is mitral valve prolapse, and it resulted in heart palpitations. Her doctor prescribed quinidine for that.

That day she had taken my dad to have his eyes examined. She was sitting in the car in the patients' parking lot of Mercy Hospital, where the eye doctor kept his office, directly across the street from Alexis's school, Sacred Heart. A woman was walking to her car when she heard my mom cry out for help. At the same time, my dad was coming out from his appointment, and he also heard her call for help. It turned out that she was having a toxic reaction to the quinidine. She lost consciousness while still in the parking lot and they rushed her inside.

I raced to the hospital and kept repeating to myself, "She's going to be okay. She's going to be okay."

When I got to the hospital parking lot I saw my brother Bill standing outside. I got out and ran for the ER. I looked over at Bill as I passed by. He didn't say a word. Inside, the medical staff was working frantically to revive Mom. Dad was trying to hold me back, but he couldn't.

I had never seen my mother look so helpless. I didn't know what I was doing or thinking, or even where I was. I can remember talking to Mom as the doctors worked on her: "Please don't leave me here alone. Please don't go. I need you, Mama."

She left us about forty-five minutes later, bringing my entire world down around me.

I remember kissing her cold face, hoping that she would, by the power of God, come back to life. I went outside and vomited into an ashtray. I never felt so alone in my entire life. After everyone left the hospital, I stayed behind. I watched as my mother's body was wrapped in a maroon blanket and placed onto a gurney, which they rolled out to the funeral home's van. I remember losing it and saying, "Don't cover her face! Don't cover her up!" I wanted to believe that the doctors had screwed up and made a horrible mistake. I wanted to believe Mom was still alive.

I followed the van to the funeral home, where they unloaded her body. I stayed there until 12:40 A.M.

I was pissed. Why hadn't she fought harder? Why hadn't the doctors saved her? Didn't she want to see Alexis grow up? Damn you, God! She was my mom, and You had to take her! How dare You take her! There was no good reason. *Fuck You, God! Fuck You! Fuck You!*

That's when I stopped believing in God.

I decided that since God only seemed to take the good people around me—my brother Andrew, my best friend Jack, my friend Mary Jane, Sister Assumpta—I would have to be bad enough that God wouldn't come for Alexis and me. That's when I officially became an atheist.

It was September, so basketball season hadn't started yet. That meant no one was sure where to find Dennis. We eventually tracked him down in San Diego with Kym Lee (aka Kym Hunt). To his credit, he flew in the next day. Keep in mind that this was at a time when Dennis was miserable in his career. Things had deteriorated in Detroit during the 1992–93 season, and there was every reason to believe things were going to get worse before they got better. Plus, he and I had officially divorced a month before Mom died.

Dennis stayed for all the services. He even got up and spoke. I don't remember what he said word for word, but it was along the lines of "Mrs. Bakes didn't see color in me. She took me in as one of her own. I loved her as if she were my own mother. She saw something in me that no one else saw. And I know that whatever I did in life, she would have loved me unconditionally."

It sounded good, even if it was mostly bullshit. My mom knew how Dennis had treated me and she did not approve. Being the good Catholic she was, perhaps she forgave him in time.

203

He knew how much my mother meant to me, so he knew how hard I would take her passing. Dennis told me, "You gotta cry, babe. You gotta let it out. Stop keeping it inside. Everything's gonna be all right now. I'm gonna take care of you, Annie, the way your mama always wanted me to. I'm never gonna hurt you."

When it was time to close the casket, I slipped my wedding ring off my finger and took hers—Mom had only a small gold band. Dennis asked what I was doing. "Mom always wanted a big diamond ring and Dad could never afford one, so now she has one," I explained. He looked at me, then he looked at my mom. Then he helped me put my diamond ring on her finger.

At some point during the rosary Dennis took an urgent phone call. That was when he found out he and Isiah Morris had been traded to the San Antonio Spurs. I think he was glad to be getting out of Detroit after all that had happened. The good days were long gone. The championship players were either breaking down or being sold off like car parts. Besides, in the Spurs, Dennis would get to play with David Robinson. What could be better? Of course, in the end, Dennis's days in San Antonio wouldn't exactly be sweetness and light. More on that later.

After the rosary Dennis came up to me and asked if I would marry him again. "There's nothing left for you in Sacramento anymore," he said. I think I was so emotionally drained from Mom's death that I couldn't muster the appropriate response. I also don't know whether he was asking me to marry him because he felt sorry for me, or whether he was trying to take advantage of my all-time emotional low.

My mother's funeral was at All Hallows Catholic Church. She had spent the last twelve years of her life working as a secretary at a predominantly black school. She used money out of her own pocket to buy shoes for some of the kids who didn't have a decent pair. She was the most decent, compassionate person I've ever known.

There wasn't an empty seat in the house. The crowd of people looked like Jesse Jackson's Rainbow Coalition. Mom cared about others, and this crowded church was proof that they cared right back. The funeral procession consisted of an amazing variety of cars, from low riders to Mercedes to hot rods to plain old station wagons. A lot of the kids from her school got up during the funeral and read special notes they had written about my mom. She touched a lot of lives and made a difference to a lot of people, but none more than me.

At the funeral I was a robot, just going through the motions, trying to take care of my dad and my brothers and poor Alexis. She had just turned five, and she was so confused. She kept asking when Nana was coming back. How far is heaven? Can I go see her? Why can't she come back? What do you mean, never? Are you gonna go away too, Mama?

About a year later Alexis started crying and saying, "I want Nana, I want Nana. I want to go to heaven and see her." I have no idea what triggered it. I fought back my own tears as I said, "No, baby, you don't want to go to heaven now. Nana wants you to grow up and live forever and make her proud. Someday baby, a long time from now, we will see Nana again, I promise."

Next to me, my mom was the most important person in Alexis's life. She helped raise Alexis and taught her all the things I didn't. They baked cookies and futzed around in the garden and played piano together. I couldn't have asked for anyone better to help raise my baby. She taught Alexis about manners, about prayer, and about love.

— — —

After my mom died I went into a severe depression. I just didn't give a damn about anything anymore, except for Alexis. I began thinking about suicide. I started drinking tequila to numb the pain. I lost thirty pounds and completely withdrew from life. I couldn't snap out of the funk I fell into.

I hid it all from Alexis. She didn't need to see her mom sliding down the drain like that. She'd already seen too much for a five-year-old, so I continued doing all the things we had done before Mom died. I used to look forward to doing those things, but now I had to force myself.

Mom's death was worse than anything Dennis ever subjected me to. He and I could fight and break up and get back together again, but Mom—my protector—was gone forever.

To make matters worse, Dennis and I tried to reconcile. I needed him badly, or so I believed at the time, and he took advantage of my emotional state. When I found out, during the course of our reconciliation, that he had a girlfriend living with him in San Antonio, I hit rock bottom.

My psychiatrist prescribed an antidepressant, and I dedicated myself to the only thing that still mattered to me: Alexis. That's why I think of Alexis as my savior—she kept me alive. She gave me a reason to keep on living. I knew I couldn't quit on her. She needed me, and I wasn't going to let her down. Now that I had finally left Dennis, Alexis had more or less lost her dad.

I had a dream, or maybe I just made it up, that I was in the afterlife. I was approaching Mom and she said, "What the hell are you doing here? I didn't raise a quitter. You get back there and take care of your little girl." Even though she was gone, she was still teaching me lessons.

Eventually my sadness was overrun by anger. I was pissed at the world. Unfortunately I was self-medicating with tequila. I was looking for any kind of shit to get into it with people. I was looking for a way to get someone pissed at me so it would give me an excuse to beat the shit out of them. Maybe I was hoping to have all that anger beaten out of me. If I was in the car alone, I would drive like a lunatic. I was out to hurt someone, anyone, but I was mainly out to hurt myself.

One night Monique and I went to a place called the Paradise Beach Club in Sacramento. When Monique went to the rest room I started talking to this dude at the bar, knowing full well that his girlfriend was just a few feet away. I needed to let out some of my frustration, and apparently I thought the best way to do that was by getting somebody pissed off at me.

The girlfriend took the bait. All of a sudden she came up from behind and shoved me. I lost my balance and dropped the two drinks I had been holding. When I regained my balance I turned and punched her as hard as I could. I felt a big rush. It was like taking a pee after you've been holding it so long it hurts. I felt so good, I wanted more. And it turned out I was just about to have my wish granted.

Two of her friends came out of nowhere and jumped on me. I remember head-butting one of them, and she let out a shriek. The other one had me from behind, and I'm not sure what my plan was in regard to her, but I didn't have to worry. Monique came rushing back from the rest room, pulled her off me, and started throttling her.

Security finally showed up and broke up the fight. They kicked Monique and me out of the bar and off the premises. The two women didn't get kicked out because no one saw the first one shove me, they only saw me nail her with a right hook. It's a lot like how they call fouls in the NBA—the guy who gets in the hidden cheap shot doesn't get called, it's the guy who retaliates who gets tossed out of the game.

My anger has finally subsided. It took a while, but I've regained my faith in God, and I'm going to church again. It was a long, hard road, but I traveled it. You gotta have faith. All I have to do is look at Alexis, and I know there's got to be a God to make something as beautiful as she is.

— — —

A month or so after Mom died, Dennis moved to San Antonio and his new team, the Spurs. He was happy because San Antonio was a lot closer to where he grew up than the Motor City was. He was going from the Bad Boys of Detroit to playing with one of the NBA's good guys—the Admiral, David Robinson. I had bizarre fantasies that some of David's decency might actually rub off on Dennis. About as close as Dennis got to having anything of David's rub off on him was pizza, when the two of them did a commercial for Pizza Hut.

Once Dennis got to San Antonio, he had a great role model in the Admiral and a coach who specialized in working with head cases. Of all the coaches Dennis has ever had, the one he should have listened to the most was John Lucas. Coach Lucas was good at dealing with "troubled" players. He himself had been troubled; he overcame a *serious* drug addiction and helped others do the same. Coach Lucas earned and deserves a lot of respect for taking responsibility for himself after making a mess out of his life.

But Dennis never wanted to listen to Coach Lucas. Hell, he doesn't want to listen to *anyone* with good sense. Dennis didn't think he had anything to learn from him. He thinks he knows it all already.

When my mom died Coach Lucas called to express his sympathy. He was very courteous and kind. He also talked to me about trying to work things out with Dennis. Coach Lucas told me how Dennis kept him up late at night talking about how much he loved me. I told him that whenever Dennis screwed up, he always had others call me on his behalf to try to apologize. Coach Lucas said he understood, but he also said that he was in San Antonio to work with Dennis, and that it really seemed like he was sincere about wanting to turn his life around.

That's how good Dennis was at fooling people. Of all the people in the world who should have been able to see through his bullshit, John Lucas should have been able to. Maybe it was because Dennis was a wife beater and a whoremonger instead of a drug addict that Coach Lucas didn't see what was going on.

I hated to see Coach Lucas leave San Antonio because I hoped he would eventually get through to Dennis. I still had hopes that he and I could repair our family. But the suits in San Antonio made their decision, and Lucas was replaced by Bob Hill. Coach Hill and Dennis got along all right, at least until the play-offs came around. Dennis had some problems with Coach Hill's strategy. Before the play-offs were over Dennis was sitting there in his socks, wondering what the Spurs would be getting for him in the impending off-season trade. The answer was Will Purdue. Dennis went over to the Bulls. Somebody got screwed. I hope they got kissed, too.

Coach Lucas was unable to change him, and Bob Hill didn't even try. And in Chicago, Phil Jackson knows better than to go there.

But the grand poo-bahs of the NBA are still fishing around for someone who can get under Dennis's hood and get him to run right. In January 1997, after he kicked Eugene Amos—the cameraman with the slow reaction time—there was some talk about the Reverend Jesse Jackson coming in to counsel Dennis. (When Eugene was later arrested for assaulting his own girlfriend, I thought it might be contagious.) I'm the first one to say Dennis needs help, but Jesse Jackson? If he can help him, I'm all for it, but I don't think Jesse does much without calling a press conference first.

— — —

In the fall of 1994 Dennis asked me to meet him in Oakland, where the Spurs were playing the Golden State Warriors. After the game Dennis, Jack Haley, and I went into the city to one of Dennis's favorite places. It was a strip bar called Centerfolds, a place Dennis frequented while in the Bay Area. By that time it didn't matter to me. The marriage was over, and his infidelities weren't my problem. As a matter of fact, with all the pressure off, we were actually having a blast. That is, until Dennis got all hooched up and started yelling to the crowd: "This is my ex-wife, but I'm gonna marry her again!" He turned to me. "Annie, will you marry me again?" He then turned back to the crowd. "Out of all the girls I've been with, this is the one that got my heart."

While Dennis carried on, I asked Jack, "So what's up with the hosebag Staci?"

"Staci loves the limelight," Jack replied. "Dennis doesn't love her. She just stays around for the lifestyle of it all."

Dennis apparently overheard us. "Staci doesn't mean anything to me," he said. "She's just easy. She's there."

Staci was a little 4'11" troll-looking bitch who, I might add, was fucking one of the Dallas Cowboys, or so the rumor went. Rumor also has it that the Cowboy paid her to have an abortion. I have no confirmation of that, however.

With his grown-up desire for firm little titties, Dennis is the only millionaire I know who is stupid enough to be seen with such a trailer-park slut. Staci put up with whatever shit Dennis did as long as he had the money to make it worth her while. If he was in a car accident and paralyzed and all his money was gone, I'd like to see Staci around then, taking care of him out of love and devotion. Hell, she'd be out of there as fast as her size 3 fuck-me-pumps could carry her.

Dennis was waxed when we got in the car to drive back to

Oakland. Jack was driving with me in the front and Dennis lying down in the back. As we crossed the Bay Bridge, Dennis announced that he had to take a piss. Genius that he is, he started to open the back door. I jumped into the backseat to stop him from trying to get out. He was trying to get his pants off and I kept telling him to hold on, we'd be back at the hotel in a minute. Just wait.

When we finally got to the hotel, Jack and I decided it was best not to use the front door. Jack went in and was going to open a side door so we could bring Dennis in. In the meantime, Dennis managed to get out of the car and take his pants and underwear off—right there in the parking lot—and he started to piss. I rushed over and stood in front of him to hide him. I wasn't much of a shield, but I tried. He peed for what seemed like an hour, and my leather boots were getting soaked. I didn't care. I just didn't want anyone to see this display.

After he finished I laid him down in the backseat and tried to get his pants back on. Jack came back and helped me get him to his feet. We carried him through the side entrance and up to his room. Jack told me that if I needed anything, he was right down the hall. I took Dennis's clothes off, washed his face, and put him to bed. I stayed with him until he fell asleep. Then I got my keys and left on my hour-and-forty-five-minute drive back to Sacramento so I'd be home in time to take Alexis to school.

The ride home went by fast. My mind was on Dennis the whole time. I was worried that I was the cause of his drinking to excess. And once again I wondered if I had done the right thing in leaving him in the first place.

— — —

Depending on who you ask, Dennis and Madonna spent either two months or six months together. I say let's split the difference and call it four. Also, depending on who you ask, either he dumped her or she dumped him. All I know is that after they crashed and burned Dennis came crawling back to me.

The whole story was incredibly devastating for me. I remember the first time I saw Dennis and Madonna together. It was on *Hard*

*Copy.* Monique was with me. I remember literally falling to the ground in slow motion. I was speechless and my entire body went numb. It had been a year since the divorce and I was glad to be free of his madness, but it still hurt to know someone else was with him. I got a sickening feeling in the pit of my stomach.

I remember Alexis running into the room and Monique turning off the TV as fast as she could, but it was too late. Alexis had already seen her daddy. Then she saw me and how wounded I looked. I pulled myself together and tried to explain about celebrities and shows like *Hard Copy*, but I'm not sure I helped much.

After I put Alexis to bed I told Monique I was going out for a walk and would be back in a little while. I lied. I walked and walked and walked for I don't know how long. I was totally oblivious to whatever was going on around me. I couldn't figure out why this was affecting me so. Why should I be bothered by Dennis being with another woman after all the years of his cheating and abuse? Now that we weren't married, it was nuts for me to care if he was sleeping with Madonna or the Queen of England for that matter.

All the shit I started getting from everybody didn't help either. "Is it true Dennis is with Madonna?" "Are they gonna have a baby?" "Did you meet her?" "Have you talked to her?" The frenzy surrounding those two was epic even by television's circus-atmosphere standards.

During their courtship Dennis never called me, and he certainly didn't call to speak to Alexis. When it was over between Madonna and the Worm in September 1994, he started calling me again. A month or so later, when the Spurs were in Sacramento to play the Kings, Dennis showed up. But not as a member of the team. Turns out he was on a fourteen-game leave of absence which had been imposed after Dennis had been suspended indefinitely for throwing a bag of ice at Coach Hill and an official after getting his second technical foul during an exhibition game.

Or maybe this was when he had a calf injury. I can't be certain. At any rate Dennis had time on his hands. (Weird Dennis note: For mysterious reasons, he has named his hands Monique and Judy.

Don't ask me why.) And since Dennis was in Sacramento and unable to play, he was out looking for me.

I was walking into America Live when a limo pulled up. A little white dude stepped out and asked me if I wanted to go for a ride. "Not in your wildest dreams," I said. Then I caught a glimpse of Dennis's face. I turned and headed toward the bar. Before I went in I lifted my short black skirt and mooned him.

A little later I was sitting at a table, having drinks with Monique and another friend. I saw Dennis come in. He was with Jack Haley, Bryne Rich, and the little white dude. Dennis and his entourage went to the bar and started drinking Jagermeister. He started sending drinks over to our table. We accepted the drinks and acknowledged them with a wave and a smile.

After I finished my second margarita I went over to the in-bar mini–basketball court and started shooting hoops with a couple of guys. Dennis was shooting nasty looks at me. Since I was pretty sure I was annoying Madonna's ex-boy toy, I kept playing. Every now and then he sent his messenger boy, Jack Haley, to ask me to join them. I declined each invitation. Eventually my margaritas wanted out, so I went to the ladies' room.

I was safely ensconced in my stall when I noticed a large black hand with painted fingernails coming over the top of the door. I was pretty sure it wasn't Sidney Poitier. As Dennis unlocked the door, I hustled to pull my pants up. Before either of us could say anything, the bouncer walked in.

"Mr. Rodman, you have to remove yourself from the ladies' room," he said with a giggle.

Dennis left without incident and I followed. Back in the bar we joined forces and spent the rest of the night partying together. We closed America Live down, then went to eat at a restaurant called Lyon's. After our meal Dennis asked if I would give him a ride back to his hotel while the others took the limo. I knew exactly where this was going.

When we got back to his hotel room we started to talk. I commented about how he always came back to me after one of his ho's dumped him. "I dumped *her*," he said, referring to the Material Girl.

"She was gonna offer me ten million dollars to father her child. She wasn't shit in bed." He had missed my point completely. Again.

He started kissing me. I kissed back, but there wasn't any passion. We were just going through the motions. We didn't actually make love that night; Dennis was having sex and I was getting a grudge fuck. Under normal circumstances I'd have made him wear a condom, but since this was after his Madonna experience, I made him wear two. Just like in the beginning of our relationship, Dennis still had time left on the shot clock when he was finished.

"I hate myself for loving you, Annie," he said. "But I can't stop!" I don't know what it was about that little speech, but it turned out to be the last straw. I knew then that I couldn't be with him anymore. I had said that a million times before, but something about what he said made this time different.

After Dennis fell asleep I got dressed and found his wallet. I took $500. I kissed him good-bye and whispered, "I'll always love you, but I'm not gonna let you continue to do this to me. I deserve better. I will never make love to you again. Oh, and by the way, I took five hundred bucks from your wallet. I think I was worth that." Call it bonus spousal support or call me a whore. I've been called worse.

Dennis woke up. As fucked up as he was, he said, "Please stay with me tonight. Don't leave me alone."

"It doesn't feel good to love someone and have them leave you when you need them the most, does it?" I replied. "Well, now you know how I felt all those times."

That was the last time I ever slept with Dennis Rodman.

# C H A P T E R        1 4

## The Fourth Quarter

DWIGHT MANLEY CLAIMS TO BE DENNIS RODMAN'S BEST FRIEND. AS HIS self-proclaimed business manager and agent, Manley is in charge of all of his money as well as his career and says he took the job because he couldn't stand to see Dennis's life and finances in such terrible shape.

Watch out, Dennis.

I think Manley created the job because he saw a sucker in Dennis. He moved on him like every other whore Dennis has been with, only being a man, Dennis listened to his line of horseshit, liked the smell of it, and turned everything over to him. Dennis is no dummy but, like I said, he trusts the wrong people.

I do not like Dwight Manley. I first met him sometime in 1995 when Alexis and I flew down to Orange County for a visit with Dennis. Dennis has his business headquarters there and, I understand, owns a house in Newport Beach. And shares it with Dwight.

A former coin collector, Manley left his wife right after meeting Dennis. Manley has been sued by various people in the past and is, at best, a shady character. He is not well liked by the NBA. I get the feeling Manley likes Dennis in a "special" way, if you get my drift. When you first meet Manley, the thing that strikes you the most is what a contradiction his last name is. And without Dennis, Mr. Dwight Manley's name would be spelled N-O-B-O-D-Y.

I certainly have an axe to grind with him, as he has been the voice in Dennis's ear speaking against me and, by association, our daughter. When Dennis and I finally got divorced, I had a little girl to take care of and a lot of bills to pay. At his request I had long since abandoned career plans and was doing what I could to pay the bills. But without training, a college degree, or just stability in having been in the same job or town for a while, I couldn't make ends meet.

I appealed to Dennis.

That's when Dwight Manley went to work. I had asked Dennis for help, and I believe he was about to give it when suddenly, *boom*, nothing. That was the icy hand of Dwight Manley striking. I was left high and dry and forced to file bankruptcy. I also had tax problems from our split and I'm still working those out. I blame Manley for Dennis's sudden hard-heartedness.

Manley has not the faintest idea who I am and what I've been to Dennis. Manley may think I'm just another of his tramps. Lord knows, if you read Dennis's book you'd think we'd spent a long weekend together. Period.

So, Dwight, now that you've read this book, know this: I've got your number, and when you screw Dennis over and run for the hills I can say, "Dennis, I told you so."

— — —

On March 18, 1996, during a game between the Chicago Bulls and the New Jersey Nets, a referee had enough of Dennis and ejected him from the game. I guess Dennis didn't like the call and decided filing a grievance or pleading with the ref to change his mind was a waste of time, so he handled his beef with typical Rodman flair: He head-butted the guy.

For those of you who aren't familiar with contact sports, a good head butt is a work of art. It requires the butter (for want of a better term) to bring that thick part of the head, where the forehead dissolves into the top of the skull, down, hard, onto the soft, vulnerable part of the buttee's forehead or even his nose. It's frowned upon it can cause the buttee serious trauma, including brain concussions and skull fractures.

Dennis has perfected his head-butting skills in other high-profile encounters during NBA games. In 1993 he butted Chicago's Stacy King (Dennis was still a Piston at the time) into submission and was awarded a one-game suspension and a seventy-five hundred dollar fine.

In 1994 John Stockton, point guard for the Utah Jazz, was another recipient of Dennis's noggin crunchers. He got only a five thousand dollar fine that time. With supply exceeding demand, the price of a good head butt was going down.

Another time he head-butted a real foe, the hapless mascot for the Spurs, a cartoon coyote, some poor joker in a polyester costume. He knocked that coyote into next week, and I'm sure that when the coyote recovered and returned to duty, he probably gave the guy with the changing hair color a wide berth.

Dennis was depressed about the scalding he was getting in the press. He would take criticism hard sometimes, despite being the cause of it all. He would always say in reference to his critics, "They're fuckin' with me. They won't get off my back." I really think he was puzzled about all the hubbub over his antics. He's like a driver who runs off the road to mow down a pedestrian, then says, "But the guy got in my way."

He started calling me at home in Sacramento. As his messages accumulated on my answering machine, I could hear the sadness and loneliness in his voice. He has countless people to turn to for everything from money and career advice to sex, drugs, and rock 'n' roll, but when he's down and wants someone who *really* knows him, he calls me.

By the tenth call I was starting to feel sorry for him. He felt like the media were ganging up on him, and he needed to talk. I was also feeling a little financial pinch and thought he might be able to help me out. So when the phone rang one morning, and I heard Dennis's familiar droning on the answering machine, I picked it up.

Dennis is a man of few words and tries not to let on what he's feeling, but I could hear his voice brighten slightly when he heard me. "What're you doin'?" he asked. Before I could answer, he said, "Where's the baby?" I always thought it was strange he still referred to Alexis, even at age seven, as "the baby." His question also told me something: By asking Alexis's whereabouts in that way, he wanted to make sure we were alone. I picked up pretty fast that he was horny.

I tried diverting the conversation. I had my agenda, he had his. "How're you doin'?" I asked. "Are you okay?" I knew all about the head-butt incident from his previous messages as well as all the TV coverage. He minimized it in his normal macho way: "I'm cool." Then we went back to his track. "What're you wearin'?" I knew where this was going, but I felt sorry for him at that moment and decided, what the hell, I'll go with the flow. "I'm wearing my cutoffs and a little tank top." I was wearing sweats.

"Where are you?" he whispered. I purred, "I'm in the bedroom. Lying on the bed. I'm thinking of you." I was in the kitchen with my feet propped up on the counter. I had the TV on and was watching *The Price Is Right*. The mute was on.

Like I said, go with the flow.

"I'm thinkin' about you, baby," Dennis continued. "You got any panties on?" I opened a Diet Coke, making sure he didn't hear the clink-fizz sound. "No, I don't." He told me he was lying on his bed. I told him I was lying on mine. He said he was naked now and he was touching himself. He asked me to touch myself.

"What're you thinkin'?" he asked. I was watching Bob Barker auction off a box of Rice-A-Roni. I thought it should go for a buck eighty-nine. I remembered Dennis's question. "Uh, I'm thinkin' how nice it would be to have you inside me," I said. The lady bidder low-balled at around a buck twenty-nine and struck out.

Suddenly it occurred to me that Dennis had another option. I asked, "Where's Staci? Why aren't you talking to her?" He didn't break stride, or stroke, if you will. "Oh, hey, I ain't messin' with that girl anymore," he replied. Then, to get us back to where he wanted to be, he said, "I miss you suckin' my dick." Okay, so Staci was out of the picture. Yeah, right.

"Yeah, well, I miss sucking it," I responded. Bob had several contestants jumping and down, and Dennis had distracted me from what was happening. I could hear the "activity" on the other end of the phone increase, and his speech took on a slightly strained tone. "Oh, baby. I wanna fuck you. Do you wanna fuck me?"

A commercial for meat tenderizer came on. I couldn't believe the coincidence. I scrunched up my face, trying not to laugh. "Yeah. Oh yeah, Dennis. I wanna fuck you."

Then I heard a thumping sound. Dennis came back on the line. "I'm hittin' the phone with it," he declared. More thumping. I guess that was the definition of phone sex.

"Are doin' yourself, baby?" he cooed. I took a swig of my Diet Coke and mustered a refreshed sigh. A few drops of the Coke spilled. "Oh, yeah. I'm really wet," I offered.

Seconds later we had liftoff. "Oh, oh! Oh fuck!" he exclaimed. By then Bob was trying to give away a living room set. I didn't like the style of furniture, but I thought one of the lamps would look good in my place. I figured I could get the conversation back on track. My track.

Dennis paused, then started talking again. Didn't ask how I was at that point. Didn't need to. He was done. We engaged in small talk. I was waiting for that perfect opportunity to bring up the money. He was hard to approach about financial matters. He'd clam up and say, "Later, let's talk about it later."

The conversation centered on me dropping everything and coming out to be with him in his time of need. I figured I was with him, at least over the phone, for his five minutes of need, and that was enough. "Dennis, I'm not twenty-three anymore," I said. "I can't just drop everything and fly out to be with you. I have responsibilities." He told me to take "the baby" over to my dad's and come to New York.

Again I refused.

The timing was bad to ask for money. I had just rebuffed him. I needed the money, but I also needed my life. I thought quickly how much I should ask for. Ten grand would have been very handy and pocket change for him. I would have settled for five. Hey, I figured a thousand bucks a minute for phone sex was steep, but the service was personalized.

I saw my opening. "We could use a little money," I noted. There, I said it. It was out in the open. Dennis clammed up, on cue. Then he muttered, "Let's talk about it later." I was toast. I knew I might as well panhandle at that point. I'd be more successful.

He continued to try to get me to come out to New York until he realized I was totally serious and not going to bend. I think I surprised him. He was so used to my flying out whenever he called. That era was officially over. I didn't turn him down with any malice or anger. He finally let it go and the conversation petered out with some "See ya laters," and we hung up.

I didn't get any money and he hadn't gotten me to come to New York, but he had gotten a fleeting thrill. I thought about Dennis in that hotel room. He's wealthy and successful, but he's all alone. He has made his choices, yet he doesn't seem to be able to deal with the storms he creates. He retreats to lick his wounds and blames everyone but himself. And when he does try to reach out for help, he twists it and never deals with the real problem. I think Dennis is a man who needs good psychiatric help but seeks escapism when he feels any heat. With that approach, he'll only get more peculiar. And worse.

Eventually the NBA spanked Dennis with a six-game suspension and a twenty thousand dollar fine for head-butting the ref in the game against the Nets. I'm sure he thought they were picking on him, just like he probably did when he kicked the cameraman and got suspended and fined. You can't head-butt and kick people and get away with it, at least not on national television.

As I went back to *The Price Is Right* and watched a little lady from somewhere in the Midwest win a red convertible, I thought about Dennis and how no one can really give him what he wants, because he doesn't even know what he wants.

Then my thoughts drifted to how tough it is to earn five grand and how I'll never use the phone in a hotel room ever again.

— — —

Last year, 1996, Dennis or Dwight Manley cooked up a little publicity stunt. During a game, the TV cameras were going to show Alexis on the sidelines, watching her daddy. I think Dennis does really love his daughter, but he tends to use her a lot to show the "sensitive other side" of his bad-boy image. While I don't doubt the sincerity of his feelings of tenderness toward her, I do question his use of Alexis to show the world what a loving, caring father he is.

Anyway, I was asked to bring Alexis down to L.A., where the Bulls were going to play the Clippers. As Alexis stayed on the sidelines, in perfect camera range, I stayed up in the nosebleed section and watched the ants scurry around on the court. At least from that distance I could pick out Dennis by his hair.

After the game Alexis and I were invited to dinner with Dennis and a group of people. The people turned out to be mostly a bunch of older, rich, snobby guys with young women on their arms, either third wives or mistresses. I think they knew Dennis from the tables in Vegas. And even though they were wealthy, they weren't famous, and they liked being around him because he was. Also with us was the ever-present weasel extraordinaire, Dwight Manley, and some blonde who was introduced as Ericka. When we sat down Ericka sat next to Dennis. At first I didn't think much of it; then I noticed Ericka really sucking up to Dennis and more or less ignoring Dwight. Hmm.

I excused myself and started to head to the ladies' room when Alexis jumped up and said she wanted to go, too. In the bathroom, Alexis looked around and whispered, "That's the lady that was in Daddy's hotel room with us today."

I was shocked. "The blonde sitting next to Daddy?"

Alexis nodded. "And you know what, Mommy? Her and Daddy were lying on the bed together, and I had to lay by myself on the other one. Her and Daddy were kissing and stuff."

I was so angry I thought I was going to have an aneurysm.

How could he do that? Make out with some cookie in front of our daughter? I knew Dennis was irresponsible, but this was too much. I recalled the incident when Dennis was in a restaurant and traded his autograph to a stranger in return for that stranger taking Alexis to the rest room, because Dennis was too fucking lazy to get his ass up and walk her to the bathroom.

On two other occasions he actually lost Alexis. He had visitation rights for the day on each of those occasions. He decided to take her to Arden Fair Mall in Sacramento. Alexis wanted me to go, too. We agreed to meet at a certain store at a certain time. When I got there two mall security cops were talking to Dennis. He had lost

Alexis. Fortunately, we found her playing with some mannequins in the store next door.

A few months later he took Alexis back to Arden Fair Mall and somehow managed to lose her in the food court. A woman found Alexis crying and figured out who she belonged to. The woman returned her to Dennis. Alexis told me the story after he dropped her off at my place at the end of the day. I could have died. And if Dennis had been within reach, he would have. I told my attorney about this, and he spoke to the judge who was handling custody matters in relation to Alexis. From that point on, Dennis had court-ordered supervised visits with Alexis. The court thought it was a good idea for a responsible adult to be with the two of them at all times.

So I shouldn't have been surprised that Dennis was making out with Ericka in front of Alexis. What next? Will he ask Alexis to hold the video camera while he frolics with another Pear? I shudder to think.

Alexis and I left the bathroom and went back to our table. I was steaming, but I kept it inside. Until the right moment. It came sooner than I expected. Dennis noticed something in the air. "What took you so long in the bathroom?" he asked. I gave him and Ericka a scathing look. "Oh, did you miss me? I didn't think you would have noticed, with that blond airhead sitting next to you."

You could have cut the tension at that table with a Ginsu knife. I asked the guy sitting next to me if he would take Alexis to get a mint. Sensing the impending train wreck about to take place at our table, he obliged.

When they had gone I lit into Dennis as well as everyone else at the table. "I know this little ho is not with Dwight, she's with Dennis." I had their attention, so I focused on Dennis. "How dare you do something so awful and cruel to your daughter! What's wrong with you? These people think anything you do is okay and cool and they'd never tell you otherwise. But I'm here to tell you that what you did, to her and to me, sucks. You're a fuckin' prick, Dennis!"

Then I aimed my sights at Ericka. "I hope you make him wear a condom, honey, 'cause he's a walking herpes sore."

That said, I left.

I found Alexis and the fellow I'd sent her out with. They were getting along great. He escorted us back to our hotel and was very nice to us. He also made it a point of telling me he did not approve of Dennis's actions. I don't remember his name, but his kindness was real. If he reads this, I want to thank him.

— — —

Dennis's appearance on *Oprah* in 1996 was more hyped than if the pope had come out and said he was dating Sharon Stone. I couldn't believe all the coverage he got for crying over his daughter. It pissed me off to no end because I knew the real story.

One day I got a call from Dennis's secretary, who told me he was going to be on *Oprah* and wondered if I would bring Alexis out to surprise him in the middle of the interview. After all of the bitterness he had shown me the previous year or so, I thought this might be a way to help soothe things between us. I didn't want to be Dennis's enemy. Despite *everything* between us, I still care about him. More important, Alexis had not seen or heard from Dennis in months. I said, sure, I'll bring Alexis out, when do you need her? The date was set and when it came, we got on the plane and flew out to Chicago, where the show is taped.

We arrived at the studio at about 11 A.M. and were escorted to a conference room that, among other things, contained gobs of food. We were nervous and picked at it a little. Alexis was puzzled. After not having contact with her father in months, she wondered why we had to come here to do so. I had no answers other than to say he was probably busy but that he loved her. I was secretly beginning to question the second half of that excuse. Dennis has a busy schedule, but he is also impulsive and has virtually unlimited resources. I *never* restricted his visitations with our daughter. Where the hell was he for a few months out of the life of that little girl? Couldn't he have at least called her? I didn't notice any news reports that his fingers had been broken playing basketball. If I sound irritated, I am.

Dennis arrived in a flurry of activity at around 12:30, with members of his entourage, production assistants, producers, and various ass-kissers scurrying around to help him find his way into the studio. They sure didn't help him find his way to his little girl, who was waiting expectantly. Despite being billed as a "surprise" when Alexis was to walk out, cross the stage, and embrace her loving father in a real Kodak moment—of course he'd have this mock look of shock and love on his face—he knew all along Alexis was in the building. Now maybe it was the producer's call not to let him see his daughter, but do you think if the Great Dennis Rodman had said, "Screw your plan. I wanna see my daughter," they would have said no? Of course not.

Three hours passed as we watched videos, and Dennis still didn't appear to say hello to Alexis. Eventually some tech person came in and attached a microphone to Alexis. Oprah's staff knew I absolutely did not want to be in the audience, so I was told I could wait in the wings while Alexis was on stage with Dennis. She was not sure what was going on, and I assured her that everything would be fine. I had been hoping Oprah would come down and say hello to us, mainly for Alexis's benefit, but she was probably busy and didn't have a chance.

Then they led us to another room, one filled with monitors so we could watch the taping. In the hallway Alexis caught a glimpse of Dennis. He looked like a heightened version of that pimpy-looking guy Huggy Bear from the show *Starsky and Hutch*. He was barefoot and covered in jewelry, and he had on a long coat, a hideous *Saturday Night Fever* shirt, and a big-ass fur hat.

Frankly, he scared Alexis.

She turned to me, her eyes wide. "Mommy, what's that on his head? He doesn't have any shoes on."

What could I say? "Oh, honey, your father is just a one-man media circus who's created a bizarre self-exploiting image of himself as an athlete-turned-renegade-pop-icon with a propensity for implying vague sexual preference." No. What I said was, "Yeah, he *is* barefoot."

As we sat in the room and watched the interview begin, Alexis had a worried look on her face. I think it was the combination of being in a strange place, seeing her dad for the first time in months, and probably Dennis's wacky-looking getup. When Oprah started asking Dennis what it was like to bone Madonna I grabbed Alexis and we went into the hallway to wait. I didn't want to hear about it, and I certainly didn't want her to hear about it.

Finally someone came for Alexis. I kissed her cheek and said, "I'll be right here, honey. You're gonna do great!" When she realized she was going to have to leave me and go see Dennis she got nervous. Oprah's production people told her it was time to go, and she started crying and wouldn't budge. She wouldn't leave my side. I must say, the assistants, producers, and others we dealt with didn't treat us with a whole lot of respect. Alexis, of course, didn't realize it, but I felt a distinct "Oh, she's the bitchy ex with his kid" attitude from the staff.

Word apparently got back to Oprah, who sent someone higher up on the ladder to convince Alexis to go out. That person lost what little tact she had pretty fast. After trying hurriedly to convince Alexis to go out, she gave up and said, "What's wrong with you? You have to go out *now*!"

That did it.

The mother bear in me emerged and I lashed out. Alexis was very upset at this point, and I felt they were ganging up on her for the sake of a man who didn't have the decency to call or come see her for months, and who's now on stage crying to Oprah about how much she means to him. I was pissed. If Dennis hadn't spent so much time in makeup and had come down to see her first, she might have been a lot more at ease. But the upshot was, if she didn't want to go out, she didn't have to go out. End of discussion.

Soon more people showed up to talk her into it. By now she really had her heels dug in. Someone mistakenly thought they could outwit my daughter. "Your daddy says he'll take you to FAO Schwarz to buy you some toys if you come out." Alexis fixed her with her trademark stubborn look. "My mommy already took me," she stated. Pretty good for a kid who came to the studio directly from the airport.

I decided that Oprah's people were fanning at the plate with Alexis, so it was time to go. She didn't want to go out on stage and that was that. We left. Though we didn't meet, I think Oprah, despite being so high-powered, is probably a decent person, but I was disappointed with the way we were treated. Had the staff done their homework with us rather than kissing Dennis's butt until their noses bled, they might have handled things differently.

When word spread about Dennis's tearful interview with Oprah and all of the bullshit commentary started up about what a sensitive guy he was, I almost kicked in my television set. Everyone with an FCC license was running that clip of Dennis's small "breakdown" over his daughter. Who knows? Maybe he was sincere, but he had to have been thinking what a shithead he'd been to her.

Life is not always what it appears to be.

— — —

Most people think of Jack Haley as Dennis's baby-sitter. And for good reason. He's more *that* than he is a legit NBA player. Jack's much more likely to have his three-piece suit retired than his jersey when he's done with the game.

Jack was just another dude who put Dennis on a pedestal. He gets a little of the spotlight shined on him by virtue of being next to Dennis, and poor Jack is willing to settle for that. I like Jack. He was nice to me and helped me deal with Dennis more than once, but I sometimes lose my respect for him because he's such a yes-man. He will do just about anything Dennis tells him to. Dennis wouldn't keep Jack around otherwise. When Dennis wanted to drink shot after shot of Jagermeister, Jack was there to cheer him on. To Jack's credit, he was willing to make sure Dennis didn't get in trouble and that he got home safely.

In a way Jack was just like the young white boys Dennis kept around the house in Michigan. They all fawned over him, making him the complete center of attention. You won't find Dennis hanging out with Michael Jordan because the spotlight would be on him, not on Dennis.

One of the many things he seems not to understand is the old saying, "What goes up must come down." He has treated a lot of people pretty shabbily on his little climb up the ladder. When he starts coming back down in the very near future, he's going to be in for a rude awakening. After Dennis is out of the league and people have grown tired of his little cross-dressing sideshow, he's going to have a hard time finding another group of hangers-on. Then what's he going to do? He's not emotionally secure enough to handle that. I won't be surprised if he calls me. And I hope he won't be surprised when he hears the click on the other end of the line.

— — —

Before Dennis was traded to the Bulls he used to talk a lot of shit about Michael Jordan. He still does. He complains that Michael is overpaid and overrated. Now, I've always liked Michael, or maybe I should say I've always liked the image he shows the public. I really don't know him as a private person, but I don't have any reason to think badly of him.

Anyway, I always used to ask Dennis why he hated Michael so much. Michael apparently loves his family and dotes on his children. Dennis would answer by saying that Michael isn't the angel he appears to be. He accuses Michael of cheating on his wife and worse, though he never explained what the worse things were.

It seems obvious to me that Dennis is simply jealous of Michael, who is, as they say, the best player of all time. Dennis has two things going for him: One, he is a hell of a good rebounder, maybe the best since Wilt Chamberlain. He may even be better than Wilt since the overall level of athleticism is higher now than it was back in Wilt's day. Two, Dennis is entertaining, in a court jester sort of way. And if he understands nothing else (which he may not), he understands that professional sports is entertainment.

Because Dennis lacks an overall game and because he is emotionally insecure and immature, it's easy to understand why he badmouths Michael. Dennis needs the limelight. That's why he does his hair the way he does. That's why he puts on wedding dresses. That's why he does all the circuslike things he does. He is still a child trying to get his mother's attention back from his sisters.

— — —

Scottie Pippen used to be one of my favorite players. That is, until I read some things about him which I'll talk about in a minute. I used to think Dennis would look like Scottie if only Dennis were more handsome. Scottie may not be Michael Jordan, but who is? Scottie was named one of the fifty best players ever. Was Dennis? Nope.

So what does Dennis think of Scottie? He thinks Scottie is just a punk. That's classic Dennis: so insecure he can't acknowledge that anyone is a better player than he is, even when the rest of the world knows it's true.

When Dennis was with the Pistons and they played Chicago one time, Dennis hit Scottie, who needed stitches. I remember Scottie being interviewed about the incident, and he was completely professional about it. "It's just part of the job," he said. He never once dissed Dennis, even though he deserved to be dissed.

Nowadays I think Scottie deserves some disrespect as well.

I don't know what Dennis thinks about his new teammate Robert Parish, but the two of them do appear to have a common interest besides basketball.

A friend gave me a 1995 *Sports Illustrated* article about Robert Parish and a bunch of other abusive athletes, Warren Moon and Mike Tyson among them. In the article, which was written by William Nack and Lester Munson, Parish is described by his ex-wife, Nancy Saad, as "a domestic terrorist." Nancy describes an incident in which Parish pushed her down a flight of stairs when she was eight months pregnant. As I read this my mouth fell wide open. I couldn't believe how similar, almost identical, my situation was to hers.

The writers had a quote from Mike Tyson: "I like to hurt women when I make love to them. I like to hear them scream with pain, to see them bleed. It gives me pleasure." Tyson also talked about when he used to beat his wife, actress Robin Givens. He said one of the best punches he ever threw was at Robin: "She flew backward, hitting every wall in the apartment." If you had substituted Dennis's name for Tyson's, I wouldn't have noticed the difference.

Later in the article the writers describe how Mark Fitzpatrick, a goalie for the Florida Panthers, once grabbed his wife, shoved her, and kicked her in the back—*when she was pregnant.* Fitzpatrick was arrested on a charge of aggravated battery on a pregnant woman, a felony. His wife filed for divorce. She said her husband had hit her many times before.

Now, if Dennis and Robert Parish ever run out of things to talk about, Dennis apparently could discuss the finer points of domestic abuse with Scottie Pippen. Scottie has been accused by both his ex-wife and an ex-fiancée of being abusive. He was arrested on a charge of domestic battery after he allegedly grabbed Yvette DeLeone, his fiancée at the time, by the arm and shoved her up against a car in the garage. Two years earlier the fiancée told the police that she suffered fractures of her right hand after Pippen threw her six feet out the front door. Scottie's ex-wife, Karen McCollum, told police that he hit and choked her one evening after she returned from telling a judge that she needed protection from him.

Pippen's handlers dismissed DeLeone as a liar. I'm not sure how they characterized McCollum, but I suspect they said she was making it up also. Yeah, and all those photos of O.J. wearing the Bruno Magli shoes were fakes, too.

Think about this: With Parish, Pippen, and Rodman, the Chicago Bulls could hold their own domestic abuse convention. Better yet, maybe they could get a group discount on a domestic abuse counselor.

The *Sports Illustrated* article mentioned lots of other athletes and cited studies that suggested athletes might be more inclined toward violence than nonathletes. As interesting as I found all of that, what resonated most in me was how similar the pattern of abuse was. I saw myself in all of the stories they told. According to the article:

> Eight to twelve million women a year are assaulted by their partners, numerous studies have shown, and these assaults have been cited as the leading cause of injuries to women from 15 to 44. In fact, more women die from or are injured at the hands of their abusers than are injured or killed in car

accidents, muggings, and rapes combined, and the numbers that make this point are most likely conservative: While 35% of emergency-room visits by women are for symptoms that may be the result of spousal abuse, as few as 5% of these victims are ever so categorized.

I was lucky to get out alive.

— — —

When my family first met Dennis they adored him. He was just a guy who had come from tough circumstances and was working to make something out of his life. They could identify with him.

Dennis seemed very fond of my mom and the two brothers he met. My other brother had moved on to San Francisco to practice law, so he didn't meet Dennis until later.

Back in 1987 he seemed to look up to my brothers. Bill used to drive this old bucket of a car around Sacramento, and there was Dennis, sitting in the passenger seat, his big arm hanging out the window with the ratty upholstery hanging down on both their heads. Dennis wasn't so status-conscious then, so he didn't care about the kind of car he was riding around in.

Bill, Matt, and Dennis used to go out to the racetrack all the time—almost every day, in fact. You've never seen Dennis laugh so much as he used to back then. That was the Dennis I fell in love with. That was the Dennis I wanted to marry. But as they say, money changes everything.

My brothers didn't care that Dennis was a professional basketball player. In fact, since Dennis was at the bottom of the pro hoops ladder and was earning only league minimum, my brothers had to loan him money on a regular basis when they were out at the track.

When Dennis and I were staying at my parents' house, he used to go into Bill and Matt's room and wake them up so they could do stuff with him. One day he went out and bought some brand-new bicycles for my brothers and my mom. Again, that was the Dennis I fell in love with. He used to think about other people. He used to do things for other people just because he felt like it.

After Dennis was reinstated to the league after being suspended for eleven games for kicking the camerman, Eugene Amos, he announced that he would play his first eleven games back for charity. But he did that after he found out I was writing this book.

Dennis likes to talk about how money doesn't mean anything to him. He can go to Vegas and lose plenty of money because it's no big deal. But at the same time he filled a lot of pages of his book whining about how underpaid he is. And he acted like a big shot, giving all that money to charity and talking about how he was willing to play the game for free. But you'll notice he does deposit most of his paychecks. I can't figure out if he's a hypocrite or just unaware of what he's saying.

I remember one night when I went for a run. Out of nowhere came Dennis and my brother Matt on two of those bikes Dennis bought. They were playing follow the leader and acting for all the world like two big kids. It was cute and endearing. I was amazed and tickled to see this man acting like such a kid. I had to laugh

Once Dennis started to become popular he stopped showing interest in my family. His betrayal absolutely crushed my brothers, who thought they had made a true friend. They were hurt but didn't complain about it. They figured the success was simply more than Dennis could handle. They rooted for him to play well and enjoyed it when he did.

After my family found out about Dennis's abusiveness, my brothers lost all respect for him, especially my brother Matt. He and I are close and fought a lot as kids. In fact, Matt was the one who taught me how to fight in the first place. At the same time he was the one who was most protective of me. I think the fact that things were kind of rough for us kids growing up helped us form a tighter bond than we would have had otherwise.

I remember one time in particular when I wanted to go with Matt and his friends to the park to play baseball. I couldn't pedal fast enough to keep up. His buddies kept saying, "Just dust her! Let's go!" But Matt slowed down and waited for me. He told me he was going to go ahead and play at the park. He told me to go back home and wait, and he'd be back to play with me in two hours. And two hours later he was back. I've never forgotten how important it is to keep your word. I've never forgotten that Matt is the kind of person who keeps his.

All of my brothers play an important role in Alexis's life. They were at her baptism; Dennis wasn't. Alexis spends two weekends a month with my oldest brother, Chris. He takes her to the theater to see plays and operas. He introduced Alexis to classical music. Can you imagine Dennis doing that? "Yo, Alexis, check this shit out, some bro named Yo-Yo Mama playin' the cello. You know what I'm sayin'?"

Chris never misses any of Alexis's special occasions, even when he has to drive from San Francisco after work. He encourages her church attendance every Sunday. Uncle Matt and Uncle Bill are equally doting and help give Alexis the feeling of family we all want. Matt calls her "Li'l Annie" because she reminds him so much of me.

These days my brother Matt would like to have Dennis's head mounted on the wall like a trophy kill. Since Matt is 6'6" and about 240 pounds he wouldn't have too hard of a time yanking Dennis's head off for the taxidermist. The notion that Dennis spent so much time beating and otherwise abusing his little sister doesn't sit well with Matt. He adores Alexis and despises Dennis for abandoning her. It will be ugly if Dennis ever runs into Matt.

— — —

After the Bulls won the NBA championship in June 1996, Dennis got a hankering to see Alexis and called with a big plan to entertain her. I listened to his sweeping itinerary and told him I'm sure Alexis would have fun, but I was worried her fragile little routine would be seriously jarred by his complicated scheme. She is a very bright, smart kid, but she's been through a lot of weirdness in her short life and has many fears and idiosyncrasies. Alexis is attached to me and though she really doesn't like to travel, she does feel an obligation to see her daddy.

With that in mind, I asked Dennis if he could come to Sacramento and spend time with her. No, he said, he wanted to show her a really great time. His plan was bigger than big: two weeks in California and Texas—Disneyland, Magic Mountain, Knott's Berry Farm, then Six Flags Over Texas. What little girl wouldn't want to do all that?

He assured me that his secretary, Tammy, would come along to supervise. I said I'd ask Alexis. She was excited but also a little scared. Even though he's her father, she's not very comfortable being alone with him. They have spent so little time together, and on a few occasions he's lost his temper and yelled at her for doing things kids do. Granted, Dennis isn't used to having kids around, and they can be trying, as any hands-on parent knows, but minimal contact and bursts of anger don't inspire confidence and trust in a little one.

Alexis wanted a trusted companion with her. She asked if she could take her dog, Kilo. Dennis cannot stand Kilo because Kilo cannot stand him, so he nixed that right off. Alexis's second choice for a familiar face to accompany her was her best friend, Molly. Dennis agreed to Molly coming, and the plans were set. Alexis and Molly were very excited to be going on this big adventure. They told me, very matter-of-factly, what they were going to do at each of the dazzling locations they were to visit. It was so cute hearing these two eight-year-olds rattle off all their planned activities: Meet Goofy, go to Splash Mountain, ride the Viper, eat cotton candy.

Dennis blew into Sacramento in a private jet owned by the Oakley sunglass company. Typical Rodman flash. Alexis and Molly boarded and off they went.

First stop, Orange County. Home of Disneyland and Knott's Berry Farm. Eighty miles north is Magic Mountain. So what did they do first? Disneyland? Knott's? No, they spent their time at one of Orange County's premier theme parks: Dwight Manley's house. There they hung out and watched Dennis watch television. Then they watched him eat. Then they watched him work out. That is, whenever he was out of bed. He usually slept in until one in the afternoon. That's about halfway through my daughter's day.

After all that excitement, Dennis decided they should just blow off the planned stops in the Los Angeles area and head straight for

Dallas and Six Flags Over Texas. Much better than Disneyland or dumb old Knott's Berry Farm.

Alexis later told me that at one point, when they actually left Dwight's house, she and Molly accompanied Dennis and Dwight somewhere in a limo. The limo made a stop (probably a strip joint), and Dennis and Dwight left the girls in the limo with the driver and disappeared for quite a while.

That's class, Dennis.

When I heard that Dennis had written off three quarters of the billed attractions I was pissed. That figures. This guy's screwed me over so long, now it's time to start doing it to his own daughter. I wanted them to come home, but Dennis insisted they'd have a blast in Texas. He gave some lame excuse about having business to attend to there. They'd come back to Orange County afterward. I grudgingly said okay.

Then secretary Tammy bailed, claiming her son was sick. I told Dennis I didn't want Alexis and Molly going to Texas without some kind of responsible supervision. Dennis dismissed that, saying they'd be just fine. Plus, he *had* to go right then.

They flew out to Dallas. Once there, Dennis went right over to his mother Shirley's place and dropped the girls off. The pressing business in Dallas turned out to be Staci, who flew in to be with Dennis. He and Staci spent a few days together, then Dennis went back to Shirley's and collected Alexis and Molly. Then he took them out on a boat for an afternoon.

They'd been to a total of zero theme parks.

The next morning Dennis and Staci dropped them at the home of one of Dennis's friends and took off for the day. Alexis said the people were very, very wealthy. She and Molly rode around on golf carts, played with the daughter of the rich people, and had lunch. That was it. Still no Goofy. Unless you count Dennis.

Dennis and Staci returned that evening, and they all flew back to Orange County in a jet he had chartered. Then they got to watch him watch some more TV, this time with Staci. Then they flew home.

When the plane landed I waited on the tarmac for Alexis and Molly. I brought Kilo, figuring it would keep Dennis from coming over to talk to me. It worked. The door to the plane opened, and Alexis leaped out and ran full tilt for me. She jumped into my arms and cried, saying how horrible the trip was. Molly followed, saying she had a pretty good time. I guess two weeks with Goofy's twin brother was Molly's cup of tea. Meanwhile, Dennis took off and headed for some golf tournament in Lake Tahoe. I imagine he had a good time. Too bad his daughter didn't.

What kind of man would get a little girl's hopes up so high, then utterly crush them?

What possessed him to take his eight-year-old daughter on the trip of a lifetime, only to sandbag her with boring rides to nowhere in limos, endless time killing while he slept or played with his girlfriend, and flying them so often as to give them jet lag?

I'm sorry I let them go. I should have known. Despite all the promises to those children, it ultimately didn't mean shit to Dennis how they felt or what happened to them or what inconveniences they suffered. After all, they're just kids.

I should have protected Alexis, but I'm in a tough position: Dennis is her father. I've never withheld her from him. He's always been free to see her and spend time with her. But this trip taught me a lesson: *Nothing* is sacred to Dennis. He may boast that he is free and that he's not afraid of anything and that he's his own man, but ponder this story of two little girls next time you read about Dennis Rodman and what a bold, empowering philosophy he has when he claims nothing gets in his way or holds him back. He's absolutely right, but at what price?

Alexis is afraid of Dennis. Not in a scary, boogeyman sense, but in the sad sense that he is truly a stranger to her. She will not take a bath when he's around, something the average eight-year-old has no problem doing in the presence of her father.

Partly because of this incident, I canceled our cable television subscription. More and more, I don't know who Dennis is anymore. His increasing weirdness and his surprise appearances on different shows, wearing odd attire and talking about everything from his pierced scrotum to doing Madonna, are things his daughter does not need to hear.

You've heard the variations of the expression "You can't have it both ways"? Dennis, you've lived your life the way you wanted and been "bad as you wanna be," but if you ever read this book, I want you to hear something your daughter does not have the courage to say to you.

Alexis once said to me, "Mommy, I don't know my daddy. He's a stranger." If you want to cry about something, Dennis, think about that. It's worth a cry.

# Postgame Wrap-Up

BEFORE I STARTED DATING MY CURRENT BOYFRIEND, TONY, I WAS seeing a man I will call BJ. BJ is a prominent man in my town and very wealthy. He has always treated me with respect. It was such a pleasant change from the past, being treated like a queen instead of a junkyard dog. The times I spent with BJ made me realize how insane Dennis is and, to some extent, how insane I was for putting up with him. Things with BJ were very good, but he was trying to work his way through a tough divorce and so we called a break for a while.

Just before we did, a mutual acquaintance of mine and Dennis's saw me and BJ at a club in Sacramento and told Dennis. I'm told he hit the roof when he found out. Why? He's made it clear he doesn't want me, by words and actions. Not that I would go back to him. I wouldn't. His jealousy is just more evidence of his instability.

When Dennis was on *Oprah* he went out of his way to thank Staci. For what? Taking his money? She's happy to do that. For not throwing his insincere gifts back in his face like I did? He's probably happy she doesn't do that. I'm sorry, but every indication is that Staci's just a gold-digging floozy. She won't leave him because she has no self-respect, and Dennis has never ended a relationship. He just burns them out and moves on. According to his secretary, he already cheats on Staci, and she cheats on him. Maybe they deserve each other. But I've wasted enough words on her.

This book will probably shock Dennis. Of all the people he has ever known, he has always thought he could depend on me. Even though he is the father of my daughter and was probably the relationship of my life, it is time to move on. I don't want to burn my bridges, but I want Dennis, and everyone else, to know what he has done. If he ever reads this book, he will feel I betrayed him. If telling the truth constitutes a betrayal, then yes, I have betrayed him.

He called me the day after it was publicly announced I had made plans to write this book. He left several messages on my answering machine, saying he was stunned and hurt that I could do this to *him*. To him? Can you believe it?

Dennis pays me nine thousand dollars a month in child support. The court ordered him to do that. It sounds like a lot and it's very helpful, but I also have to pay taxes on it. I end up with a little over six thousand. I work several part-time jobs to supplement my income. Dennis probably makes a million bucks a month *or more.*

By the way, the child support was originally ten thousand a month. I needed money to pay outstanding bills and taxes, and Dwight Manley "generously" arranged a loan and took the payback out of the ten thousand dollars, so I get nine thousand instead. I'm only telling you these numbers to put things in perspective and set the record straight. I don't want anything else from Dennis Rodman. I don't want anything from *any* man. Except respect. I deserve that much.

Alexis and I have a good life and are doing fine on our own. But it still bothers me that Dennis did this to his own daughter. He hated his father for running out on him as a kid, and then he turns around and does it to his own child. She deserves a father, but she deserves a good one, not Dennis. No amount of money sent every month is an acceptable substitute for a good dad. My heart aches for Alexis because she wants a father so badly. Like all children, Alexis is innocent in every sense of the word. She doesn't care that her daddy is famous or that he's on TV or in the movies. To her, Dennis is just the dad who hurt her mom and then left. She just wants a daddy to play catch with her and take her camping and skating. She just wants a daddy who will pick her up and hold her when she scrapes her knee or when she has a bad dream.

I don't regret that I left Dennis, but I do regret that Alexis doesn't have a dad. But Dennis screwed up so royally that it would have been far worse to stay with him. Now all I can do is my best to see that my daughter is taken care of and raised properly.

In the past ten years I've discovered a lot about myself and about life. I have a man in my life with whom I enjoy spending time, but if I'm not with Alexis, I have found that I prefer to be alone. I enjoy the peace and freedom of my own thoughts.

Probably the most important thing I've learned is one should never, ever, ever take abuse and not do something to stop it. There are many men out there who treat the women in their lives like garbage. Those men are sick, and *they* are the garbage. No one has the right to treat a fellow human being that way, let alone someone you supposedly love.

One last thought to women in abusive, hurtful relationships: Get the hell out.

Find a way, *any* way, to escape. I was wrong to keep going back. You think your man will change? He won't. You think he'll start respecting you? He won't. You think your life will get better if you can just make it until tomorrow? It won't unless you *take action*.

If your man won't acknowledge his abusive behavior and won't get help, leave or ask *him* to leave. Start caring about *yourself.* It's *okay* to do that.

I can't emphasize this enough: **Don't put up with it. Ever.**

The following is an excerpt from

# YOU CAN RUN BUT YOU CAN'T HIDE
## The Secret Diary of My Life with George Foreman

by Cynthia Lewis Foreman with Stuart White
available from Dove Books in September 1997

## PROLOGUE

IT HAS BECOME SOMETHING OF A LITERARY CLICHE, OR perhaps a journalistic one, to say of an event or an episode in a person's life that what had been a dream turned into a nightmare.

But my marriage to George Foreman did exactly that.

It had been everything I dreamt about. To fall in love with and marry a man I not only admired, but one who was adored and respected by the whole world as a champion boxer. Then to have that love apparently returned and transformed into marriage. There was nothing more I could have wished for at that moment.

Headline writers would dub us the Lady and the Champ. But I would come to privately think of us as Beauty and the Beast.

For I had been Miss Teenage Black America—and therefore tasted my own tiny slice of celebrity cake, earned my own Warholian fifteen minutes of fame. In the eyes of the world I had been proclaimed officially beautiful, although I never especially felt that way about myself.

George Foreman was famous. I was still young enough to believe in the American ideal of marriage and in my own particular interpretation of it. I felt that if I married this man whom I had come to love, then I could put myself in the background and help him to achieve whatever future goals he held.

I was a devout Christian and knew that George was, too—or that he professed to be. Together in our shared Christian belief, I was sure we could live a happy and productive life together.

What an innocent fool I was. I would soon grow up the hard way. I would soon see the slimy underbelly of public men and their private vices. I would soon learn that, without love, fame, riches, position, and public acclaim count for naught.

I would also learn what individuals and cults can do when they pervert the Christian religion that I so love. But at the time I was naive. I genuinely believed that George Foreman would love and care for me, as I loved and was ready to care for him. I should have known better. It is said you cannot build happiness on the unhappiness of others, and that was what I was attempting.

This man had already been involved with my mother, and I eventually married him despite her despair, her humiliation, and the tearful protests that fell upon my deaf ears.

The next three years would prove just what a fool I was. Since writing this book I have become acquainted with an old saying about boxing: They can run, but they can't hide.

I believe it's attributed to Joe Louis, who, ironically, became a good friend of mine. It means that in the boxing ring there are four rope walls and no cover. However fast your footwork, there is no place to hide from the lashing fists of the superior fighter.

Well, I could run, too—but I couldn't hide. Each home in which I lived with George was my boxing ring. Inside it I was the hunted opponent who could dodge and wave and feint all she wished, but who could not ultimately escape the physical and mental punishment of the kind of that particular ring—George Foreman.

We've come to roll our eyes and sniff a little at the word *abuse*. The so-called "abuse excuse" is pretty well discredited now, certainly in criminal trials. Yet the brutal truth is that according to recent figures, at least two million women a year are being abused by their spouses, lovers, and boyfriends in the United States. It happens every minute of every day and night of the week, all over America.

It is going on from the mansions of Beverly Hills to the shacks of Mississippi, from elegant estates on Long Island to high-rise projects in Chicago.

It's happening now behind those closed net curtains on your street, behind that door in your apartment block. And the culprits are of every ethnic, racial, and religious persuasion—black, white, Hispanic, Native American, Chinese, Japanese, Korean, Jewish,

Protestant, Catholic, Southern Baptist, Buddhist, and Muslim—no one can claim immunity or exclusion from the sin of wife battering.

And it isn't just about black eyes, bruised ribs, broken teeth, and—in the most extreme cases—a trip to the morgue, although that is how it commonly manifests itself. This abuse also sneers its corrosive message from the withheld pay packet and the dime-counting, penny-pinching state in which many women are kept, even as they struggle to put meals on the table and shoes on their children's feet.

This abuse echoes painfully from the constant belittling, the verbal scorn, the paranoia directed at them, the lack of respect and the downright indifference that so many women endure hour by miserable hour, each lousy day of their lives.

I accept, too, that on occasion, it is the wife who inflicts all of the above on a male spouse. Partners in gay relationships suffer in this way as well, no doubt. But the terrible, shameful majority of this kind of treatment is meted out by men on women. By the technically stronger, on the usually weaker.

So I believe that it's important that women read this book and see that they are not alone; to let them privately compare notes with another casebook from household Hell.